# ZOOT SUIT
## and
## Other
## Plays

## LUIS
## VALDEZ

Arte Publico Press
Houston
Texas
1992

# Acknowledgements

This volume is made possbile through a grant from the National Endowment for the Arts, a federal agency, and the Ford Foundation.

The following people and institutions were instrumental in the development of this collection of plays:

El Teatro Campesino

*Zoot Suit*

The Mark Taper Forum. The Rockefeller Foundation, The Shubert Organization, Alice McGrath, George Shibly, Ben Margolis, The Leyvas Family, The 38th St. Club.

*Bandido!*

NEA Theater Program, AT&T On Stage.

*I Don't Have to Show You No Stinking Badges!*

Lila Wallace-Reader's Digest Foundation, Charles Duggan, Los Angeles Theatre Center.

For reprint rights contact: Arte Público Press

*Recovering the past, creating the future*

Arte Público Press
University of Houston
452 Cullen Performance Hall
Houston, TX 77204-2004

Cover design by Mark Piñón
Cover illustration by Ignacio Gómez

Zoot Suit & Other Plays / Luis Valdez
     p. cm.
     Contents: Zoot Suit–Bandido!–I don't have to show you no stinking badges!
     ISBN 978-1-55885-048-4
     1. Mexican Americans–Drama. I. Title
PS3572.A387Z6    1992                         91-4z1789
812'.54–dc20                                      CIP

11 12 13 14 15 16 17            20 19 18 17 16 15 14

To my lovely wife and co-worker, Lupe Trujillo Valdez

# Contents

# INTRODUCTION

It is a pleasure to introduce the reader to *Zoot Suit, Bandido!* and *I Don't Have to Show You No Stinking Badges!*, as well as to their celebrated creator, Luis Miguel Valdez. These plays have never been published before and are an important addition to the growing corpus of Valdez's writings that have been preserved for future theater artists, students, scholars and the general reader. These three plays represent only a fraction of Valdez's astounding output since he first began writing plays in college.

For some, Luis Valdez needs no introduction; for others, his name may only be associated with his more widely seen films and television programs. No other individual has made as important an impact on Chicano theater as Luis Valdez. He is widely recognized as the leading Chicano director and playwright who, as the founder of El Teatro Campesino (Farmworker's Theatre) in 1965, inspired a national movement of theater troupes dedicated to the exposure of socio-political problems within the Chicano communities of the United States. His output includes plays, poems, books, essays, films and videos, all of which deal with the Chicano and Mexican experience in the U.S. Before discussing the plays in this collection, I would like to briefly trace the director/playwright's development, placing him and these plays in their historical context.

From Flatbed Trucks to Hollywood Sound Stages:
The Evolution of Luis Valdez

Luis Valdez was born to migrant farmworker parents in Delano, California, on June 26, 1940, the second in a family of ten children. Although his early schooling was constantly interrupted as his family followed the crops, he managed to do well in school. By the age of twelve, he had developed an interest in puppet shows, which he would stage for neighbors and friends. While still in high school he appeared regularly on a local television program, foreshadowing the work in film and video which would later give him his widest audience. After high school, Valdez entered San Jose State College where his interest in theater fully developed.

Valdez's first full-length play, *The Shrunken Head of Pancho Villa,* was produced by San Jose State College in 1964, setting the young artist's feet firmly in the theater. Following graduation in 1964, Valdez worked with the San Francisco Mime Troupe before founding El Teatro Campesino. Valdez became the Artistic Director as well as resident playwright for this raggle-taggle troupe of striking farmworkers, creating and performing brief comedia-like sketches called "*actos*" about the need for a farmworker's union. The *acto* became the signature style for the Teatro and Valdez, inspiring many other teatros to emulate this type of broad, farcical and presentational political theater based on improvisations of socio-political issues.

Within a matter of months El Teatro Campesino was performing away from the fields, educating the general public about the farmworkers' struggle and earning revenue for the Union. By 1967 Valdez decided to leave the ranks of the union in order to focus on his theater rather than on the demands of a struggling labor organization. As a playwright, Valdez could now explore issues relevant to the Chicano beyond the fields; as a director, he could begin to develop a core of actors no longer committed to one cause and one style alone.

Although he and his troupe were working collectively from the beginning, the individual playwright in Valdez was anxious to emerge. Discussing the process of writing plays outside of the group, Valdez recalled: "I used to work on them with a sense of longing, wanting more time to be able to sit down and write." In 1967, the playwright did sit down and write, creating what he termed a *"mito,"* or myth, that condemned the Vietnam war, titled *Dark Root of a Scream.* This contemporary myth takes place during a wake for a Chicano who died in Vietnam, an ex-community leader who should have stayed home and fought the battle in the barrio. The dead soldier becomes symbolic of all Chicanos who fought in a war that the playwright himself objected to. "I refused to go to Vietnam," Valdez said twenty years later, "but I encountered all the violence I needed on the home front: people were killed by the farmworkers' strike."

In 1968 the Teatro was awarded an Obie, off-Broadway's highest honor, and the following year Valdez and his troupe gained international exposure at the *Theatre des Nations* at Nancy, France. In 1970 Valdez wrote his second *mito*, *Bernabé*. This one act play is the tale of a *loquito del pueblo* (village idiot), Bernabé, who is in love with La Tierra (The Earth) and wants to marry her. La Tierra is portrayed as a *soldadera*, one of the women who followed and supported the troops during the Mexican Revolution of 1910.

*Bernabé* is a wonderfully written play that brings together myth and history, contemporary figures and historical icons. The allegorical figure of La Luna, brother to La Tierra, is portrayed as a Zoot Suiter. This is Valdez's first theatrical exploration of this 1940's Chicano renegade, foreshadowing one of his most powerful characters, El Pachuco, in *Zoot Suit. Bernabé* tells its audience that Chicanos not only have a history of struggle but *are* that struggle. Bernabé "marries" La Tierra and becomes a whole person; he symbolically represents all men who love and respect the earth.

Also in 1970, even as Valdez, the playwright, was scripting his individual statement about the Chicano and his relationship to the earth, Valdez, the director, was guiding the collective creation of an *acto* dealing with the war in Vietnam: *Soldado Razo* (*Buck Private*). *Soldado Razo* carefully explored some of the reasons young Chicanos were willing to go fight in Vietnam. Reflecting the influences of Bertholt Brecht's theories, the playwright uses the allegorical figure of La Muerte (Death) as a constant presence narrating the action, continually reminding his audience that this is theater and that the soldier's death is inevitable.

*Soldado Razo* complemented and expanded the earlier *mito*, *Dark Root of a Scream*, looking at the same issue but from a different viewpoint and in a distinct style. In Valdez's words, the *acto* "is the Chicano through the eyes of man," whereas the *mito* "is the Chicano through the eyes of God," exploring the Chicanos' roots in Mayan philosophy, science, religion and art. While *Soldado Razo* methodically demonstrates the eventual death of its central figure, *Dark Root of a Scream* begins after a soldier's death, exploring the cause from a mythical distance.

In 1971 the troupe moved to its permanent home base in the rural village of San Juan Bautista, California, where the Teatro established itself as a resident company. During this period Valdez began to explore the idea of adapting the traditional Mexican *corridos*, or ballads, to the stage. A singer would sing the songs and the actors would act them out, adding dialogue from the corridos' texts. Sometimes the singer/narrator would verbalize the text while the actors mimed the physical actions indicated by the song. These simple movements were stylized, enhancing the musical rhythms and adding to the unique combination of elements. The *corrido* style was to appear again, altered to suit the needs of a broader theatrical piece, *La Carpa de los Rasquachis* (*The Tent of the Underdogs*).

Developed over a period of years, *La carpa de los Rasquachis* stunned the audience at the Fourth Annual Chicano Theater Festival in San Jose, California in 1973. This production became the hallmark of the Teatro for several years, touring the United States and Europe many times to great critical acclaim. This piece is epic in scope, following a Cantinflas-like (read "Mexico's Charlie Chaplin") Mexican character from his crossing the border into the U.S. and the subsequent indignities to which he is exposed until his death.

*La carpa de los Rasquachis* brought together a Valdezian aesthetic that could be defined as raucous, lively street theater with deep socio-political and spiritual roots. The style combined elements of the *acto, mito* and *corrido* with an almost constant musical background as a handful of actors revealed the action in multiple roles with minimal costumes, props and set changes. This was the apogee of Valdez's "poor theater," purposely based on the early twentieth-century Mexican tent shows, otherwise known as "carpas."

In an effort to define his neo-Mayan philosophy, Valdez wrote a poem, *Pensamiento Serpentino,* in 1973. The poem describes a way of thinking that was determining the content of Valdez's evolving dramaturgy. The poem begins:

> *Teatro*
> *eres el mundo*
> *y las paredes de los*
> buildings *más grandes*
> *son* nothing but scenery.

Later in the poem Valdez describes and revives the Mayan philosophy of "In Lak Ech" which translates as "*Tú eres mi otro yo /* You are my other me." The phrase represents the following philosophy:

> Tú eres mi otro yo / You are my other me.
> Si te hago daño a ti / If I do harm to you,
> Me hago daño a mí mismo /I do harm to myself;
> Si te amo y respeto / If I love and respect you,
> Me amo y respeto yo / I love and respect myself.

In the opening lines Valdez describes Chicano theater as a reflection of the world; a universal statement about what it is to be a Chicano in the United States. Recognizing the many injustices the Chicano has suffered in this country, the poet nonetheless attempts to revive a non-violent response. Valdez creates a distinct vision of a "cosmic people" whose destiny is finally being realized as Chicanos who are capable of love rather than hate, action rather than words.

While *La carpa de los Rasquachis* continued to tour, Valdez made another crucial change in his development by writing *Zoot Suit* and co-producing it with the Center Theatre Group of Los Angeles. Once again at the vanguard, Valdez began the mainstreaming of Chicano theater, or, for some observers, "the infiltration of the regional theaters."

The director/playwright did not abandon El Teatro Campesino by getting involved with a major regional theater. The Teatro was still touring and *Zoot Suit* was co-produced by both theater organizations, thus including the Teatro in all negotiations and contracts. But this was a first step towards an individual identity that Valdez had previously rejected by working in a collective.

As advertised in the Los Angeles press, "On July 30, 1978, the Second Zoot Suit Riot begins," and it did. *Zoot Suit* played to sold-out houses for eleven months—breaking all previous records for Los Angeles theater. While the Los Angeles production continued to run, another production opened in New York on March 25, 1979, the first (and only) Chicano play to open on Broadway. Although audiences were enthusiastic, the New York critics were not, and the play was closed after a four-week run. Hurt, but undaunted, Valdez could have the satisfaction that the play continued to be the biggest hit ever in Los Angeles and a motion picture contract had been signed.

*Zoot Suit* marked an important turning point in Valdez's relationship with El Teatro Campesino as he began to write for actors outside the group. This experience introduced Valdez to the Hollywood Latino and non-Latino talent pool, suddenly bringing him into contact with a different breed of artist. With a large population of professionals at his disposal, Valdez's vision had to expand. No longer surrounded by sincere, but sometimes limited talent, Valdez could explore any avenue of theater he desired. The success of the Los Angeles run of *Zoot Suit* enabled our playwright/director to move more seriously into filmmaking. Valdez adapted and directed *Zoot Suit* as a motion picture in 1981.

The collaboration with a non-Hispanic theater company and subsequent move into Hollywood film making was inevitable for Valdez; the natural course for a man determined to reach as many people as possible with his message and with his art. Theater was his life's work, it was in his blood, but so was the fascinating world of film and video.

With the financial success of *Zoot Suit*, Valdez purchased an old packing house in San Juan Bautista and had it converted into a theater for the company. This new playhouse and administrative complex was inaugurated in 1981 with a production of David Belasco's 1905 melodrama *Rose of the Rancho*, adapted by Valdez. This old fashioned melodrama was an ideal play for San Juan Bautista, because it was based on actual historical figures and events that had

occurred in that town in the nineteenth century. Played as a revival of the melodrama genre, the play could be taken for face
value, a tongue-in-cheek taste of history replete with stereotypes
and misconceptions.

The experiment with *Rose of the Rancho* served as a kind of mo-
tivation for Valdez, inspiring him to write the second play in this
collection, *Bandido!* which he then directed in 1982 in the Teatro's
theater. This was Valdez's personal adaptation of the melodrama
genre but with a distinctly Valdezian touch as we will see later.

Valdez wrote and directed *Corridos* for the 1983 season, producing this elaboration of the earlier exercises in San Francisco's
Marine's Memorial Theater, a large house that was filled to capac-
ity for six months. The San Francisco production garnered eleven
awards from the Bay Area Theater Critics Circle before moving on
to residencies in San Diego and Los Angeles.

All of his interaction in Hollywood and his own sense of history inspired Valdez to write the final play in this collection, *I Don't
Have to Show You No Stinking Badges!*, first produced by El Teatro
Campesino and the Los Angeles Theatre Center in 1986. This production represented the beginning of yet another phase for Valdez
and his company. El Teatro Campesino was no longer a full-time
core of artists, living and creating collectively under Valdez's direction. Instead, the company began to contract talent only for the
rehearsal and performance period. El Teatro Campesino became
a producing company with Valdez at the helm as Artistic Director and writer. After great success in Los Angeles, *Badges!* was
co-produced with the San Diego Repertory Theater and the Burt
Reynolds Dinner Theatre in Jupiter, Florida. While the Teatro
continued to produce, Valdez began to focus his efforts more on
writing and directing films.

Valdez directed "La Bamba," the sleeper hit of the summer of
1987, finally opening up the doors that had been so difficult to pen-
etrate for so many years. "When I drove up to the studio gate,"
Valdez related, following the success of his film, "the guard at the
gate told me that the pastries were taken to a certain door. The
only other Mexican he ever saw delivered the pastries." That same
year our playwright adapted and directed the earlier *Corridos* into
a PBS version titled "Corridos: Tales of Passion and Revolution,"
starring Linda Rondstadt and featuring himself as narrator. This
production won the Peabody Award, the Pulitzer Prize of broad-
casting.

Following the success of "La Bamba" and "Corridos," Valdez
continued to work on other projects for television and film as he

also look his position as the leading Chicano filmmaker in Hollywood. Ever the activist, Valdez helped form the Latino Writers Group, which he hoped would pressure the studios to produce films written by Latinos. "The embryo is the screenplay," he said. "The embryo, in fact, is what is written on the page. This is where you begin to tell the difference between a stereotype and reality."

In 1991, Valdez adapted and directed *La Pastorela*, or *Shepherd's Play* for a great performances segment on PBS. This television production is based on the traditional Christmas play, which El Teatro Campesino has produced in the mission at San Juan Bautista for many years. That same year, Valdez and his wife, Lupe, co-scripted a motion picture based on the life of Frida Kahlo, for production in 1992. Plans were also underway for a revival of *Bandido!* in San Juan Bautista during the 1992 season as well as a re-mounting of *Zoot Suit* for a national tour.

Valdez's impressive career can be separated into the following four periods: Phase One, the director/playwright of the original group of farmworkers; Phase Two, a Teatro Campesino independent of the Union; Phase Three, a professional Teatro and co-productions such as *Zoot Suit*; and the current, Fourth Phase, Luis Valdez, the filmmaker alongside El Teatro Campesino, professional productions across the country and community-professional productions at home.

Cutting through the News: *Zoot Suit*

*Zoot Suit* is the logical culmination of all that Valdez had written before, combining elements of the *acto*, *mito* and *corrido* in a spectacular documentary play with music. Unlike any of his previous plays or *actos*, however, *Zoot Suit* is based on historical fact, not a current crisis.

By illuminating an actual incident in the history of Chicano-Anglo relations in Los Angeles, *Zoot Suit* does not have the immediacy of an *acto* about today's headlines. The politically aware will know that the police brutality and injustices rendered in this play are still happening; others may lose the point. Most significantly, this play illuminates events that had a major impact on the Chicano community of Los Angeles during World War II, incidents that are carefully ignored by most high school history books.

Like the *acto*, *Zoot Suit* exposes social ills in a presentational style. It is a play that is closer to the docu-drama form, owing more to Brecht than to Odets as the action reveals the events surrounding the infamous Sleepy Lagoon Murder Trial of 1942. By employing a narrator, Valdez is discarding a totally representational style in favor of this more direct contact with his audience. El Pachuco's almost constant presence, underscoring Henry's inner thoughts and tribulations, skillfully captivates the audience and serves as a continual commentator on the action.

Just as La Muerte did in *Soldado Razo*, El Pachuco will stop the action entirely in order to make a point, telling Henry (and the audience) to listen again when the judge rules that the "zoot haircuts will be retained throughout the trial for purposes of identification ... " It is a kind of "instant replay" that is only used once for maximum effect. Countering the figure of El Pachuco is the allegorical character of The Press which descends directly from the *acto* as well.

Like the *corrido*, there is a musical underscoring in *Zoot Suit*, placing the events in a historical context by employing the music of the period. El Pachuco sings some of the songs, as in a *corrido*, setting the mood through lyrics such as those that introduce the "Saturday Night Dance" in Act One, Scene Seven. While El Pachuco sings, the actors dance to the rhythms he creates, transforming from youthful fun to vengeful intensity gone wild by the end of the scene.

Some of the songs are original while others are traditional Latin or Anglo-American tunes, such as Glenn Miller's "In The Mood." Unlike the *corrido*, in which the music was played by live musicians, however, the music is pre-recorded. The choreography is also more like that of a musical comedy during the dance numbers, staged with historical authenticity to enhance the theatricality and further engage the audience.

Most importantly, this play places the Chicanos in a historical context that identifies them as "American," by showing that they, too, danced the swing as well as the mambo. Valdez is telling his audience that the Chicanos' taste for music can be as broad as anyone's. He is also revealing a cross-culturalism in the Chicanos' language, customs and myths. As Valdez so emphatically stated when this play first appeared, "this is an *American* play," attempting to dispel previous notions of separatism from the society at large. He is also reminding us that Americans populate The Americas, not just the U.S.

Valdez will not ignore his indigenous American ancestors, either, employing elements of the *mito* very subtly when the Pachuco is stripped of his zoot suit and remains covered only by an indigenous loincloth. This image suggests the sacrificial "god" of the Aztecs, stripped bare before his heart is offered to the cosmos. It is a stunning moment in the play, when the cocky Pachuco is reduced to bare nakedness in piercing contrast to his treasured "drapes." He may be naked, but he rises nobly in his bareness, dissolving into darkness. He will return, and he does.

The character of El Pachuco also represents the Aztec concept of the "*nahual,*" or other self as he comes to Henry's support during the solitary scene in prison. Henry is frightened, stripped emotionally bare in his cell and must rely on his imagination to recall the spirit of El Pachuco in order to survive. The strength he receives from his other self is determined by his ability to get in touch with his *nahual.*

The documentary form of the play is influenced by the Living Newspaper style, a documentary theater that exposed current events during the 1930's through dramatizations of those events. The use of newspapers for much of the set decoration, as well as the giant front page backdrop through which El Pachuco cuts his way at the top of the play is an effective metaphor for the all-pervading presence of the press. When Dolores Reyna hangs newspapers on the clothesline instead of actual laundry, the comment is complete.

Like most of Valdez's works, this play dramatizes a Chicano family in crisis. Henry Reyna is the central figure, but he is not alone. His *familia* is the link with the Chicano community in the audience, a continuing reminder that the Chicano *is* a community. Unlike the members of his family, however, Henry's alter-ego brings another dimension to this misunderstood figure. El Pachuco represents an inner attitude of defiance determining Henry's actions most of the time. El Pachuco is reminiscent at times of the Diablo and Diabla characters that permeated the *corridos*, motivating the characters' hapless choices as in Medieval morality plays.

El Pachuco's advice is not based on a moral choice, as in the *corridos*, but rather, on judgments of character. Mostly, El Pachuco represents the defiance against the system that identifies and determines the pachuco character. Sometimes, Henry does not take El Pachuco's advice, choosing instead to do what he thinks is right. At times, Henry has no choice, whether he listens to his alter-ego or to another part of himself, he will still get beaten. Interestingly, El Pachuco is sometimes more politically astute than the defendants themselves, allowing Henry an awareness his fellows do not have. In other instances, such as when the boys debate whether to confide in George, the boys' instincts are better for the whole and Henry must ignore El Pachuco's advice.

Now available in video, the motion picture of *Zoot Suit* is a vivid record of elements of the original stage production, because it was filmed in the Aquarius Theatre in Hollywood where it had played. The motion picture recreates and reconstructs the play. At times we watch the action unfolding as if we, too, are one of the hundreds sitting in the audience, watching the play; then suddenly the characters are in a realistic setting, as in a sound stage and we are enveloped in social realism. Just as the Pachuco continually reminds the audience that "this is just a play" in the stage version, the film also prompts us to remember that this is a *demonstration of actual events*, urging us to think about it as we watch the action moving back and forth between realities. *Zoot Suit* is also a rewriting of history, as is the central issue of the next play, *Bandido!*

Rewriting History: *Bandido!*

*Bandido!* is an exploration and expurgation of old clichés about the early California bandits. Valdez's intent is to alter history by demonstrating his version of the exploits of one Tiburcio Vásquez, the last man to be publicly hanged in California. The play is therefore didactic like an *acto* or a docu-drama but goes beyond those forms to become a "melodrama within a play." The playwright creates a construct in which audience sees Vásquez through different eyes. Vásquez is sympathetic when observed through the playwright's eyes and a stereotype when seen through history's distorted characterization.

The key to a successful production of *Bandido!* lies in an understanding of the satiric nature within the form of the play. Valdez's introductory notes state the challenge to director and actors most clearly: "The contrast of theatrical styles between the realism of the jail and the *trompe l'oleil* of the melodrama is purely intentional and part of the theme of the play ... their combined reality must be a metaphor—and not a facile cliché—of the Old West." The actors must therefore represent real people in the jail scenes and stereotypes of those characters and others in the melodramatic scenes.

Valdez is no stranger to stereotypes, as is illustrated in one of the playwright's most enduring *actos*, *Los vendidos* (*The Sellouts*), which he first wrote in 1967. In this very funny and popular *acto*, the playwright turns stereotyping around, making the audience reassess their attitudes about various Chicano and Mexican "types." We laugh, but also understand that the characteristics exposed are a reflection of Anglo perceptions and, yes, even sometimes our own biases as Chicanos. In both *Los vendidos* and *Bandido!* the playwright is portraying these characters *with a clear understanding that they are stereotypes*.

The characterization of Tiburcio Vásquez will vary according to the point of view of who is re-creating him on stage. If he is perceived as "real" in the jail scenes and a stereotype in the melodrama, the audience will distinguish the playwright's bias. They might also understand that their own biases come from the Hollywood stereotype of a "bandido." The actor, too, must delight in demonstrating the exaggeration, commenting upon his character even as he explores the exaggerations. This is a Brechtian acting technique, asking the actor to have an opinion about his character's actions and choices. Within the construct of the melodrama within the play, this can be effectively displayed.

Valdez clearly thinks of Vásquez as a social bandit, a gentleman who never killed anyone but who was forced into a life of crime by the Anglo invaders of his homeland. The playwright's goal here is to make Tiburcio Vásquez more than a romantic figure cloaked in evil, to present us with a reason for his actions instead of only the results.

Valdez's first play, *The Shrunken Head of Pancho Villa*, featured a young Chicano social bandit named Joaquín, symbolic of that better known "*bandido*," Joaquín Murrieta. Labelled a pachuco by the police, Joaquín steals from the rich to give to the poor. Neither Joaquín nor Vásquez are clearly understood by the authorities, but they fascinate their communities. As Pico says to Vásquez in the second act: "You've given all of us Californios twenty years of secret vicarious revenge."

*The Shrunken Head of Pancho Villa* offers hope for the community through unified social action, although the fate of *Bandido!*'s central figure is predetermined by history. Valdez knows that nobody can change the inequities of the past, but offers the suggestion that the future can be altered for the better, if misrepresentations of the Chicano are altered.

It is not that Valdez is attempting to completely whitewash Vásquez, either. When the Impresario asks him, "Are you comic or tragic, a good man or a bad man?" Vásquez responds: "All of them." To which the playwright might respond: "Aren't we *all* comic and tragic, good and bad?" It is perhaps the degree of evil that fascinates our playwright here, that degree always determined by who is being asked. Thus, the opposing views of this comic, tragic, good and bad man.

Valdez's style here is reminiscent of Luigi Pirandello, the Italian playwright and novelist whose works often turn reality inside out, leaving the reader or observer to ponder the nature of reality. Again, the Impresario states the obvious when he tells Vásquez,

"Reality and theater don't mix, sir," as we watch a play that is watching its own melodrama.

Above all, *Bandido!* is *theatrical*, offering the audience a delightful mixture of songs and dances that narrate the story as in the *corrido*, as well as characters that can be hissed or cheered as they would have been in the nineteenth century. Melodramas were extremely popular in Mexican theaters and *carpas* of the nineteenth and early twentieth centuries in this country, a fact that histories of U.S. theater neglect to report. In other words, the genre belongs to all of us.

What makes this play truly Valdezian, however, is the fact that it is not simply a play presenting us with villains and heroes in conflict. The conflict is the melodrama itself—the distortion the Impresario wants to present for profit. "The public will only buy tickets to savour the evil in your soul," he tells Vásquez, a truism that cannot be denied. It is more fun to watch the villain than the hero in an old fashioned melodrama. In Valdez's play, however, the villain is the Impresario, precursor to a legion of Hollywood producers. If history cannot be changed in either *Zoot Suit* or *Bandido!*, the next play looks to the future as the only hope.

Searching for Reality: *I Don't Have to Show You No Stinking Badges!*

The Valdezian questioning of reality reaches its pinnacle in *I Don't Have to Show You No Stinking Badges!* In this play the playwright presents us with a world that resembles a hall of mirrors, sometimes catching this picture, other times another view. One never knows for certain if what we are observing is real or an illusion. Instead of *Bandido!*'s "Melodrama within a play," we are now given a much more complex vision as Valdez explores the different levels of reality between the world of the stage and the realm of television. Like *Zoot Suit*, this play was written for a fully-equipped theater. Furthermore, it requires a realistic set, designed to look like a television studio setting, including video monitors hanging above the set to help the audience understand its transformation into a "live studio audience."

*Badges!* focuses on a middle-aged Chicano couple who have made their living as "King and Queen of the Hollywood Extras," playing non-speaking roles as maids, gardeners and the like. The couple have been very successful, having put their daughter through medical school and their son into Harvard. They have, in effect, accomplished the American Dream, with a suburban home complete with swimming pool, family room and microwave.

The major conflict arises when Sonny, alienated from the Ivy League reality, comes home from Harvard unexpectedly and announces that he has dropped-out. To make matters worse, he decides he will become a Hollywood actor. His parents, his girlfriend and the audience know his fate will be the same as his parents', playing "on the hyphen" in bit parts as thieves, drug addicts and rapists. Or will he? Like *Zoot Suit*, *I Don't Have to Show You No Stinking Badges!* does not give a distinct ending, but rather, leaves the solution up to the audience members to decide.

While *Zoot Suit* takes us from a presentational style to a representational style as a play, *Bandido!* explores both styles transferring from the "real" Tiburcio Vásquez to the melodramatic version: Vásquez through the eyes of Luis Valdez and Vásquez through the eyes of Hollywood and dime novels. *Badges!*, on the other hand, takes us on a much more involved journey, by remodeling the theater to look like an actual television studio with all of the paraphernalia of the medium. To add to the effect, when the action begins it begins as an actual taping in progress.

As soon as the action begins in *Badges!*, we begin to think of it as a play, performed in the style of a sit-com, not a taping, but rather, a *play*, until the final scene. This is when it becomes difficult to tell if what we are seeing is a part of Buddy and Consuelo's "sitcom," or if what we are witnessing is Sonny's "sit-com," or his "play," existing only in his mind.

Just as we saw Tiburcio Vásquez attempting to write the true version of his story, we now see Sonny Villa recreating his reality. "Is it real, or is it Memorex?" he asks, underscoring the premise of the play itself. Are we, the audience, a "live studio audience?" Are they really taping this? Did Sonny really rob a fast food restaurant? Questions mount as we watch Sonny's transformation, his angst or his drama.

What is real to Sonny is the fact that he must find himself within this society, the son of parents whose very existence has depended on portraying the marginalized "other." When Connie tells her son "I'd rather play a maid than *be* a maid," she makes a point but cannot escape the fact that maids are all she ever will play. Sonny knows that he, too, will not be given greater opportunities unless he writes and directs his own material, to his standards and not some Hollywood advertising agency's.

From melodrama-within-a-play to video-within-a-play, the playwright takes us on theatrical explorations that offer no easy solutions. The earliest *actos* offered clearly defined action: "Join the union," "Boycott grapes," etc. But what to do about distorted history or negative portrayals of Chicanos in the media? Can any of us, as Sonny Villa proposes to do, write and produce films and videos that cut through the biases of generations? Only a select few will ever have that opportunity and Luis Valdez is one of them.

Ultimately, these three plays present us with different aspects of the playwright himself. Valdez is the Pachuco of Broadway, the social bandit of the media and the brilliant student who will change the face of Hollywood portrayals of his people. He laughs at himself as much as at historians and Hollywood in these plays, exploding myths by creating others, transforming the way in which Chicanos and Chicanas view themselves within the context of this society. Each of these plays is finally about a search for identity through the playwright's quest for what is reality—past, present and future. "How can we know who we are," he continually asks, "if we do not know who we were?"

In the twenty-six years since he founded El Teatro Campesino, Luis Valdez has made an odyssey few theater artists in the United States can claim. This course could not have been predicted, yet the journey was inevitable. Yes, Valdez has gone from the fields of Delano to the migrant labor of a theater artist, to the even more complex world of Broadway and Hollywood. But he has never forgotten his roots, has never abandoned the beauty of his languages, both *Inglés* and Spanish.

Nor has he forgotten about his people's troubles and triumphs.

Valdez taught us to laugh at ourselves as we worked to improve the conditions in our barrios and in our nation. In particular, he urges us to embrace life with all of the vigor we can muster in the midst of seemingly insurmountable obstacles. May these plays inspire others to follow in his footsteps.

Jorge Huerta, Ph.D.
Professor of Theatre
University of California, San Diego

# ZOOT SUIT

# CHARACTERS

EL PACHUCO
HENRY REYNA

His Family:
ENRIQUE REYNA
DOLORES REYNA
LUPE REYNA
RUDY REYNA

His Friends:
GEORGE SHEARER
ALICE BLOOMFIELD

His Gang:
DELLA BARRIOS
SMILEY TORRES
JOEY CASTRO
TOMMY ROBERTS
ELENA TORRES
BERTHA VILLARREAL

The Downey Gang:
RAFAS
RAGMAN
HOBO
CHOLO
ZOOTER
GÜERA
HOBA
BLONDIE
LITTLE BLUE

Detectives:
LIEUTENANT EDWARDS
SERGEANT SMITH

The Press:
PRESS
CUB REPORTER
NEWSBOY

The Court:
JUDGE F.W. CHARLES

BAILIFF

The Prison:

GUARD

The Military:

BOSUN'S MATE
SAILORS
MARINE
SWABBIE
MANCHUKA
SHORE PATROLMAN

Others:

GIRLS
PIMP
CHOLO

# SETTING

*The giant facsimile of a newspaper front page serves as a drop curtain.*

*The huge masthead reads:  LOS ANGELES HERALD EX-PRESS Thursday, June 3, 1943.*

*A headline cries out: ZOOT-SUITER HORDES INVADE LOS ANGELES. US NAVY AND MARINES ARE CALLED IN.*

*Behind this are black drapes creating a place of haunting shadows larger than life.  The somber shapes and outlines of pachuco images hang subtly, black on black, against a back-ground of heavy fabric evoking memories and feelings like an old suit hanging forgotten in the depths of a closet somewhere, sometime ... Below this is a sweeping, curving place of levels and rounded corners with the hard, ingrained brilliance of countless spit shines, like the memory of a dance hall.*

# ACT ONE

## PROLOGUE

*A switchblade plunges through the newspaper. It slowly cuts a
rip to the bottom of the drop. To the sounds of "Perdido" by Duke
Ellington,* EL PACHUCO *emerges from the slit.* HE *adjusts his
clothing, meticulously fussing with his collar, suspenders, cuffs.* HE
*tends to his hair, combing back every strand into a long luxurious
ducktail, with infinite loving pains. Then* HE *reaches into the slit
and pulls out his coat and hat.* HE *dons them. His fantastic costume
is complete. It is a zoot suit.* HE *is transformed into the very image
of the pachuco myth, from his pork-pie hat to the tip of his four-foot
watch chain. Now* HE *turns to the audience. His three-soled shoes
with metal taps click-clack as* HE *proudly, slovenly, defiantly makes
his way downstage.* HE *stops and assumes a pachuco stance.*

PACHUCO:

¿Que le watcha a mis trapos, ese?
¿Sabe qué, carnal?
Estas garras me las planté porque
Vamos a dejarnos caer un play, ¿sabe?
(HE *crosses to center stage, models his clothes.*)
Watcha mi tacuche, ese. Aliviánese con mis calcos,
     tando,
lisa, tramos, y carlango, ese.
(*Pause.*)
Nel, sabe qué, usted está muy verdolaga. Como se me
     hace
que es puro square.
(EL PACHUCO *breaks character and addresses
the audience in perfect English.*)
Ladies and gentlemen
the play you are about to see
is a construct of fact and fantasy.
The Pachuco Style was an act in Life
and his language a new creation.
His will to be was an awesome force
eluding all documentation ...
A mythical, quizzical, frightening being

precursor of revolution
Or a piteous, hideous heroic joke
deserving of absolution?
I speak as an actor on the stage.
The Pachuco was existential
for he was an Actor in the streets
both profane and reverential.
It was the secret fantasy of every bato
in or out of the Chicanada
to put on a Zoot Suit and play the Myth
más chucote que la chingada.
(*Puts hat back on and turns.*)
¡Pos órale!
(*Music. The newspaper drop flies.* EL PACHUCO *begins
    his chuco stroll upstage, swinging his watch chain.*)


..................... 1. ZOOT SUIT .....................

*The scene is a barrio dance in the forties.* PACHUCOS *and*
PACHUCAS *in zoot suits and pompadours.*

*They are members of the* 38TH STREET GANG, *led by*
HENRY REYNA, *21, dark, Indian-looking, older than his years,
and* DELLA BARRIOS, *20, his girlfriend in miniskirt and finger-
tip coat. A* SAILOR *called* SWABBIE *dances with his girlfriend*
MANCHUKA *among the* COUPLES. *Movement. Animation.* EL
PACHUCO *sings.*

PACHUCO:

    PUT ON A ZOOT SUIT, MAKES YOU FEEL REAL
        ROOT
    LOOK LIKE A DIAMOND, SPARKLING, SHINING
    READY FOR DANCING
    READY FOR THE BOOGIE TONIGHT!
    (*The* COUPLES, *dancing, join the* PACHUCO *in
    exclaiming the last term of each line in the next verse.*)
    THE HEPCATS UP IN HARLEM WEAR THAT DRAPE
        SHAPE
    COMO LOS PACHUCONES DOWN IN L.A.
    WHERE HUISAS IN THEIR POMPADOURS LOOK
        REAL KEEN

ON THE DANCE FLOOR OF THE BALLROOMS
DONDE BAILAN SWING.

YOU BETTER GET HEP TONIGHT
AND PUT ON THAT ZOOT SUIT!

(*The* DOWNEY GANG, *a rival group of pachucos enters up-stage left. Their quick dance step becomes a challenge to* 38TH STREET.)

DOWNEY GANG: Downey ... ¡Rifa!
HENRY: (*Gesturing back.*) ¡Toma! (*The music is hot.* EL PA-CHUCO *slides across the floor and momentarily breaks the tension.* HENRY *warns* RAFAS, *the leader of the* DOWNEY GANG, *when* HE *sees him push his brother* RUDY.) ¡Rafas!
PACHUCO: (*Sings.*)

TRUCHA, ESE LOCO, VAMOS AL BORLO
WEAR THAT CARLANGO, TRAMOS Y TANDO
DANCE WITH YOUR HUISA
DANCE TO THE BOOGIE TONIGHT!

'CAUSE THE ZOOT SUIT IS THE STYLE IN CAL-
IFORNIA
TAMBIÉN EN COLORADO Y ARIZONA
THEY'RE WEARING THAT TACUCHE EN EL PASO
Y EN TODOS LOS SALONES DE CHICAGO

YOU BETTER GET HEP TONIGHT
AND PUT ON THAT ZOOT SUIT!

.................. 2. THE MASS ARRESTS ..................

*We hear a siren, then another, and another. It sounds like gangbusters. The dance is interrupted.* COUPLES *pause on the dance floor.*

PACHUCO: Trucha, la jura. ¡Pélenle! (*Pachucos start to run out, but* DETECTIVES *leap onstage with drawn guns. A* CUB REPORTER *takes flash pictures.*)
SGT. SMITH: Hold it right there, kids!

LT. EDWARDS: Everybody get your hands up!

RUDY: Watcha! This way! (RUDY *escapes with some others.*)

LT. EDWARDS: Stop or I'll shoot! (EDWARDS *fires his revolver
into the air. A number of pachucos and their girlfriends
freeze. The cops round them up.* SWABBIE, *an American
sailor, and* MANCHUKA, *a Japanese-American dancer,
are among them.*)

SGT. SMITH: ¡Ándale! (*Sees* SWABBIE.) You! Get out of here.

SWABBIE: What about my girl?

SGT. SMITH: Take her with you. (SWABBIE *and* MANCHUKA
*exit.*)

HENRY: What about my girl?

LT. EDWARDS: No dice, Henry. Not this time. Back in line.

SGT. SMITH: Close it up!

LT. EDWARDS: Spread! (*The* PACHUCOS *turn upstage in a line
with their hands up. The sirens fade and give way to
the sound of a teletype. The* PACHUCOS *turn and form
a lineup, and the* PRESS *starts shooting pictures as* HE
*speaks.*)

PRESS: The City of the Angels, Monday, August 2, 1942. The Los
Angeles Examiner, Headline:

THE LINEUP: (*In chorus.*)    Death Awakens Sleepy Lagoon
(*Breath.*) LA Shaken by Lurid "Kid" Murder.

PRESS: The City of the Angels, Monday, August 2, 1942. The Los
Angeles Times Headline:

THE LINEUP: One Killed, Ten Hurt in Boy Wars: (*Breath.*) Mexican Boy Gangs Operating Within City.

PRESS: The City of the Angels, August 2, 1942. Los Angeles Herald Express Headline:

THE LINEUP: Police Arrest Mexican Youths. Black Widow Girls
in Boy Gangs.

PRESS: The City of the Angels ...

PACHUCO: (*Sharply.*) El Pueblo de Nuestra Señora la Reina de
los Ángeles de Porciúncula, pendejo.

PRESS: (*Eyeing the* PACHUCO *cautiously.*) The Los Angeles Daily
News Headline:

BOYS IN THE LINEUP: Police Nab 300 in Roundup.

GIRLS IN THE LINEUP: Mexican Girls Picked Up in Arrests.

LT. EDWARDS: Press Release, Los Angeles Police Department:
A huge showup of nearly 300 boys and girls rounded up
by the police and sheriff's deputies will be held tonight
at eight o'clock in Central Jail at First and Hill Street.
Victims of assault, robbery, purse snatching, and similar

crimes are asked to be present for the identification of suspects.

PRESS: Lieutenant ... ? (EDWARDS *poses as the* PRESS *snaps a picture.*)

LT. EDWARDS: Thank you.

PRESS: Thank you. (SMITH *gives a signal, and the lineup moves back, forming a straight line in the rear, leaving* HENRY *up front by himself.*)

LT. EDWARDS: Move! Turn! Out! (*As the rear line moves off to the left following* EDWARDS, SMITH *takes* HENRY *by the arm and pulls him downstage, shoving him to the floor.*)

..................... 3. PACHUCO YO .....................

SGT. SMITH: Okay, kid, you wait here till I get back. Think you can do that? Sure you can. You pachucos are regular tough guys. (SMITH *exits.* HENRY *sits up on the floor.* EL PACHUCO *comes forward.*)

HENRY: Bastards. (HE *gets up and paces nervously. Pause.*) ¿Ese? ¿Ese?

PACHUCO: (*Behind him.*) ¿Qué pues, nuez?

HENRY: (*Turning.*) Where the hell you been, ese?

PACHUCO: Checking out the barrio. Qué desmadre, ¿no?

HENRY: What's going on, ese? This thing is big.

PACHUCO: The city's cracking down on pachucos, carnal. Don't you read the newspapers? They're screaming for blood.

HENRY: All I know is they got nothing on me. I didn't do anything.

PACHUCO: You're Henry Reyna, ese—Hank Reyna! The snarling juvenile delinquent. The zootsuiter. The bitter young pachuco gang leader of 38th Street. That's what they got on you.

HENRY: I don't like this, ese. (*Suddenly intense.*) I DON'T LIKE BEING LOCKED UP!

PACHUCO: Calmantes montes, chicas patas. Haven't I taught you to survive? Play it cool.

HENRY: They're going to do it again, ese! They're going to charge me with some phony rap and keep me until they make something stick.

PACHUCO: So what's new?

HENRY: (*Pause.*) I'm supposed to report for the Navy tomorrow. (THE PACHUCO *looks at him with silent disdain.*) You don't want me to go, do you?

PACHUCO: Stupid move, carnal.

HENRY: (*Hurt and angered by* PACHUCO*'s disapproval.*) I've got to do something.

PACHUCO: Then hang tough. Nobody's forcing you to do shit.

HENRY: I'm forcing me, ese—ME, you understand?

PACHUCO: Muy patriotic, eh?

HENRY: Yeah.

PACHUCO: Off to fight for your country.

HENRY: Why not?

PACHUCO: Because this ain't your country. Look what's happening all around you. The Japs have sewed up the Pacific. Rommel is kicking ass in Egypt but the Mayor of L.A. has declared all-out war on Chicanos. On you! ¿Te curas?

HENRY: Órale.

PACHUCO: Qué mamada, ¿no? Is that what you want to go out and die for? Wise up. These bastard paddy cops have it in for you. You're a marked man. They think you're the enemy.

HENRY: (*Refusing to accept it.*) Screw them bastard cops!

PACHUCO: And as soon as the Navy finds out you're in jail again, ya estuvo, carnal. Unfit for military duty because of your record. Think about it.

HENRY: (*Pause.*) You got a frajo?

PACHUCO: Simón. (HE *pulls out a cigarette, hands it to* HENRY, *lights it for him.* HENRY *is pensive.*)

HENRY: (*Smokes, laughs ironically.*) I was all set to come back a hero, see? Me la rayo. For the first time in my life I really thought Hank Reyna was going someplace.

PACHUCO: Forget the war overseas, carnal. Your war is on the homefront.

HENRY: (*With new resolve.*) What do you mean?

PACHUCO: The barrio needs you, carnal. Fight back! Stand up to them with some style. Show the world a Chicano has balls. Hang tough. You can take it. Remember, Pachuco Yo!

HENRY: (*Assuming the style.*) Con safos, carnal.

................ 4. THE INTERROGATION ................

*The* PRESS *enters, followed by* EDWARDS *and* SMITH.

PRESS: (*To the audience.*) Final Edition; The Los Angeles Daily
News. The police have arrested twenty-two members of
the 38th Street Gang, pending further investigation of various charges.

LT. EDWARDS: Well, son, I was hoping I wouldn't see you in here
again.

HENRY: Then why did you arrest me?

LT. EDWARDS: Come on, Hank, you know why you're here.

HENRY: Yeah. I'm a Mexican.

LT. EDWARDS: Don't give me that. How long have I known you?
Since '39?

HENRY: Yeah, when you got me for stealing a car, remember?

LT. EDWARDS: All right. That was a mistake. I didn't know it
was your father's car. I tried to make it up to you. Didn't
I help you set up the youth club?

SGT. SMITH: They turned it into a gang, Lieutenant. Everything
they touch turns to shit.

LT. EDWARDS: I remember a kid just a couple of years back.
Head boy at the Catholic Youth Center. His idea of fun
was going to the movies. What happened to that nice kid,
Henry?

PRESS: He's "Gone With The Wind," trying to look like Clark
Gable.

SGT. SMITH: Now he thinks he's Humphrey Bogart.

PACHUCO: So who are you, puto? Pat O'Brien?

LT. EDWARDS: This is the wrong time to be anti-social, son. This
country's at war, and we're under strict orders to crack
down on all malcontents.

SGT. SMITH: Starting with all pachucos and draft dodgers.

HENRY: I ain't no draft dodger.

LT. EDWARDS: I know you're not. I heard you got accepted by
the Navy. Congratulations. When do you report?

HENRY: Tomorrow?

SGT. SMITH: Tough break!

LT. EDWARDS: It's still not too late, you know. I could still release
you in time to get sworn in.

HENRY: If I do what?

LT. EDWARDS: Tell me, Henry, what do you know about a big gang fight last Saturday night, out at Sleepy Lagoon?

PACHUCO: Don't tell 'em shit.

HENRY: Which Sleepy Lagoon?

LT. EDWARDS: You mean there's more than one? Come on, Hank, I know you were out there. I've got a statement from your friends that says you were beaten up. Is that true? Were you and your girl attacked?

HENRY: I don't know anything about it. Nobody's ever beat me up.

SGT. SMITH: That's a lie and you know it. Thanks to your squealer friends, we've got enough dope on you to indict for murder right now.

HENRY: Murder?

SGT. SMITH: Yeah, murder. Another greaser named José Williams.

HENRY: I never heard of the bato.

SGT. SMITH: Yeah, sure.

LT. EDWARDS: I've been looking at your record, Hank. Petty theft, assault, burglary, and now murder. Is that what you want? The gas chamber? Play square with me. Give me a statement as to what happened at the Lagoon, and I'll go to bat for you with the Navy. I promise you.

PACHUCO: If that ain't a line of gabacho bullshit, I don't know what is.

LT. EDWARDS: Well?

PACHUCO: Spit in his pinche face.

SGT. SMITH: Forget it, Lieutenant. You can't treat these animals like people.

LT. EDWARDS: Shut up! I'm thinking of your family, Hank. Your old man would be proud to see you in the Navy. One last chance, son. What do you say?

HENRY: I ain't your son, cop.

LT. EDWARDS: All right, Reyna, have it your way. (EDWARDS *and* PRESS *exit.*)

PACHUCO: You don't deserve it, ese, but your going to get it anyway.

SGT. SMITH: All right, muchacho, it's just me and you now. I hear tell you pachucos wear these monkey suits as a kind of armor. Is that right? How's it work? This is what you zooters need—a little old-fashioned discipline.

HENRY: Screw you, flatfoot.

SGT. SMITH: You greasy son of a bitch. What happened at the Sleepy Lagoon? Talk! Talk! Talk! (SMITH *beats* HENRY *with a rubber sap.* HENRY *passes out and falls to the floor, with his hands still handcuffed behind his back.* DO-LORES *his mother appears in a spot upstage, as he falls.*)

DOLORES: Henry! (*Lights change. Four* PACHUCO COUPLES *enter, dancing a 40's pasodoble (two-step) around* HENRY *on the floor, as they swing in a clothesline of newspaper sheets. Music.*)

PACHUCO:

Get up and escape, Henry ...
leave reality behind
with your buenas garras
muy chamberlain
escape through the barrio streets of your mind
through a neighborhood of memories
all chuckhole lined
and the love
and the pain
as fine as wine ...
(HENRY *sits up, seeing his mother* DOLORES *folding newspaper sheets like clothes on a clothesline.*)


DOLORES: Henry?

PACHUCO: It's a lifetime ago, last Saturday night ... before Sleepy Lagoon and the big bad fight.

DOLORES: Henry!

PACHUCO: Tu mamá, carnal. (HE *recedes into the background.*)

DOLORES: (*At the clothesline.*) Henry, ¿hijo? Ven a cenar.

HENRY: (*Gets up off the floor.*) Sorry, jefita, I'm not hungry. Besides, I got to pick up Della. We're late for the dance.

DOLORES: Dance? In this heat? Don't you muchachos ever think of anything else? God knows I suffer la pena negra seeing you go out every night.

HENRY: This isn't just any night, jefa. It's my last chance to use my tacuche.

DOLORES: Tacuche? Pero tu padre ...

HENRY: (*Revealing a stubborn streak.*) I know what mi 'apá said, 'amá. I'm going to wear it anyway.

DOLORES: (*Sighs, resigns herself.*) Mira, hijo. I know you work hard for your clothes. And I know how much they mean

to you. Pero por diosito santo, I just don't know what you
see en esa cochinada de "soot zoot."

HENRY: (*Smiling.*) Drapes, 'amá, we call them drapes.

DOLORES: (*Scolding playfully.*) Ay sí, drapes, muy funny, ¿verdad? And what do the police call them, eh? They've put
you in jail so many times. ¿Sabes qué? I'm going to send
them all your clothes!

HENRY: A qué mi 'amá. Don't worry. By this time next week,
I'll be wearing my Navy blues. Okay?

DOLORES: Bendito sea Dios. I still can't believe you're going off
to war. I almost wish you were going back to jail.

HENRY: ¡Órale! (LUPE REYNA, *16, enters dressed in a short skirt
and baggy coat. She is followed by* DELLA BARRIOS, *17,
dressed more modestly.* LUPE *hides behind a newspaper
sheet on the line.*)

LUPE: Hank! Let's go, carnal. Della's here.

HENRY: Della ... Órale, esa. What are you doing here? I told
you I was going to pick you up at your house.

DELLA: You know how my father gets.

HENRY: What happened?

DELLA: I'll tell you later.

DOLORES: Della, hija, buenas noches. How pretty you look.

DELLA: Buenas noches. (DOLORES *hugs* DELLA, *then spots*
LUPE *hiding behind the clothesline.*)

DOLORES: (*To* LUPE.) ¿Oye y tú? What's wrong with you? What
are you doing back there.

LUPE: Nothing, 'amá.

DOLORES: Well, come out then.

LUPE: We're late, 'amá.

DOLORES: Come out, te digo. (LUPE *comes out exposing her
extremely short skirt.* DOLORES *gasps.*) ¡Válgame Dios!
Guadalupe, are you crazy? Why bother to wear anything?

LUPE: Ay, 'amá, it's the style. Short skirt and fingertip coat. Huh,
Hank?

HENRY: Uh, yeah, 'amá.

DOLORES: ¿Oh sí? And how come Della doesn't get to wear the
same style?

HENRY: No ... that's different. No, chale.

ENRIQUE: (*Off.*) ¡VIEJA!

DOLORES: Ándale. Go change before your father sees you.

ENRIQUE: I'm home. (*Coming into the scene.*) Buenas noches,
everybody. (*All respond.* ENRIQUE *sees* LUPE.) ¡Ay, jijo!
Where's the skirt?!

LUPE: It's here.

ENRIQUE: Where's the rest of it?

DOLORES: She's going to the dance.

ENRIQUE: ¿Y a mí qué me importa? Go and change those clothes. Ándale.

LUPE: Please, 'apá?

ENRIQUE: No, señorita.

LUPE: Chihuahua, I don't want to look like a square.

ENRIQUE: ¡Te digo que no! I will not have my daughter looking like a ...

DOLORES: Like a puta ... I mean, a pachuca.

LUPE: (*Pleading for help.*) Hank ...

HENRY: Do what they say, sis.

LUPE: But you let Henry wear his drapes.

ENRIQUE: That's different. He's a man. Es hombre.

DOLORES: Sí, that's different. You men are all alike. From such a stick, such a splinter. De tal palo, tal astillota.

ENRIQUE: Natural, muy natural, and look how he came out. ¡Bien macho! Like his father. ¿Verdad, m'ijo?

HENRY: If you say so, jefito.

ENRIQUE: (*To* DELLA.) Buenas noches.

DELLA: Buenas noches.

HENRY: 'Apá, this is Della Barrios.

ENRIQUE: Mira, mira ... So this is your new girlfriend, eh? Muy bonita. Quite a change from the last one.

DOLORES: Ay, señor.

ENRIQUE: It's true. What was her name?

DELLA: Bertha?

ENRIQUE: That's the one. The one with the tattoo.

DOLORES: Este hombre. We have company.

ENRIQUE: That reminds me. I invited the compadres to the house mañana.

DOLORES: ¿Que qué?

ENRIQUE: I'm buying a big keg of cerveza to go along with the menudo.

DOLORES: Oye, ¿cuál menudo?

ENRIQUE: (*Cutting him off.*) ¡Qué caray, mujer! It isn't every day a man's son goes off to fight for his country. I should know. Della, m'ija, when I was in the Mexican Revolution, I was not even as old as my son is.

DOLORES: N'ombre, don't start with your revolution. We'll be here all night.

HENRY: Yeah, jefe, we've got to go.

LUPE: (*Comes forward. She has rolled down her skirt.*) 'Apá, is this better?

ENRIQUE: Bueno. And you leave it that way.

HENRY: Órale, pues. It's getting late. Where's Rudy?

LUPE: He's still getting ready. Rudy! (RUDY REYNA, *19, comes downstage in an old suit made into a tachuche.*)

RUDY: Let's go everybody. I'm ready.

ENRIQUE: Oye, oye, ¿y tú? What are you doing with my coat?

RUDY: It's my tachuche, 'apá.

ENRIQUE: ¡Me lleva la chingada!

DOLORES: Enrique ... ¡por el amor de Dios!

ENRIQUE: (*To* HENRY.) You see what you're doing? First that one and now this one. (*To* RUDY.) Hijo, don't go out like that. Por favor. You look like an idiot, pendejo.

RUDY: Órale, Hank. Don't I look all right?

HENRY: Nel, ese, you look fine. Watcha. Once I leave for the service, you can have my tachuche. Then you can really be in style. ¿Cómo la ves?

RUDY: Chale. Thanks, carnal, but if I don't join the service myself, I'm gonna get my own tachuche.

HENRY: You sure? I'm not going to need it where I'm going. ¿Tú sabes?

RUDY: Are you serious?

HENRY: Simón.

RUDY: I'll think about it.

HENRY: Pos, no hay pedo, ese.

ENRIQUE: ¿Cómo que pedo? Nel, ¿Simón? Since when did we stop speaking Spanish in this house? Have you no respect?

DOLORES: Muchachos, muchachos, go to your dance. (HENRY *starts upstage.*)

HENRY: Buenas noches ... (ENRIQUE *holds out his hand.* HENRY *stops, looks, and then returns to kiss his father's hand. Then* HE *moves to kiss his* MOTHER *and* RUDY *in turn kisses* ENRIQUE's *hand.* ENRIQUE *says "Buenas Noches" to each of his sons.*)

HENRY: Órale, we'd better get going ... (*General "goodbyes" from everybody.*)

ENRIQUE: (*As* RUDY *goes past him.*) Henry! Don't let your brother drink beer.

RUDY: Ay, 'apá. I can take care of myself.

DOLORES: I'll believe that when I see it. (SHE *kisses him on the nose.*)

LUPE: Ahí te watcho, 'amá.

ENRIQUE: ¿Que qué?

LUPE: I mean, I'll see you later. (HENRY, DELLA, LUPE *and* RUDY *turn upstage. Music starts.*)

ENRIQUE: Mujer, why didn't you let me talk?

DOLORES: (*Sighing.*) Talk, señor, talk all you want. I'm listening. (ENRIQUE *and* DOLORES *exit up right.* RUDY *and* LUPE *exit up left. Lights change. We hear hot dance music.* HENRY *and* DELLA *dance at center stage.* EL PACHUCO *sings.*)

PACHUCO:

> CADA SÁBADO EN LA NOCHE
> YO ME VOY A BORLOTEAR
> CON MI LINDA PACHUCONA
> LAS CADERAS A MENEAR
>
> ELLA LE HACE MUY DE AQUELLAS
> CUANDO EMPIEZA A GUARACHAR
> AL COMPÁS DE LOS TIMBALES
> YO ME SIENTO PETATEAR

(*From upstage right, three pachucos now enter in a line, moving to the beat. They are* JOEY CASTRO, *17;* SMILEY TORRES, *23; and* TOMMY ROBERTS, *19, Anglo. They all come downstage left in a diagonal.*)

> LOS CHUCOS SUAVES BAILAN RUMBA
> BAILAN LA RUMBA Y LE ZUMBAN
> BAILAN GUARACHA SABROSÓN
> EL BOTECITO Y EL DANZÓN!

(*Chorus repeats, the music fades.* HENRY *laughs and happily embraces* DELLA.)

...................... 5. THE PRESS ......................

*Lights change.* EL PACHUCO *escorts* DELLA *off right.* THE PRESS *appears at upstage center.*

PRESS: Los Angeles Times: August 8, 1942.

*A* NEWSBOY *enters, lugging in two more bundles of newspapers, hawking them as he goes.* PEOPLE *of various walks of life*

*enter at intervals and buy newspapers. They arrange themselves in
the background reading.*

NEWSBOY: EXTRA! EXTRAAA! READ ALL ABOUT IT.
SPECIAL SESSION OF L.A. COUNTY GRAND
JURY CONVENES. D.A. CHARGES CONSPIRACY IN
SLEEPY LAGOON MURDER. EXTRAAA! (*A* CUB RE-
PORTER *emerges and goes to the* PRESS, *as* LIEU-
TENANT EDWARDS *enters.*)

CUB REPORTER: Hey, here comes Edwards! (EDWARDS *is be-
seiged by the* PRESS, *joined by* ALICE BLOOMFIELD,
*26, a woman reporter.*)

PRESS: How about it, Lieutenant? What's the real scoop on the
Sleepy Lagoon? Sex, violence ...

CUB REPORTER: Marijuana?

NEWSBOY: Read all about it! Mexican Crime Wave Engulfs L.A.

LT. EDWARDS: Slums breed crime, fellas. That's your story.

ALICE: Lieutenant. What exactly is the Sleepy Lagoon?

CUB REPORTER: A great tune by Harry James, doll. Wanna
dance? (ALICE *ignores the* CUB.)

LT. EDWARDS: It's a reservoir. An old abandoned gravel pit, really. It's on a ranch between here and Long Beach. Serves
as a swimming hole for the younger Mexican kids.

ALICE: Because they're not allowed to swim in the public plunges?

PRESS: What paper are you with, lady? The Daily Worker?

LT. EDWARDS: It also doubles as a sort of lovers' lane at night—
which is why the gangs fight over it. Now they've finally
murdered somebody.

NEWSBOY: EXTRA! EXTRA! ZOOT-SUITED GOONS OF
SLEEPY LAGOON!

LT. EDWARDS: But we're not going to mollycoddle these young-
sters any more. And you can quote me on that.

PRESS: One final question, Lieutenant. What about the 38th
Street Gang—weren't you the first to arrest Henry Reyna?

LT. EDWARDS: I was. And I noticed right away the kid had great
leadership potential. However ...

PRESS: Yes?

LT. EDWARDS: You can't change the spots on a leopard.

PRESS: Thank you, sir. (PEOPLE *with newspapers crush them and
throw them down as they exit.* EDWARDS *turns and exits.*
ALICE *turns towards* HENRY *for a moment.*)

NEWSBOY: EXTRA, EXTRA. READ ALL ABOUT THE MEX-
ICAN BABY GANGSTERS. EXTRA, EXTRA.

THE PRESS *and* CUB REPORTER *rush out happily to file
their stories. The* NEWSBOY *leaves, hawking his papers.* ALICE
*exits, with determination. Far upstage,* ENRIQUE *enters with a
rolling garbage can.* HE *is a street sweeper. During the next scene*
HE *silently sweeps up the newspapers, pausing at the last to read
one of the news stories.*


............... 6. THE PEOPLE'S LAWYER ...............


JOEY: ¡Chale, ese, chale! Qué pinche agüite.
SMILEY: Mexican Baby Gangsters?!
TOMMY: Zoot-suited goons! I knew it was coming. Every time
    the D.A. farts, they throw us in the can.
SMILEY: Pos, qué chingados, Hank. I can't believe this. Are they
    really going to pin us with a murder rap? I've got a wife
    and kid, man!
JOEY: Well, there's one good thing anyway. I bet you know that
    we've made the headlines. Everybody knows we got the
    toughest gang in town.
TOMMY: Listen to this, pip squeak. The biggest heist he ever
    pulled was a Tootsie Roll.
JOEY: (*Grabbing his privates.*) Here's your Tootsie Roll, ese.
TOMMY: What, that? Get my microscope, Smiley.
JOEY: Why don't you come here and take a little bite, joto.
TOMMY: Joto? Who you calling a joto, maricón?
JOEY: You, white boy. Did I ever tell you, you got the finest little
    duck ass in the world.
TOMMY: No, you didn't tell me that, culero. (JOEY *and* TOMMY
    *start sparring.*)
SMILEY: (*Furious.*) Why don't you batos knock it off?
HENRY: (*Cool.*) Cálmenla.
SMILEY: ¡Pinches chavalos! (*The batos stop.*)
JOEY: We're just cabuliando, ese.
TOMMY: Simón, ese. Horsing around. (*He gives* JOEY *a final
    punch.*)
SMILEY: (*With deep self-pity.*) I'm getting too old for this pedo,
    Hank. All this farting around con esos chavalillos.
HENRY: Relax, carnal. No te agüites.
SMILEY: You and me have been through a lot, Hank. Parties,
    chingazos, jail. When you said let's join the pachucada, I
    joined the pachucada. You and me started the 38th, bato.

I followed you even after my kid was born, but what now, carnal? This pinche pedo is serious.

TOMMY: He's right, Hank. They indicted the whole gang.

JOEY: Yeah, you know the only one who ain't here is Rudy. (HENRY *turns sharply.*) He was at the Sleepy Lagoon too, ese. Throwing chingazos.

HENRY: Yeah, but the cops don't know that, do they? Unless one of us turned stoolie.

JOEY: Hey, ese, don't look at me. They beat the shit out of me, but that's all they got. Shit.

TOMMY: That's all you got to give. (*Laughs.*)

HENRY: Okay! Let's keep it that way. I don't want my carnalillo pulled into this. And if anybody asks about him, you batos don't know nothing. You get me?

SMILEY: Simón.

TOMMY: Crazy.

JOEY: (*Throwing his palms out.*) Say, Jackson, I'm cool. You know that.

HENRY: There's not a single paddy we can trust.

TOMMY: Hey, ese, what about me?

HENRY: You know what I mean.

TOMMY: No, I don't know what you mean. I'm here with the rest of yous.

JOEY: Yeah, but you'll be the first one out, cabrón.

TOMMY: Gimme a break, maníaco. ¡Yo soy pachuco!

HENRY: Relax, ese. Nobody's getting personal with you. Don't I let you take out my carnala? Well, don't I?

TOMMY: Simón.

HENRY: That's because you respect my family. The rest of them paddies are after our ass.

PACHUCO: Talk about paddies, ese, you got company. (GEORGE SHEARER *enters upstage right and comes down. HE is a middle-aged lawyer, strong and athletic, but with the slightly frazzled look of a people's lawyer.*)

GEORGE: Hi, boys.

HENRY: Trucha!

GEORGE: My name is George Shearer. I've been retained by your parents to handle your case. Can we sit and talk for a little bit? (*Pause. The* BOYS *eye* GEORGE *suspiciously. HE slides a newspaper bundle a few feet upstage.*)

PACHUCO: Better check him out, ese. He looks like a cop.

HENRY: (*To the* GUYS, *sotto voce.*) Pónganse al alba. Este me huele a chota.

GEORGE: What was that? Did you say I could sit down? Thank you. (HE *pulls a bundle upstage.* HE *sits.*) Okay, let me get your names straight first. Who's José Castro?

JOEY: Right here, ese. What do you want to know?

GEORGE: We'll get to that. Ismael Torres?

SMILEY: (*Deadpan.*) That's me. But they call me Smiley.

GEORGE: (*A wide grin.*) Smiley? I see. You must be Thomas Roberts.

TOMMY: I ain't Zoot Suit Yokum.

GEORGE: Which means you must be Henry Reyna.

HENRY: What if I am. Who are you?

GEORGE: I already told you, my name's George Shearer. Your parents asked me to come.

HENRY: Oh yeah? Where did they get the money for a lawyer?

GEORGE: I'm a People's Lawyer, Henry.

SMILEY: People's Lawyer?

JOEY: Simón, we're people.

TOMMY: At least they didn't send no animal's lawyer.

HENRY: So what does that mean? You doing this for free or what?

GEORGE: (*Surprise turning to amusement.*) I try not to work for free, if I can help it, but I do sometimes. In this case, I expect to be paid for my services.

HENRY: So who's paying you? For what? And how much?

GEORGE: Hey, hey, hold on there. I'm supposed to ask the questions. You're the one going on trial, not me.

PACHUCO: Don't let him throw you, ese.

GEORGE: I sat in on part of the Grand Jury. It was quite a farce, wasn't it? Murder one indictment and all.

SMILEY: You think we stand a chance?

GEORGE: There's always a chance, Smiley. That's what trials are for.

PACHUCO: He didn't answer your question, ese.

HENRY: You still didn't answer my question, mister. Who's paying you? And how much?

GEORGE: (*Getting slightly peeved.*) Well, Henry, it's really none of your damned business. (*The* BOYS *react.*) But for whatever it's worth, I'll tell you a little story. The first murder case I ever tried, and won incidentally, was for a Filipino. I was paid exactly three dollars and fifty cents plus a pack of Lucky Strike cigarettes, and a note for a thousand dollars—never redeemed. Does that answer your question?

HENRY: How do we know you're really a lawyer?

GEORGE: How do I know you're Henry Reyna? What do you really mean, son? Do you think I'm a cop?

HENRY: Maybe.

GEORGE: What are you trying to hide from the cops? Murder? (*The* BOYS *react.*) All right! Aside from your parents, I've been called into this case by a citizens committee that's forming in your behalf, Henry. In spite of evidence to the contrary, there are some people out there who don't want to see you get the shaft.

HENRY: ¿Sabes qué, mister? Don't do us any favors.

GEORGE: (*Starting to leave.*) All right, you want another lawyer? I'll talk to the Public Defender's office.

JOEY: (*Grabbing his briefcase.*) Hey, wait a minute, ese. Where are you going?

TOMMY: De cincho se le va a volar la tapa.

JOEY: Nel, este bolillo no sabe nada.

GEORGE: (*Exploding.*) All right, kids, cut the crap!

SMILEY: (*Grabs his briefcase and crosses to* HENRY.) Let's give him a break, Hank. (SMILEY *hands the briefcase to* GEORGE.)

GEORGE: Thank you. (HE *starts to exit. Stops.*) You know, you're making a big mistake. I wonder if you know who your friends are? You boys are about to get a mass trial. You know what that is? Well, it's a new one on me too. The Grand Jury has indicted you all on the same identical crime. Not just you four. The whole so-called 38th Street Gang. And you know who the main target is? You, Henry, because they're saying you're the ringleader. (*Looks around at the* GUYS.) And I suppose you are. But you're leading your buddies here down a dead-end street. The D.A.'s coming after you, son, and he's going to put you and your whole gang right into the gas chamber. (GEORGE *turns to leave.* SMILEY *panics.* JOEY *and* TOMMY *react with him.*)

SMILEY/JOEY/TOMMY: (*All together.*) Gas chamber! But we didn't do nothing! We're innocent!

HENRY: ¡Cálmenla! (*The batos stop in their tracks.*) Okay. Say we believe you're a lawyer, what does that prove? The press has already tried and convicted us. Think you can change that?

GEORGE: Probably not. But then, public opinion comes and goes, Henry. What matters is our system of justice. I believe it works, however slowly the wheels may grind. It could

be a long uphill fight, fellas, but we can make it. I know
we can. I've promised your parents the best defense I'm
capable of. The question is, Henry, will you trust me?

HENRY: Why should I? You're a gringo.

GEORGE: (*Calmly, deliberately.*) ¿Cómo sabes?

TOMMY: (*Shocked.*) Hey, you speak Spanish?

GEORGE: Más o menos.

JOEY: You mean you understood us a while ago?

GEORGE: More or less.

JOEY: (*Embarrassed.*) ¡Híjole, qué gacho, ese!

GEORGE: Don't worry. I'm not much on your pachuco slang.
The problem seems to be that I look like an Anglo to you.
What if I were to tell you that I had Spanish blood in my
veins? That my roots go back to Spain, just like yours?
What if I'm an Arab? What if I'm a Jew? What difference
does it make? The question is, will you let me help you?
(*Pause.* HENRY *glances at the* PACHUCO.)

PACHUCO: ¡Chale!

HENRY: (*Pause.*) Okay!

SMILEY: Me too!

JOEY: Same here!

TOMMY: ¡Órale!

GEORGE: (*Eagerly.*) Okay! Let's go to work. I want to know exactly what happened right from the beginning. (GEORGE
*sits down and opens his briefcase.*)

HENRY: Well, I think the pedo really started at the dance last
Saturday night ... (*El* PACHUCO *snaps his fingers and
we hear dance music. Lights change.* GEORGE *exits.*)

··········· 7. THE SATURDAY NIGHT DANCE ···········

SWABBIE *and* MANCHUKA *come running onstage as the
barrio dance begins to take shape.* HENRY *and the batos
move upstage to join other* PACHUCOS *and* PACHUCAS *coming in.* HENRY *joins* DELLA BARRIOS; JOEY *teams up with*
BERTHA VILLARREAL, TOMMY *picks up* LUPE REYNA; *and*
SMILEY *escorts his wife* ELENA TORRES. *They represent the*
38TH STREET *neighborhood. Also entering the dance comes the*
DOWNEY GANG, *looking mean.* RUDY *stands upstage, in the
background, drinking a bottle of beer.* EL PACHUCO *sings.*

PACHUCO:

CUANDO SALGO YO A BAILAR
YO ME PONGO MUY CATRÍN
LAS HUISITAS TODAS GRITAN, DADDY
VAMOS A BAILAR EL SWING!


(*The* COUPLES *dance. A lively swing number. The music comes to a natural break and shifts into a slow number.* BERTHA *approaches* HENRY *and* DELLA *downstage on the dance floor.*)

BERTHA: Ese, ¡surote! How about a dance for old time's sake? No te hagas gacho.
HENRY: (*Slow dancing with* DELLA.) Sorry, Bertha.
BERTHA: Is this your new huisa? This little fly chick?
DELLA: Listen, Bertha ...
HENRY: (*Stops her.*) Chale. She's just jealous. Beat it, Bertha.
BERTHA: Beat it yourself. Mira. You got no hold on me, cabrón. Not any more. I'm as free as a bird.
SMILEY: (*Coming up.*) Ese, Hank, that's the Downey Gang in the corner. You think they're looking for trouble?
HENRY: There's only a couple of them.
BERTHA: That's all we need.
SMILEY: Want me to alert the batos?
HENRY: Nel, be cool.
BERTHA: Be cool? Huy, yu, yui. Forget it, Smiley. Since he joined the Navy, this bato forgot the difference between being cool and being cool-O. (*She laughs and turns but* HENRY *grabs her angrily by the arm.* BERTHA *pulls free and walks away cool and tough. The music changes and the beat picks up.* EL PACHUCO *sings as the* COUPLES *dance.*)
PACHUCO:

CUANDO VOY AL VACILÓN
Y ME METO YO A UN SALÓN
LAS CHAVALAS GRITAN, PAPI VENTE
VAMOS A BAILAR DANSÓN!


(*The dance turns Latin. The music comes to another natural break and holds.* LUPE *approaches* HENRY *on the dance floor.*)

LUPE: Hank. Rudy's at it again. He's been drinking since we got here.

HENRY: (*Glancing over at* RUDY.) He's okay, sis, let the carnal enjoy himself.

RUDY: (*Staggering over.*) ¡Ese, carnal!

HENRY: What you say, brother?

RUDY: I'm flying high, Jackson. Feeling good.

LUPE: Rudy, if you go home drunk again, mi 'apá's going to use you for a punching bag. (RUDY *kisses her on the cheek and moves on.*)

DELLA: How are you feeling?

HENRY: Okay.

DELLA: Still thinking about Bertha?

HENRY: Chale, ¿qué traes? Listen, you want to go out to the Sleepy Lagoon? I've got something to tell you.

DELLA: What?

HENRY: Later, later.

LUPE: You better tell Rudy to stop drinking.

HENRY: Relax, sis. If he gets too drunk, I'll carry him home. (*Music picks up again.* EL PACHUCO *sings a third verse.*)

PACHUCO:

> TOCAN MAMBO SABROSÓN
> SE ALBOROTA EL CORAZÓN
> Y CON UNA CHAVALONA VAMOS
> VAMOS A BAILAR EL MAMBO

(*The* COUPLES *do the mambo. In the background,* RUDY *gets into an argument with* RAFAS, *the leader of the* DOWNEY GANG. *A fight breaks out as the music comes to a natural break.* RAFAS *pushes* RUDY, *half drunk, onto the floor.*)

RAFAS: ¡Y a ti qué te importa, puto!

RUDY: (HE *falls.*) ¡Cabrón!

HENRY: (*Reacting immediately.*) Hey! (*The whole dance crowd tenses up immediately, splitting into separate camps. Batos from* 38TH *clearly outnumber the* GUYS *from* DOWNEY.)

RAFAS: He started it, ese. El comenzó a chingar conmigo.

RUDY: You chicken shit, ese! Tú me haces la puñeta, ¡pirujo!

RAFAS: Come over here and say that, puto!

HENRY: (*Pulling* RUDY *behind him.*) ¡Agüítala, carnal! (*Faces* RAFAS.) You're a little out of your territory, ¿que no Rafas?

RAFAS: It's a barrio dance, ese. We're from the barrio.

HENRY: You're from Downey.

RAFAS: Vale madre. ¡Downey Rifa!

DOWNEY GANG: ¡SIMÓN!

RAFAS: What are you going to do about it?

HENRY: I'm going to kick your ass. (*The* TWO SIDES *start to attack each other.*) ¡Cálmenla! (ALL *stop.*)

RAFAS: (*Pulls out a switchblade.*) You and how many batos?

HENRY: Just me and you, cabrón. That's my carnalillo you started pushing around, see? And nobody chinga con mi familia without answering to me, ese! Hank Reyna! (HE *pulls out another switchblade.*)

BERTHA: ALL-RIGHT!

HENRY: Let's see if you can push me around like you did my little brother, ese. Come on ... COME ON! (*They knife fight.* HENRY *moves in fast. Recoiling,* RAFAS *falls to the floor.* HENRY*'s blade is at his throat.* EL PACHUCO *snaps his fingers. Everyone freezes.*)

PACHUCO: Qué mamada, Hank. That's exactly what the play needs right now. Two more Mexicans killing each other. Watcha ... Everybody's looking at you.

HENRY: (*Looks out at the audience.*) Don't give me that bullshit. Either I kill him or he kills me.

PACHUCO: That's exactly what they paid to see. Think about it. (EL PACHUCO *snaps again. Everybody unfreezes.*)

HENRY: (*Kicks* RAFAS.) Get out of here. ¡Píntate!

BERTHA: What?

GÜERA: (RAFAS'*girlfriend runs forward.*)    Rafas.    ¡Vámonos! (SHE *is stopped by other* DOWNEY *batos.*)

RAFAS: Está suave. I'll see you later.

HENRY: Whenever you want, cabrón. (*The* DOWNEY GANG *retreats, as the* 38TH *razzes them all the way out. Insults are exchanged.* BERTHA *shouts "¡Chinga tu madre!" and they are gone. The* 38TH *whoops in victory.*)

SMILEY: Órale, you did it, ese! ¡Se escamaron todos!

TOMMY: We sure chased those jotos out of here.

BERTHA: I could have beat the shit out of those two rucas.

JOEY That pinche Rafas is yellow without his gang, ese.

LUPE: So why didn't you jump out there?

JOEY Chale, Rudy ain't my baby brother.

RUDY: (*Drunk.*) Who you calling a baby, pendejo? I'll show you who's a baby!

JOEY: Be cool, ese.

TOMMY: Man, you're lucky your brother was here.

BERTHA: Why? He didn't do nothing. The old Hank would have slit Rafas' belly like a fat pig.

HENRY: Shut your mouth, Bertha!

RUDY: ¿Por qué, carnal? You backed down, ese. I could have taken that sucker on by myself.

HENRY: That's enough, Rudy. You're drunk.

DELLA: Hank, what if Rafas comes back with all his gang?

HENRY: (*Reclaiming his leadership.*) We'll kill the sons of bitches.

JOEY: ¡Órale! ¡La 38th rifa! (*Music. Everybody gets back with furious energy.* EL PACHUCO *sings.*)

PACHUCO:

> DE LOS BAILES QUE MENTÉ
> Y EL BOLERO Y EL BEGUÍN
> DE TODOS LOS BAILES JUNTOS
> ME GUSTA BAILAR EL SWING! HEY!
> (*The dance ends with a group exclamation: HEY!*)

.................. 8. EL DÍA DE LA RAZA ..................

*The* PRESS *enters upstage level, pushing a small hand truck piled high with newspaper bundles. The batos and rucas on the dance floor freeze in their final dance positions.* EL PACHUCO *is the only one who relaxes and moves.*

PRESS: October 12, 1942: Columbus Day. Four Hundred and Fiftieth Anniversary of the Discovery of America. Headlines!

*In their places, the* COUPLES *now stand straight and recite a headline before exiting. As they do so, the* PRESS *moves the bundles of newspapers on the floor to outline the four corners of a jail cell.*

SMILEY/ELENA: President Roosevelt Salutes Good Neighbors In Latin America. (SMILEY *and* ELENA *exit.*)

TOMMY/LUPE: British Begin Drive to Oust Rommel From North Africa. (TOMMY *and* LUPE *exit.*)

RUDY/CHOLO: Japs In Death Grip On Pacific Isles. (RUDY *and* CHOLO *exit.* PRESS *tosses another bundle.*)

ZOOTER/LITTLE BLUE: Web Of Zoot Crime Spreads. (ZOOTER *and* LITTLE BLUE *exit.*)

MANCHUKA/SWABBIE: U.S. Marines Land Bridgehead On Guadalcanal. (MANCHUKA *and* SWABBIE *exit.*)

JOEY/BERTHA: First Mexican Braceros Arrive In U.S.A. (JOEY *and* BERTHA *exit.*)

DELLA: Sleepy Lagoon Murder Trial Opens Tomorrow. (DELLA *and the* PRESS *exit. As they exit,* GEORGE *and* ALICE *enter upstage left.* HENRY *is center, in a "cell" outlined by four newspaper bundles left by the* PRESS.)

GEORGE: Henry? How you doing, son? Listen, I've brought somebody with me that wants very much to meet you. I thought you wouldn't mind. (ALICE *crosses to* HENRY.)

ALICE: Hello! My name is Alice Bloomfield and I'm a reporter from the Daily People's World.

GEORGE: And ... And, I might add, a red hot member of the ad hoc committee that's fighting for you guys.

ALICE: Oh, George! I'd hardly call it fighting, for Pete's sake. This struggle has just barely begun. But we're sure going to win it, aren't we, Henry?

HENRY: I doubt it.

GEORGE: Oh come on, Henry. How about it, son? You all set for tomorrow? Anything you need, anything I can get for you?

HENRY: Yeah. What about the clean clothes you promised me? I can't go to court looking like this.

GEORGE: You mean they didn't give them to you?

HENRY: What?

GEORGE: Your mother dropped them off two days ago. Clean pants, shirt, socks, underwear, the works. I cleared it with the Sheriff last week.

HENRY: They haven't given me nothing.

GEORGE: I'm beginning to smell something around here.

HENRY: Look, George, I don't like being like this. I ain't dirty. Go do something, man!

GEORGE: Calm down. Take it easy, son. I'll check on it right now. Oh! Uh, Alice?

ALICE: I'll be okay, George.

GEORGE: I'll be right back. (HE *exits.*)

ALICE: (*Pulling out a pad and pencil.*) Now that I have you all to myself, mind if I ask you a couple of questions?

HENRY: I got nothing to say.

ALICE: How do you know? I haven't asked you anything yet. Relax. I'm from the progressive press. Okay? (HENRY *stares at her, not knowing quite how to react.* ALICE *sits on a bundle and crosses her goodlooking legs.* HENRY *concentrates on that.*) Now. The regular press is saying the Pachuco Crime Wave is fascist inspired—any thoughts about that?

HENRY: (*Bluntly.*) No.

ALICE: What about the American Japanese? Is it true they are directing the subversive activities of the pachucos from inside the relocation camps? (HENRY *turns to the* PACHUCO *with a questioning look.*)

PACHUCO: This one's all yours, ese.

HENRY: Look, lady, I don't know what the hell you're talking about.

ALICE: I'm talking about you, Henry Reyna. And what the regular press has been saying. Are you aware you're in here just because some bigshot up in San Simeon wants to sell more papers? It's true.

HENRY: So?

ALICE: So, he's the man who started this Mexican Crime Wave stuff. Then the police got into the act. Get the picture? Somebody is using you as a patsy.

HENRY: (*His machismo insulted.*) Who you calling a patsy?

ALICE: I'm sorry, but it's true.

HENRY: (*Backing her up.*) What makes you so goddamned smart?

ALICE: (*Starting to get scared and trying not to show it.*) I'm a reporter. It's my business to know.

PACHUCO: Puro pedo. She's just a dumb broad only good for you know what.

HENRY: Look, Miss Bloomfield, just leave me alone, all right? (HENRY *moves away.* ALICE *takes a deep breath.*)

ALICE: Look, let's back up and start all over, okay? Hello. My name is Alice Bloomfield, and I'm not a reporter. I'm just somebody that wants very much to be your friend. (*Pause. With sincere feeling.*) Can you believe that?

HENRY: Why should I?

ALICE: Because I'm with you.

HENRY: Oh, yeah? Then how come you ain't in jail with me?

ALICE: (*Holding her head up.*) We are all in jail, Henry. Some of us just don't know it.

PACHUCO: Mmm, pues. No comment. (*Pause.* HENRY *stares at her, trying to figure her out.* ALICE *tries a softer approach.*)

ALICE: Believe it or not, I was born in Los Angeles just like you. But for some strange reason I grew up here, not knowing very much about Mexicans at all. I'm just trying to learn.

HENRY: (*Intrigued, but cynical.*) What?

ALICE: Little details. Like that tattooed cross on your hand. Is
that the sign of the pachuco? (HENRY *covers his right
hand with and automatic reflex, then* HE *realizes what he
has done.*)

HENRY: (*Smiles to himself, embarrassed.*) Órale.

ALICE: Did I embarrass you? I'm sorry. Your mother happened
to mention it.

HENRY: (*Surprised.*) My mother? You talked to my jefita?

ALICE: (*With enthusiasm.*) Yes! And your father and Lupe and
Rudy. The whole family gave me a helluva interview.
But your mother was sensational. I especially liked her
story about the midnight raid. How the police rushed
into your house with drawn guns, looking for you on some
trumped up charge, and how your father told them you
were already in jail ... God, I would have paid to have
seen the cops' faces.

HENRY: (*Hiding his sentiment.*) Don't believe anything my jefa
tells you. (*Then quickly.*) There's a lot she doesn't know.
I'm no angel.

ALICE: I'll just bet you're not. But you have been taken in for
suspicion a dozen times, kept in jail for a few days, then
released for lack of evidence. And it's all stayed on your
juvenile record.

HENRY: Yeah, well I ain't no punk, see.

ALICE: I know. You're an excellent mechanic. And you fix all
the guys' cars. Well, at least you're not one of the lumpen
proletariat.

HENRY: The lumpen what?

ALICE: Skip it. Let's just say you're a classic social victim.

HENRY: Bullshit.

ALICE: (*Pause. A serious question.*) Are you saying you're guilty?

HENRY: Of what?

ALICE: The Sleepy Lagoon Murder.

HENRY: What if I am?

ALICE: Are you?

HENRY: (*Pause, a serious answer.*) Chale. I've pulled a lot of
shit in my time, but I didn't do that. (GEORGE *re-enters
flushed and angry, trying to conceal his frustration.*)

GEORGE: Henry, I'm sorry, but dammit, something's coming off
here, and the clothes have been withheld. I'll have to
bring it up in court.

HENRY: In court?

GEORGE: They've left me no choice.

ALICE: What's going on?

HENRY: It's a set up, George. Another lousy set up!

GEORGE: It's just the beginning, son. Nobody said this was going to be a fair fight. Well, if they're going to fight dirty, so am I. Legally, but dirty. Trust me.

ALICE: (*Passionately.*) Henry, no matter what happens in the trial, I want you to know I believe you're innocent. Remember that when you look out, and it looks like some sort of lynch mob. Some of us ... a lot of us ... are right there with you.

GEORGE: Okay, Alice, let's scram. I've got a million things to do. Henry, see you tomorrow under the big top, son. Good luck, son.

ALICE: Thumbs up, Henry, we're going to beat this rap! (ALICE *and* GEORGE *exit.* EL PACHUCO *watches them go, then turns to* HENRY.)

PACHUCO: "Thumbs up, Henry, we're going to beat this rap." You really think you're going to beat this one, ese?

HENRY: I don't want to think about it.

PACHUCO: You've got to think about it, Hank. Everybody's playing you for a sucker. Wake up, carnal!

HENRY: Look, bato, what the hell do you expect me to do?

PACHUCO: Hang tough. (*Grabs his scrotum.*) Stop going soft.

HENRY: Who's going soft?

PACHUCO: (*Incisively.*) You're hoping for something that isn't going to happen, ese. These paddies are leading you by the nose. Do you really believe you stand a chance?

HENRY: (*Stubborn all the more.*) Yeah. I think I got a chance.

PACHUCO: Just because that white broad says so?

HENRY: Nel, ese, just because Hank Reyna says so.

PACHUCO: The classic social victim, eh?

HENRY: (*Furious but keeping his cool.*) Mira, ese. Hank Reyna's no loser. I'm coming out of this on top. ¿Me entiendes, Mendez? (HE *walks away with a pachuco gait.*)

PACHUCO: (*Forcefully.*) Don't try to out-pachuco ME, ese! We'll see who comes out on top. (HE *picks up a bundle of newspapers and throws it upstage center. It lands with a thud.*) Let's go to court!

.............. 9. OPENING OF THE TRIAL ..............

*Music. The* JUDGE's *bench, made up of more newspaper bundles piled squarely on a four-wheeled hand truck is pushed in by the batos. The* PRESS *rides it in, holding the State and Federal Flags. A* BAILIFF *puts in place a hand cart: the* JUDGE's *throne. From the sides, spectators enter, including* HENRY's *family and friends:* ALICE, DELLA, BERTHA, ELENA.

PRESS: The largest mass trial in the history of Los Angeles County opens this morning in the Superior Court at ten A.M. The infamous Sleepy Lagoon Murder case involves sixty-six charges against twenty-two defendants with seven lawyers pleading for the defense, two for the prosecution. The District Attorney estimates that over a hundred witnesses will be called and has sworn—I quote—"to put an end to Mexican baby gangsterism." End quote.

BAILIFF: (*Bangs a gavel on the bench.*) The Superior Court of the State of California. In and For the County of Los Angeles. Department forty-three. The honorable F. W. Charles, presiding. All rise! (JUDGE CHARLES *enters. All rise.* EL PACHUCO *squats. The* JUDGE *is played by the same actor that portrays* EDWARDS.)

JUDGE: Please be seated. (*All sit.* PACHUCO *stands.*) Call this case, Bailiff.

BAILIFF: (*Reading from a sheet.*) The people of the State of California Versus Henry Reyna, Ismael Torres, Thomas Roberts, Jose Castro and eighteen other ... (*Slight hesitation.*) ... pa-coo-cos.

JUDGE: Is Counsel for the Defense present?

GEORGE: (*Rises.*) Yes, Your Honor.

JUDGE: Please proceed. (*Signals the* PRESS.)

PRESS: Your Honor ...

GEORGE: (*Moving in immediately.*) If the Court please, it was reported to me on Friday that the District Attorney has absolutely forbidden the Sheriff's Office to permit these boys to have clean clothes or haircuts. Now, it's been three months since the boys were arrested ...

PRESS: (*Jumping in.*) Your Honor, there is testimony we expect to develop that the 38th Street Gang are characterized by their style of haircuts ...

GEORGE: Three months, Your Honor.

PRESS: ... the thick heavy heads of hair, the ducktail comb, the pachuco pants ...

GEORGE: Your Honor, I can only infer that the Prosecution ... is trying to make these boys look disreputable, like mobsters.

PRESS: Their appearance is distinctive, Your Honor. Essential to the case.

GEORGE: You are trying to exploit the fact that these boys look foreign in appearance! Yet clothes like these are being worn by kids all over America.

PRESS: Your Honor ...

JUDGE: (*Bangs the gavel.*) I don't believe we will have any difficulty if their clothing becomes dirty.

GEORGE: What about the haircuts, Your Honor?

JUDGE: (*Ruling.*) The zoot haircuts will be retained throughout the trial for purposes of identification of defendants by witnesses.

PACHUCO: You hear that one, ese? Listen to it again. (*Snaps. JUDGE repeats automatically.*)

JUDGE: The zoot haircuts will be retained throughout the trial for purposes of identification of defendants by witnesses.

PACHUCO: He wants to be sure we know who you are.

JUDGE: It has been brought to my attention the Jury is having trouble telling one boy from another, so I am going to rule the defendants stand each time their names are mentioned.

GEORGE: I object. If the Prosecution makes an accusation, it will mean self-incrimination.

JUDGE: (*Pause.*) Not necessarily. (*To* PRESS.) Please proceed.

GEORGE: (*Still trying to set the stage.*) Then if the Court please, might I request that my clients be allowed to sit with me during the trial so that I might consult with them?

JUDGE: Request denied.

GEORGE: May I inquire of Your Honor, if the defendant Thomas Robert might rise from his seat and walk over to counsel table so as to consult with me during the trial?

JUDGE: I certainly will not permit it.

GEORGE: You will not?

JUDGE: No. This is a small courtroom, Mr. Shearer. We can't have twenty-two defendants all over the place.

GEORGE: Then I object. On the grounds that that is a denial of the rights guaranteed all defendants by both the Federal and State constitutions.

JUDGE: Well, that is your opinion. (*Gavel.*) Call your first witness.

PRESS: The prosecution calls Lieutenant Sam Edwards of the Los Angeles Police Department.

PACHUCO: (*Snaps. Does double take on* JUDGE.) You know what. We've already heard from that bato. Let's get on with the defense. (*Snaps.* PRESS *sits.* GEORGE *stands.*)

GEORGE: The defense calls Adela Barrios.

BAILIFF: (*Calling out.*) Adeela Barreeos to the stand. (DELLA BARRIOS *comes forth out of the spectators.* BERTHA *leans forward.*)

BERTHA: (*Among the spectators.*) Don't tell 'em nothing. (*The* BAILIFF *swears in* DELLA *silently.*)

PACHUCO: Look at your gang. They do look like mobsters. Se watchan bien gachos. (HENRY *looks at the batos, who are sprawled out in their places.*)

HENRY: (*Under his breath.*) Come on, Batos, sit up.

SMILEY: We're tired, Hank.

JOEY: My butt is sore.

TOMMY: Yeah, look at the soft chairs the jury's got.

HENRY: What did you expect? They're trying to make us look bad. Come on! Straighten up.

SMILEY: Simón, batos, Hank is right.

JOEY: ¡Más alba nalga!

TOMMY: Put some class on your ass.

HENRY: Sit up! (*They all sit up.*)

GEORGE: State your name please.

DELLA: Adela Barrios. (*She sits.*)

GEORGE: Miss Barrios, were you with Henry Reyna on the night of August 1, 1942?

DELLA: Yes.

JUDGE: (*To* HENRY.) Please stand. (HENRY *stands.*)

GEORGE: Please tell the court what transpired that night.

DELLA: (*Pause. Takes a breath.*) Well, after the dance that Saturday night, Henry and I drove out to the Sleepy Lagoon about eleven-thirty.

·················· 10. SLEEPY LAGOON ··················

*Music: THE HARRY JAMES THEME. EL PACHUCO creates the scene. The light changes. We see a shimmering pattern of light*

*on the floor growing to the music. It becomes the image of the*
*Lagoon. As the music soars to a trumpet solo,* HENRY *reaches out*
*to* DELLA, *and she glides to her feet.*

DELLA: There was a full moon that night, and as we drove up
to the Lagoon we noticed right away the place was empty
... (*A pair of headlights silently pulls in from the black*
*background upstage center.*) Henry parked the car on the
bank of the reservoir and we relaxed. (*Headlights go off.*)
It was such a warm, beautiful night, and the sky was so
full of stars, we couldn't just sit in the car. So we got out,
and Henry took my hand ... (HENRY *stands and takes*
DELLA's *hand.*) We went for a walk around the Lagoon.
Neither of us said anything at first, so the only sounds we
could hear were the crickets and the frogs ... (*Sounds of*
*crickets and frogs, then music faintly in the background.*)
When we got to the other side of the reservoir, we began
to hear music, so I asked Henry, what's that?

HENRY: Sounds like they're having a party.

DELLA: Where?

HENRY: Over at the Williams' Ranch. See the house lights.

DELLA: Who lives there?

HENRY: A couple of families. Mexicanos. I think they work on
the ranch. You know, their name used to be Gonzales,
but they changed it to Williams.

DELLA: Why?

HENRY: I don't know. Maybe they think it gives 'em more class.
(*We hear Mexican music.*) Ay, jijo. They're probably cel-
ebrating a wedding or something.

DELLA: As soon as he said wedding, he stopped talking and we
both knew why. He had something on his mind, something he was trying to tell me without sounding like a
square.

HENRY: Della ... what are you going to do if I don't come back
from the war?

DELLA: That wasn't the question I was expecting, so I answered
something dumb, like I don't know, what's going to keep
you from coming back?

HENRY: Maybe wanting too much out of life, see? Ever since
I was a kid, I've had this feeling like there's a big party
going on someplace, and I'm invited, but I don't know
how to get there. And I want to get there so bad, I'll even
risk my life to make it. Sounds crazy, huh? (DELLA *and*

HENRY *kiss.  They embrace and then* HENRY *speaks haltingly.*) If I get back from the war ... will you marry me?

DELLA: Yes! (SHE *embraces him and almost causes them to topple over.*)

HENRY: ¡Órale! You'll knock us into the Lagoon. Listen, what about your old man? He ain't going to like you marrying me.

DELLA: I know. But I don't care. I'll go to hell with you if you want me to.

HENRY: ¿Sabes qué? I'm going to give you the biggest Pachuco wedding L.A. has ever seen. (*Another pair of headlights comes in from the left.* DELLA *goes back to her narration.*)

DELLA: Just then another car pulled up to the Lagoon. It was Rafas and some drunk guys in a gang from Downey. They got out and started to bust the windows on Henry's car. Henry yelled at them, and they started cussing at us. I told Henry not to say anything, but he cussed them back!

HENRY: You stay here, Della.

DELLA: Henry, no! Don't go down there! Please don't go down there!

HENRY: Can't you hear what they're doing to my car?

DELLA: There's too many of them. They'll kill you!

HENRY: ¡Chale! (HENRY *turns and runs upstage, where he stops in a freeze.*)

DELLA: Henry! Henry ran down the back of the Lagoon and attacked the gang by himself. Rafas had about ten guys with him and they jumped on Henry like a pack of dogs. He fought them off as long as he could, then they threw him on the ground hard and kicked him until he passed out ... (*Headlights pull off.*) After they left, I ran down to Henry and held him in my arms until he came to. And I could tell he was hurt, but the first thing he said was ...

PACHUCO: Let's go into town and get the guys. (*Music: Glen Miller's "In the Mood."* HENRY *turns to the batos and they stand.* SMILEY, JOEY *and* TOMMY *are joined by* RUDY, BERTHA, LUPE *and* ELENA, *who enter from the side. They turn downstage in a body and freeze.*)

DELLA: It took us about an hour to go into town and come back. We got to the Lagoon with about eight cars, but the Downey gang wasn't there.

JOEY: Órale, ¿pos qué pasó? Nobody here.

SMILEY: Then let's go to Downey.

THE BOYS: (*Ad lib.*) Let's go!

HENRY: ¡Chale! ¡Chale! (*Pause. They all stop.*) Ya estuvo. Everybody go home. (*A collective groan from* THE BOYS.) Go home!

DELLA: That's when we heard music coming from the Williams' Ranch again. We didn't know Rafas and his gang had been there too, causing trouble. So when Joey said . . .

JOEY: Hey, there's a party! Bertha, let's crash it.

DELLA: We all went there yelling and laughing. (*The group of batos turns upstage in a mimetic freeze.*) At the Williams' Ranch they saw us coming and thought we were the Downey Gang coming back again . . . They attacked us. (*The group now mimes a series of tableaus showing the fight.*) An old man ran out of the house with a kitchen knife and Henry had to hit him. Then a girl grabbed me by the hair and in a second everybody was fighting! People were grabbing sticks from the fence, bottles, anything! It all happened so fast, we didn't know what hit us, but Henry said let's go!

HENRY: ¡Vámonos! Let's get out of here.

DELLA: And we started to back off . . . Before we got to the cars, I saw something out of the corner of my eye . . . It was a guy. He was hitting a man on the ground with a big stick. (EL PACHUCO *mimes this action.*) Henry called to him, but he wouldn't stop. He wouldn't stop . . . He wouldn't stop . . . He wouldn't stop . . . (DELLA *in tears, holds* HENRY *in her arms. The batos and rucas start moving back to their places, quietly.*) Driving back in the car, everybody was quiet, like nothing had happened. We didn't know José Williams had died at the party that night and that the guys would be arrested the next day for murder. (HENRY *separates from her and goes back to stand in his place.* DELLA *resumes the witness stand.*)

## . . . . . . . . . 11. THE CONCLUSION OF THE TRIAL . . . . . . . .

*Lights change back to courtroom, as* JUDGE CHARLES *bangs his gavel. Everyone is seated back in place.*

GEORGE: Your witness.

PRESS: (*Springing to the attack.*) You say Henry Reyna hit the man with his fist. (*Indicates* HENRY *standing.*) Is this the Henry Reyna?

DELLA: Yes. I mean, no. He's Henry, but he didn't ...

PRESS: Please be seated. (HENRY *sits.*) Now, after Henry Reyna
hit the old man with his closed fist, is that when he pulled
the knife?

DELLA: The old man had the knife.

PRESS: So Henry pulled one out, too?

GEORGE: (*Rises.*) Your Honor, I object to counsel leading the
witness.

PRESS: I am not leading the witness.

GEORGE: You are.

PRESS: I certainly am not.

GEORGE: Yes, you are.

JUDGE: I would suggest, Mr. Shearer, that you look up during the
noon hour just what a leading question is?

GEORGE: If the Court please, I am going to assign that remark of
Your Honor as misconduct.

JUDGE: (*To* PRESS.) Proceed.   (GEORGE *crosses back to his
chair.*)

PRESS: Where was Smiley Torres during all this? Is it not true that
Smiley Torres grabbed a woman by the hair and kicked her
to the ground? Will Smiley Torres please stand? (SMILEY
*stands.*) Is this the man?

DELLA: Yes, it's Smiley, but he ...

PRESS: Please be seated. (SMILEY *sits.* PRESS *picks up a two-by-
four.*) Wasn't José Castro carrying a club of some kind?

GEORGE: (*On his feet again.*) Your Honor, I object! No such
club was ever found. The Prosecution is implying that
this two-by-four is associated with my client in some way.

PRESS: I'm not implying anything, Your Honor, I'm merely using
this stick as an illustration.

JUDGE: Objection overruled.

PRESS: Will José Castro please stand? (JOEY *stands.*) Is this
man who was carrying a club? (DELLA *refuses to answer.*)
Answer the question please.

DELLA: I refuse.

PRESS: You are under oath. You can't refuse.

JUDGE: Answer the question, young lady.

DELLA: I refuse.

PRESS: Is this the man you saw hitting another man with a two-
by-four? Your Honor ...

JUDGE: I order you to answer the question.

GEORGE: Your Honor, I object. The witness is obviously afraid her testimony will be manipulated by the Prosecution.

PRESS: May I remind the court that we have a signed confession from one José Castro taken while in jail ...

GEORGE: I object. Those were not confessions! Those are statements. They are false and untrue, Your Honor, obtained through beatings and coercion of the defendants by the police!

JUDGE: I believe the technical term is admissions, Mr. Prosecutor. Objection sustained. (*Applause from spectators.*) At the next outburst, I will clear this courtroom. Go on, Mr. Prosecutor.

PRESS: Sit down please. (JOEY *sits.* GEORGE *goes back to his seat.*) Is Henry Reyna the leader of the 38TH Street Gang? (HENRY *stands.*)

DELLA: Not in the sense that you mean.

PRESS: Did Henry Reyna, pachuco ringleader of the 38th Street Gang, willfully murder José Williams?

DELLA: No. They attacked us first.

PRESS: I didn't ask for your comment.

DELLA: But they did, they thought we were the Downey gang.

PRESS: Just answer my questions.

DELLA: We were just defending ourselves so we could get out of there.

PRESS: Your Honor, will you instruct the witness to be cooperative.

JUDGE: I must caution you, young lady, answer the questions or I'll hold you in contempt.

PRESS: Was this the Henry Reyna who was carrying a three-foot lead pipe?

GEORGE: I object!

JUDGE: Overruled.

DELLA: No.

PRESS: Was it a two-foot lead pipe?

GEORGE: Objection!

JUDGE: Overruled.

DELLA: No!

PRESS: Did he kick a women to the ground?

DELLA: No, he was hurt from the beating.

PRESS: Sit down. (HENRY *sits.*) Did Tommy Roberts rip stakes from a fence and hit a man on the ground?

GEORGE: Objection!

JUDGE: Overruled.

DELLA: I never saw him do anything.

PRESS: Did Joey Castro have a gun?

GEORGE: Objection!

JUDGE: Overruled. (JOEY *stands*.)

PRESS: Sit down. (JOEY *sits*.) Did Henry Reyna have a blackjack in his hand? (HENRY *stands*.)

DELLA: No.

PRESS: A switchblade knife?

DELLA: No.

PRESS: A two-by-four?

DELLA: No.

PRESS: Did he run over to José Williams, hit him on the head and kill him?

DELLA: He could barely walk, how could he run to any place?

PRESS: (*Moving in for the kill*.) Did Smiley Torres? (*The batos stand and sit as their names are mentioned*.) Did Joey Castro? Did Tommy Roberts? Did Henry Reyna? Did Smiley Torres? Did Henry Reyna? Did Henry Reyna? Did Henry Reyna kill José Williams?!

DELLA: No, no, no!

GEORGE: (*On* HIS *feet again*.) Your Honor, I object! The Prosecution is pulling out objects from all over the place, none of which were found at Sleepy Lagoon, and none of which have been proven to be associated with my clients in any way.

JUDGE: Overruled.

GEORGE: If Your Honor please, I wish to make an assignment of misconduct!

JUDGE: We have only had one this morning. We might as well have another now.

GEORGE: You have it, Your Honor.

JUDGE: One more remark like that and I'll hold you in contempt. Quite frankly, Mr. Shearer, I am getting rather tired of your repeated useless objections.

GEORGE: I have not made useless objections.

JUDGE: I am sorry. Somebody is using ventriloquism. We have a Charlie McCarthy using Mr. Shearer's voice.

GEORGE: I am going to assign that remark of Your Honor as misconduct.

JUDGE: Fine. I would feel rather bad if you did not make an assignment of misconduct at least three times every session. (*Gavel*.) Witness is excused. (DELLA *stands*.) However,

I am going to remand her to the custody of the Ventura
State School for Girls for a period of one year ...

HENRY: What?

JUDGE: ... to be held there as a juvenile ward of the State. Bailiff?

GEORGE: If the court please ... If the court please ... (BAILIFF
*crosses to* DELLA *and takes her off left.*)

JUDGE: Court is in recess until tomorrow morning. (JUDGE
*retires.* PRESS *exits.* HENRY *meets* GEORGE *halfway
across center stage. The rest of the batos stand and stretch
in the background.*)

GEORGE: Now, Henry, I want you to listen to me, please. You've
got to remember he's the judge, Hank. And this is his
courtroom.

HENRY: But he's making jokes, George, and we're getting screwed!

GEORGE: I know. I can't blame you for being bitter, but believe
me, we'll get him.

HENRY: I thought you said we had a chance.

GEORGE: (*Passionately.*) We do! This case is going to be won on
appeal.

HENRY: Appeal? You mean you already know we're going to lose?

PACHUCO: So what's new?

GEORGE: Don't you see, Henry, Judge Charles is hanging himself
as we go. I've cited over a hundred separate cases of misconduct by the bench, and it's all gone into the record.
Prejudicial error, denial of due process, inadmissible evidence, hearsay ...

HENRY: ¿Sabes qué, George? Don't tell me any more. (HENRY
*turns.* ALICE *and* ENRIQUE *approach him.*)

ALICE: Henry ... ?

HENRY: (*Turns furiously.*) I don't want to hear it, Alice! (HENRY
*sees* ENRIQUE, *but neither father nor son can think of
anything to say.* HENRY *goes back upstage.*)

ALICE: George, is there anything we can do?

GEORGE: No. He's bitter, and he has a right to be. (JUDGE
CHARLES *pounds his gavel. All go back to their places
and sit.*)

JUDGE: We'll now hear the Prosecution's concluding statement.

PRESS: Your Honor, ladies and gentlemen of the jury. What you
have before you is a dilemma of our times. The City of
Los Angeles is caught in the midst of the biggest, most
terrifying crime wave in its history. A crime wave that
threatens to engulf the very foundations of our civic well-
being. We are not only dealing with the violent death of

one José Williams in a drunken barrio brawl. We are dealing with a threat and danger to our children, our families,
our homes. Set these pachucos free, and you shall unleash
the forces of anarchy and destruction in our society. Set
these pachucos free and you will turn them into heroes.
Others just like them must be watching us at this very
moment. What nefarious schemes can they be hatching
in their twisted minds? Rape, drugs, assault, more violence? Who shall be their next innocent victim in some
dark alley way, on some lonely street? You? You? Your
loved ones? No! Henry Reyna and his Latin juvenile co-
horts are not heroes. They are criminals, and they must be
stopped. The specific details of this murder are irrelevant
before the overwhelming danger of the pachuco in our
midst. I ask you to find these zoot-suited gangsters guilty
of murder and to put them in the gas chamber where they
belong. (*The* PRESS *sits down.* GEORGE *rises and takes
center stage.*)

GEORGE: Ladies and gentlemen of the jury, you have heard me
object to the conduct of this trial. I have tried my best to
defend what is most precious in our American society—a
society now at war against the forces of racial intolerance
and totalitarian injustice. The prosecution has not pro-
vided one witness that actually saw, with his own eyes,
who actually murdered José Williams. These boys are
not the Downey gang, yet the evidence suggests that they
were attacked because the people at the ranch thought
they were. Henry Reyna and Della Barrios were victims
of the same bunch. Yes, they might have been spoiling
for a revenge—who wouldn't under the circumstances—
but not with the intent to conspire to commit murder. So
how did Jose Williams die? Was it an accident? Was it
manslaughter? Was it murder? Perhaps we may never
know. All the prosecution has been able to prove is that
these boys wear long hair and zoot suits. And all the rest
has been circumstantial evidence, hearsay and war hys-
teria. The prosecution has tried to lead you to believe
that they are some kind of inhuman gangsters. Yet they
are Americans. Find them guilty of anything more serious than a juvenile bout of fisticuffs, and you will con-
demn all American youth. Find them guilty of murder,
and you willl murder the spirit of racial justice in America. (GEORGE *sits down.*)

JUDGE: The jury will retire to consider its verdict. (*The* PRESS *stands and starts to exit with the* BAILIFF. *EL PACHUCO snaps. All freeze.*)

PACHUCO: Chale. Let's have it. (*Snaps again. The* PRESS *turns and comes back again.*)

JUDGE: Has the jury reached a verdict?

PRESS: We have, Your Honor.

JUDGE: How say you?

PRESS: We find the defendants guilty of murder in the first and second degrees.

JUDGE: The defendants will rise. (*The batos come to their feet.*) Henry Reyna, José Castro, Thomas Roberts, Ismael Torres, and so forth. You have been tried by a jury of your peers and found guilty of murder in the first and second degrees. The Law prescribes the capital punishment for this offense. However, in view of your youth and in consideration of your families, it is hereby the judgement of this court that you be sentenced to life imprisonment ...

RUDY: No!

JUDGE: ... and sent to the State Penitentiary at San Quentin. Court adjourned. (*Gavel.* JUDGE *exits.* DOLORES, ENRIQUE *and family go to* HENRY. BERTHA *crosses to* JOEY; LUPE *goes to* TOMMY. ELENA *crosses to* SMILEY. GEORGE *and* ALICE *talk.*)

DOLORES: ¡Hijo mío! ¡Hijo de mi alma! (BAILIFF *comes down with a pair of handcuffs.*)

BAILIFF: Okay, boys. (HE *puts the cuffs on* HENRY. RUDY *comes up.*)

RUDY: ¿Carnal? (HENRY *looks at the* BAILIFF, *who gives him a nod of permission to spend a moment with* RUDY. HENRY *embraces him with the cuffs on.* GEORGE *and* ALICE *approach.*)

GEORGE: Henry? I can't pretend to know how you feel, son. I just want you to know that our fight has just begun.

ALICE: We may have lost this decision, but we're going to appeal immediately. We're going to stand behind you until your name is absolutely clear. I swear it!

PACHUCO: What the hell are they going to do, ese? They just sent you to prison for life. Once a Mexican goes in, he never comes out.

BAILIFF: Boys? (*The* BOYS *exit with the* BAILIFF. *As they go* ENRIQUE *calls after them.*)

ENRIQUE: (*Holding back tears.*) Hijo. Be a man, hijo. (*Then to his family.*) Vámonos ... ¡Vámonos! (*The family leaves and* EL PACHUCO *slowly walks to center stage.*)

PACHUCO: We're going to take a short break right now, so you can all go out and take a leak, smoke a frajo. Ahí los watcho. (HE *exits up center and the newspaper backdrop comes down.*)

# ACT TWO

## PROLOGUE

*Lights up and* EL PACHUCO *emerges from the shadows. The newspaper drop is still down. Music.*

PACHUCO:

    Watchamos pachucos
    los batos
    the dudes
    street-corner warriors who fought and moved
    like unknown soldiers in wars of their own
    El Pueblo de Los was the battle zone
    from Sleepy Lagoon to the Zoot Suit wars
    when Marines and Sailors made their scores
    stomping like Nazis on East L.A. ...
    pero ¿saben qué?
    That's later in the play. Let's pick it up in prison.
    We'll begin this scene
    inside the walls of San Quintín.

..................... 1. SAN QUENTIN .....................

*A bell rings as the drop rises.* HENRY, JOEY, SMILEY *and* TOMMY *enter accompanied by a* GUARD.

GUARD: All right, people, lock up. (BOYS *move downstage in four directions. They step into "cells" simply marked by shadows of bars on the floor in their separate places. Newspaper handcarts rest on the floor as cots. Sound of cell doors closing. The* GUARD *paces back and forth upstage level.*)

HENRY:

San Quentin, California

March 3, 1943

Dear Family:

Coming in from the yard in the evening, we are quickly locked up in our cells. Then the clank and locking of the doors leaves one with a rather empty feeling. You are standing up to the iron door, waiting for the guard to come along and take the count, listening as his footsteps fade away in the distance. By this time there is a tense stillness that seems to crawl over the cellblock. You realize you are alone, so all alone.

PACHUCO: This all sounds rather tragic, doesn't it?

HENRY: But here comes the guard again, and he calls out your number in a loud voice ...

GUARD: (*Calls numbers;* BOYS *call name.*) 24–545

HENRY: Reyna!

GUARD: 24–546

JOEY: Castro!

GUARD: 24–547

TOMMY: Roberts!

GUARD: 24–548

SMILEY: Torres! (GUARD *passes through dropping letters and exits up left.*)

HENRY: You jump to your feet, stooping to pick up the letter ...

JOEY: (*Excited.*) Or perhaps several letters ...

TOMMY: You are really excited as you take the letters from the envelope.

SMILEY: The censor has already broken the seal when he reads it.

HENRY: You make a mental observation to see if you recognize the handwriting on the envelope.

SMILEY: (*Anxious.*) It's always nice to hear from home ...

JOEY: Or a close comrade ...

TOMMY: Friends that you know on the outside ...

HENRY: Or perhaps it's from a stranger. (*Pause. Spotlight at upstage center.* ALICE *walks in with casual clothes on. Her hair is in pigtails, and she wears a pair of drapes.* SHE *is cheerful.*)

...................... 2. THE LETTERS ......................

Dear Boys,

Announcing the publication (mimeograph) of the Appeal News, your very own newsletter, to be sent to you twice a month for the purpose of keeping you reliably informed of everything—the progress of the Sleeping Lagoon Defense Committee (We have a name now) and, of course, the matter of your appeal.

Signed,
Your editor
Alice Bloomfield.

(*Music. "Perdido" by Duke Ellington.* ALICE *steps down and sits on the lip of the upstage level. The* BOYS *start swinging the bat, dribbling the basketball, shadow-boxing and exercising.* ALICE *mimes typing movements and we hear the sounds of a typewriter. Music fades.* ALICE *rises.*)
ALICE: The Appeal News Volume I, Number I, April 7, 1943.

Boys,

You can, you must, and you will help us on the outside by what you do on the inside. Don't forget, what you do affects others. You have no control over that. When the time comes, let us be proud to show the record.

Signed,
Your editor.

(*Music up again. The* BOYS *go through their activities.* ALICE *moves downstage center and the music fades.*)
SMILEY: (*Stepping toward her.*)

April 10, 1943

Dear Miss Bloomfield,

I have discovered from my wife that you are conducting door-to-door fund-raising campaigns in Los Angeles. She doesn't want to tell you, but she feels bad about doing such a thing. It's not our custom to go around the neighborhoods asking for money.

ALICE: (*Turning toward* SMILEY.)

> Dear Smiley,
>
> Of course, I understand your feelings ...

SMILEY: (*Adamant.*) I don't want my wife going around begging.
ALICE: It isn't begging—it's fund-raising.
SMILEY: I don't care what you call it. If that's what it's going to take, count me out.
ALICE: All right. I won't bother your wife if she really doesn't want me to. Okay? (SMILEY *looks at her and turns back to his upstage position. Music. The batos move again.* TOMMY *crosses to* ALICE. *Another fade.*)
TOMMY:

> April 18, 1943
>
> Dear Alice,
>
> Trying to find the words and expression to thank you for your efforts in behalf of myself and the rest of the batos makes me realize what a meager vocabulary I possess ...

ALICE:

> Dear Tommy,
>
> Your vocabulary is just fine. Better than most.

TOMMY: Most what?
ALICE: People.
TOMMY: (*Glances at* HENRY.) Uh, listen, Alice. I don't want to be treated any different than the rest of the batos, see? And don't expect me to talk to you like some square Anglo, some pinche gabacho. You just better find out what it means to be Chicano, and it better be pretty damn quick.
ALICE: Look, Tommy, I didn't ...
TOMMY: I know what you're trying to do for us and that's reet, see? Shit. Most paddies would probably like to to see us locked up for good. I been in jail a couple of times before, but never nothing this deep. Strange, ain't it, the trial in Los? I don't really know what happened or why. I don't give a shit what the papers said. We didn't do half the things I read about. I also know that I'm in here just because I hung around with Mexicans ... or pachucos. Well, just remember this, Alicia ... I grew up right alongside most of these batos, and I'm pachuco too. Simón, esa,

you better believe it! (*Music up. Movement.* TOMMY *returns to his position.* HENRY *stands.* ALICE *turns toward him, but* HE *walks over to* THE PACHUCO, *giving her his back.*)

JOEY: (*Stepping forward anxiously.*)

May 1, 1943

Dear Alice ... Darling!

I can't help but spend my time thinking about you. How about sending us your retra—that is, your photograph? Even though Tommy would like one of Rita Hayworth—he's always chasing Mexican skirts (Ha! Ha!)—I'd prefer to see your sweet face any day.

ALICE: (*Directly to him.*)

Dear Joey,

Thank you so much. I really appreciated receiving your letter.

JOEY: That's all reet, Grandma! You mind if I call you Grandma?
ALICE: Oh, no.
JOEY: Eres una ruca de aquellas.
ALICE: I'm a what?
JOEY: Ruca. A fine chick.
ALICE: (*Pronounces the word.*) Ruca?
JOEY: De aquellas. (*Makes a cool gesture, palms out at hip level.*)
ALICE: (*Imitating him.*) De aquellas.
JOEY: All reet! You got it. (*Pause.*) P.S. Did you forget the photograph?
ALICE: (SHE *hands it to him.*)

Dearest Joey,

Of course not. Here it is, attached to a copy of the Appeal News. I'm afraid it's not exactly a pin-up.

JOEY: (*Kissing the photo.*) Alice, honey, you're a doll! (JOEY *shows the photo to* TOMMY *then* SMILEY, *who is curious enough to come into the circle.* ALICE *looks at* HENRY, *but* HE *continues to ignore her.*)
ALICE: (*Back at center.*) The Appeal News, Volume I, Number 3, May 5, 1943.

Dear Boys,

Feeling that el Cinco de Mayo is a very appropriate day—the CIO radio program, "Our Daily Bread," is devoting the entire time this evening to a discussion of discrimination against Mexicans in general and against you guys in particular.

*Music up. The repartee between* ALICE *and the batos is now friendly and warm. Even* SMILEY *is smiling with* ALICE. *They check out her "drapes."*

........... 3. THE INCORRIGIBLE PACHUCO ...........

HENRY *stands at downstage left, looks at the group, then decides to speak.*

HENRY:

May 17, 1943

Dear Miss Bloomfield,

I understand you're coming up to Q this weekend, and I would like to talk to you—in private. Can you arrange it?
*(The batos turn away, taking a hint.)*

ALICE: *(Eagerly.)* Yes, yes, I can. What can I do for you, Henry? (HENRY *and* ALICE *step forward toward each other.* EL PACHUCO *moves in.)*

HENRY: For me? ¡Ni madre!

ALICE: *(Puzzled.)* I don't understand.

HENRY: I wanted you to be the first to know, Alice. I'm dropping out of the appeal.

ALICE: *(Unbelieving.)* You're what?

HENRY: I'm bailing out, esa. Dropping out of the case, see?

ALICE: Henry, you can't!

HENRY: Why can't I?

ALICE: Because you'll destroy our whole case! If we don't present a united front, how can we ask the public to support us?

HENRY: That's your problem. I never asked for their support. Just count me out.

ALICE: *(Getting nervous, anxious.)* Henry, please, think about what you're saying. If you drop out, the rest of the boys will probably go with you. How can you even think of dropping out of the appeal? What about George and all the people that have contributed their time and money in the past few months? You just can't quit on them!

HENRY: Oh no? Just watch me.

ALICE: If you felt this way, why didn't you tell me before?

HENRY: Why didn't you ask me? You think you can just move in and defend anybody you feel like? When did I ever ask you to start a defense committee for me? Or a newspaper? Or a fundraising drive and all that other shit? I don't need defending, esa. I can take care of myself.

ALICE: But what about the trial, the sentence. They gave you life imprisonment?

HENRY: It's my life!

ALICE: Henry, honestly—are you kidding me?

HENRY: You think so?

ALICE: But you've seen me coming and going. Writing to you, speaking for you, traveling up and down the state. You must have known I was doing it for you. Nothing has come before my involvement, my attachment, my passion for this case. My boys have been everything to me.

HENRY: My boys? My boys! What the hell are we—your personal property? Well, let me set you straight, lady, I ain't your boy.

ALICE: You know I never meant it that way.

HENRY: You think I haven't seen through your bullshit? Always so concerned. Come on, boys. Speak out, boys. Stand up for your people. Well, you leave my people out of this! Can't you understand that?

ALICE: No, I can't understand that.

HENRY: You're just using Mexicans to play politics.

ALICE: Henry, that's the worst thing anyone has ever said to me.

HENRY: Who are you going to help next—the Colored People?

ALICE: No, as a matter of fact, I've already helped the Colored People. What are you going to do next—go to the gas chamber?

HENRY: What the hell do you care?

ALICE: I don't!

HENRY: Then get the hell out of here!

ALICE: (*Furious.*) You think you're the only one who doesn't want to be bothered? You ought to try working in the Sleepy Lagoon defense office for a few months. All the haggling, the petty arguments, the lack of cooperation. I've wanted to quit a thousand times. What the hell am I doing here?

They're coming at me from all sides. You're too senti-
mental and emotional about this, Alice. You're too cold
hearted, Alice. You're collecting money and turning it
over to the lawyers, while the families are going hungry.
They're saying you can't be trusted because you're a Com-
munist, because you're a Jew. Okay! If that's the way
they feel about me, then to hell with them! I hate them
too. I hate their language, I hate their enchiladas, and
I hate their goddamned mariachi music! (*Pause. They
look at each other.* HENRY *smiles, then* ALICE—*feeling
foolish—and they both break out laughing.*)

HENRY: All right! Now you sound like you mean it.

ALICE: I do.

HENRY: Okay! Now we're talking straight.

ALICE: I guess I have been sounding like some square paddy chick.
But, you haven't exactly been Mister Cool yourself... ese.

HENRY: So, let's say we're even Steven.

ALICE: Fair enough. What now?

HENRY: Why don't we bury the hatchet, you know what I mean?

ALICE: Can I tell George you'll go on with the appeal?

HENRY: Yeah. I know there's a lot of people out there who are
willing and trying to help us. People who feel that our
conviction was an injustice. People like George ... and
you. Well, the next time you see them, tell them Hank
Reyna sends his thanks.

ALICE: Why don't you tell them?

HENRY: You getting wise with me again?

ALICE: If you write an article—and I know you can—we'll publish
it in the People's World. What do you say?

PACHUCO: Article! Pos who told you, you could write, ese?

HENRY: (*Laughs.*) Chale.

ALICE: I'm serious. Why don't you give it a try?

HENRY: I'll think about it. (*Pause.*) Listen, you think you and I
could write each other ... outside the newsletter?

ALICE: Sure.

HENRY: Then it's a deal. (*They shake hands.*)

ALICE: I'm glad we're going to be communicating. I think we're
going to be very good friends. (ALICE *lifts her hands to*
HENRY'*s shoulder in a gesture of comradeship.* HENRY
*follows her hand, putting his on top of hers.*)

HENRY: You think so?

ALICE: I know so.

GUARD: Time, miss.

ALICE: I gotta go. Think about the article, okay? (SHE *turns to the* BOYS.) I gotta go, boys.

JOEY: Goodbye, Grandma! Say hello to Bertha.

SMILEY: And to my wife!

TOMMY: Give my love to Lupe!

GUARD: Time!

ALICE: I've got to go. Goodbye, goodbye. (ALICE *exits, escorted by the* GUARD *upstage left. As* SHE *goes,* JOEY *calls after her.*)

JOEY: See you, Grandma.

TOMMY: (*Turning to* JOEY *and* SMILEY.) She loves me.

PACHUCO: Have you forgotten what happened at the trial? You think the Appeals Court is any different? Some paddy judge sitting in the same fat-ass judgment of your fate.

HENRY: Come on, ese, give me a break!

PACHUCO: One break, coming up! (HE *snaps his fingers. The* GUARD *blows his whistle.*)

GUARD: Rec time! (*The batos move upstage to the upper level. Music. The* BOYS *mime a game of handball against the backdrop. During the game,* GEORGE *enters at stage right and comes downstage carrying his briefcase. The* GUARD *blows a whistle and stops the game.*)

GUARD: Reyna, Castro, Roberts, Torres!—You got a visitor.

.................. 4. MAJOR GEORGE ..................

*The* BOYS *turn and see* GEORGE. *They come down enthusiastically.*

JOEY: ¡Óra-leh! ¡Ese, Cheer!

SMILEY: George!

GEORGE: Hi, guys! (*The* BOYS *shake his hand, pat him on the back.* HENRY *comes to him last.*) How are you all doing? You boys staying in shape?

JOEY: Ese, you're looking at the hero of the San Quentin athletic program. Right, batos? (HE *shadowboxes a little.*)

TOMMY: Ten rounds with a busted ankle.

JOEY: ¡Simón! And I won the bout, too. I'm the terror of the flyweights, ese. The killer fly!

TOMMY: They got us doing everything, Cheer. Baseball, basketball.

SMILEY: Watch repairing.

GEORGE: (*Impressed.*) Watch repairing?

SMILEY: I'm also learning to improve my English and arithmetic.

GEORGE: Warden Duffy has quite a program. I hear he's a good man?

JOEY: Simón, he's a good man. We've learned our lesson ... Well, anyway, I've learned my lesson, boy. No more pachuquismo for me. Too many people depending on us to help out. The raza here in Los. The whole Southwest. Mexico, South America! Like you and Grandma say, this is the people's world. If you get us out of here, I figure the only thing I could do is become a union organizer. Or go into major league baseball.

GEORGE: Baseball?

JOEY: Simón, ese. You're looking at the first Mexican Babe Ruth. Or maybe, "Babe Root." Root! You get it?

TOMMY: How about "Baby Zoot"?

JOEY: Solid, Jackson.

GEORGE: Babe Zooter!

JOEY: Solid tudee, that's all reet, ese.

GEORGE: What about you, Henry? What have you been doing?

HENRY: Time, George, I've been doing time.

TOMMY: Ain't it the truth?

SMILEY: Yeah, George! When you going to spring us out of here, ese?

HENRY: How's the appeal coming?

GEORGE: (*Getting serious.*) Not bad. There's been a development I have to talk to you about. But other than that ...

HENRY: Other than what?

SMILEY: (*Pause.*) Bad news?

GEORGE: (*Hedging.*) It all depends on how you look at it, Smiley. It really doesn't change anything. Work on the brief is going on practically day and night. The thing is, even with several lawyers on the case now, it'll still be several months before we file. I want to be honest about that.

HENRY: (*Suspiciously.*) Is that the bad news?

GEORGE: Not exactly. Sit down, boys. (*Pause.* HE *laughs to himself.*) I really don't mean to make such a big deal out of this thing. Fact is I'm still not quite used to the idea myself. (*Pause.*) You see ... I've been drafted.

JOEY: Drafted?

TOMMY: Into the Army?

SMILEY: You?

GEORGE: That's right. I'm off to war.

JOEY: But ... you're old, Cheer.

HENRY: (*A bitter edge.*) Why you, George? Why did they pick on you?

GEORGE: Well, Henry, I wouldn't say they "picked" on me. There's lots of men my age overseas. After all, it is war time and ...

HENRY: And you're handling our appeal.

GEORGE: (*Pause.*) We have other lawyers.

HENRY: But you're the one who knows the case!

GEORGE: (*Pause.*) I knew you were going to take this hard. Believe me, Henry, my being drafted has nothing to do with your case. It's just a coincidence.

HENRY: Like our being in here for life is a coincidence?

GEORGE: No, that's another ...

HENRY: Like our being hounded every goddam day of our life is a coincidence?

GEORGE: Henry ... (HENRY *turns away furiously. There is a pause.*) It's useless anger, son, believe me. Actually, I'm quite flattered by your concern, but I'm hardly indispensable.

HENRY: (*Deeply disturbed.*) What the hell are you talking about, George?

GEORGE: I'm talking about all the people trying to get you out. Hundreds, perhaps thousands. Alice and I aren't the only ones. We've got a heck of a fine team of lawyers working on the brief. With or without me, the appeal will be won. I promise you that.

HENRY: It's no use, George.

GEORGE: I realize all that sounds pretty unconvincing under the circumstances, but it's true.

HENRY: Those bastard cops are never going to let us out of here. We're here for life and that's it.

GEORGE: You really believe that?

HENRY: What do you expect me to believe?

GEORGE: I wish I could answer that, son, but that's really for you to say.

GUARD: Time, Counselor.

GEORGE: Coming. (*Turns to the other* BOYS.) Listen, boys, I don't know where in the world I'll be the day your appeal is won—and it will be won—whether it's in the Pacific somewhere or in Europe or in a hole in the ground ... Take care of yourselves.

TOMMY: See you around, George.

SMILEY: So long, George.

JOEY: 'Bye, Cheer.

GEORGE: Yeah. See you around. (*Pause.*) Goodbye, Henry. Good luck and God bless you.

HENRY: God bless you, too, George. Take care of yourself.

TOMMY: Say, George, when you come back from the war, we're going to take you outa town and blast some weed.

JOEY: We'll get you a pair of buns you can hold in your hands!

GEORGE: I may just take you up on that. (*The* GUARD *escorts* GEORGE *out, then turns back to the* BOYS.)

GUARD: All right, new work assignments. Everybody report to the jute mill. Let's go. (SMILEY, JOEY *and* TOMMY *start to exit.* HENRY *hangs back.*) What's the matter with you, Reyna? You got lead in your pants? I said let's go.

HENRY: We're supposed to work in the mess hall.

GUARD: You got a new assignment.

HENRY: Since when?

GUARD: Since right now. Get going!

HENRY: (*Hanging back.*) The warden know about this?

GUARD: What the hell do you care? You think you're something special? Come on, greaseball. Move!

HENRY: Make me, you bastard!

GUARD: Oh yeah. (*The* GUARD *pushes* HENRY. HENRY *pushes back. The batos react, as the* GUARD *traps* HENRY *with his club around the chest. The* BOYS *move to* HENRY's *defense.*) Back!

HENRY: (*To the batos.*) Back off! BACK OFF! Don't be stupid.

GUARD: Okay, Reyna, you got solitary! Bastard, huh? Into the hole! (HE *pushes* HENRY *onto center stage. Lights down. A single spot.*) Line, greaseballs. Move out! (*As they march.*) Quickly, quickly. You're too slow. Move, move, move. (*The* BOYS *exit with the* GUARD.)

........................ 5. SOLITARY ........................

*A lone saxophone sets the mood.*

PACHUCO: Too bad, ese. He set you up again.

HENRY: (*Long pause.* HE *looks around.*) Solitary, ese ... they
    gave me solitary. (HE *sits down on the floor, a forlorn
    figure.*)
PACHUCO: Better get used to it, carnal. That's what this stretch
    is going to be about, see? You're in here for life, bato.
HENRY: I can't accept it, ese.
PACHUCO:

> You've got to, Hank ...
> only this reality is real now,
> only this place is real,
> sitting in the lonely cell of your will ...

HENRY: I can't see my hands.
PACHUCO:

> Then tell your eyes to forget the light, ese
> Only the hard floor is there, carnal
> Only the cold hard edge of this reality
> and there is no time ...
> Each second is a raw drop of blood from your brain
> that you must swallow
> drop by drop
> and don't even start counting
> or you'll lose your mind ...

HENRY: I've got to know why I'm here, ese! I've got to have a
    reason for being here.
PACHUCO: You're here, Hank, because you chose to be—because
    you protected your brother and your family. And nobody
    knows the worth of that effort better than you, ese.
HENRY: I miss them, ese ... my jefitos, my carnalillo, my sis ...
    I miss Della.
PACHUCO: (*A spot illuminates* HENRY's *family standing upstage;*
    EL PACHUCO *snaps it off.*)

> Forget them!
> Forget them all.
> Forget your family and the barrio
> beyond the wall.

HENRY: There's still a chance I'll get out.
PACHUCO: Fat chance.
HENRY: I'm talking about the appeal!
PACHUCO: And I'm talking about what's real! ¿Qué traes, Hank?
    Haven't you learned yet?

HENRY: Learned what?
PACHUCO:

> Not to expect justice when it isn't there.
> No court in the land's going to set you free.
> Learn to protect your loves by binding them
> in hate, ese! Stop hanging on to false hopes.
> The moment those hopes come crashing down,
> you'll find yourself on the ground foaming at
> the mouth. ¡Como loco!

HENRY: (*Turning on him furiously.*) ¿Sabes qué? Don't tell me
any more. I don't need you to tell me what to do. Fuck off!
FUCK OFF! (HENRY *turns away from* EL PACHUCO.
*Long pause. An anxious, intense moment.* EL PACHUCO
*shifts gears and breaks the tension with a satirical twist.*
HE *throws his arms out and laughs.*)
PACHUCO:

> ¡Órale pues!
> Don't take the pinche play so seriously, Jesús!
> Es puro vacilón!
> Watcha.

(HE *snaps his fingers. Lights change. We hear the sounds of the
city.*)

> This is Los, carnal.
> You want to see some justice for pachucos?
> Check out what's happening back home today.
> The Navy has landed, ese—
> on leave with full pay
> and war's breaking out in the streets of L.A.!

.................. 6. ZOOT SUIT RIOTS ...................

*We hear music: the bugle call from "Bugle Call Rag." Suddenly
the stage is awash in colored lights. The city of Los Angeles appears
in the background in a panoramic vista of lights tapering into the
night horizon.* SAILORS *and* GIRLS *jitterbug on the dance floor.
It is the Avalon Ballroom. The music is hot, the dancing hotter.* EL
PACHUCO *and* HENRY *stand to the side.*

*The scene is in dance and mostly pantomime. Occasionally
words are heard over the music which is quite loud. On the floor*

*are two* SAILORS (SWABBIE *is one.*) *and a* MARINE *dancing with the* GIRLS. *A* SHORE PATROLMAN *speaks to the* CIGARETTE GIRL. *A* PIMP *comes on and watches the action.* LITTLE BLUE *and* ZOOTER *are also on the floor.* RUDY *enters wearing* HENRY*'s zoot suit with* BERTHA *and* LUPE. LUPE *takes their picture, then all three move up center to the rear of the ballroom.* CHOLO *comes in down center, sees them and moves up stage. All four make an entrance onto the dance floor.*

*The* MARINE *takes his girl aside after paying her.* SHE *passes the money to the* PIMP. *The* SAILORS *try to pick up on* LUPE *and* BERTHA, *and* CHOLO *pushes one back. The* SAILORS *complain to the* SHORE PATROL, *who throws* CHOLO *out the door down center. There is an argument that* RUDY *joins. The* SAILORS *go back to* BERTHA *and* LUPE *who resist.* CHOLO *and* RUDY *go to their defense and a fight develops.* ZOOTER *and* LITTLE BLUE *split.* CHOLO *takes the* GIRLS *out and* RUDY *pulls a knife. He is facing the three* SAILORS *and the* MARINE, *when* THE PACHUCO *freezes the action.*

PACHUCO: (*Forcefully.*) Órale, that's enough! (EL PACHUCO *takes* RUDY*'s knife and with a tap sends him off-stage.* RUDY *exits with the* GIRLS. EL PACHUCO *is now facing the angry* SERVICEMEN. *He snaps his fingers. The* PRESS *enters quickly to the beeping sound of a radio broadcast.*)

PRESS: Good evening, Mr. and Mrs. North and South America and all the ships at sea. Let's go to press. FLASH. Los Angeles, California, June 3, 1943. Serious rioting broke out here today as flying squadrons of Marines and soldiers joined the Navy in a new assault on zooter-infested districts. A fleet of twenty taxicabs carrying some two hundred servicemen pulled out of the Naval Armory in Chavez Ravine tonight and assembled a task force that invaded the eastside barrio. (*Unfreeze. The following speeches happen simultaneously.*)

MATE: You got any balls in them funny pants, boy?

SAILOR: He thinks he's tough ...

SWABBIE: How about it, lardhead? You a tough guy or just a draft dodger?

PRESS: The Zoot Suiters, those gamin' dandies ...

PACHUCO: (*Cutting them off.*) Why don't you tell them what I really am, ese, or how you've been forbidden to use the very word ...

PRESS: We are complying in the interest of the war.
PACHUCO: How have you complied?
PRESS: We're using other terms.
PACHUCO: Like "pachuco" and "zoot suiter?"
PRESS: What's wrong with that? The Zoot Suit Crime Wave is
      even beginning to push the war news off the front page.
PACHUCO:

> The Press distorted the very meaning of the word "zoot
>     suit."
> All it is for you guys is another way to say Mexican.
> But the ideal of the original chuco
> was to look like a diamond
> to look sharp
> hip
> bonaroo
> finding a style of urban survival
> in the rural skirts and outskirts
> of the brown metropolis of Los, cabrón.

PRESS: It's an afront to good taste.
PACHUCO: Like the Mexicans, Filipinos and blacks who wear
      them.
PRESS: Yes!
PACHUCO: Even the white kids and the Wops and the Jews are
      putting on the drape shape.
PRESS: You are trying to outdo the white man in exaggerated white
      man's clothes!
PACHUCO:

> Because everybody knows
> that Mexicans, Filipinos and Blacks
> belong to the huarache
> the straw hat and the dirty overall.

PRESS: You savages weren't even wearing clothes when the white
      man pulled you out of the jungle.
MARINE: My parents are going without collars and cuffs so you
      can wear that shit.
PRESS: That's going too far, too goddamned far and it's got to be
      stopped!
PACHUCO: Why?
PRESS: Don't you know there's a war on? Don't you fucking well
      know you can't get away with that shit? What are we fight-

ing for if not to annihilate the enemies of the American way of life?

MATE: Let's tear it off his back!

SAILORS / MARINE: Let's strip him! Get him! (Etc.)

PRESS: KILL THE PACHUCO BASTARD! ! (*Music: "American Patrol" by Glenn Miller. The* PRESS *gets a searchlight from upstage center while the* FOUR SERVICEMEN *stalk* EL PACHUCO.)

SAILOR: Heh, zooter. Come on, zooter!

SWABBIE: You think you're more important than the war, zooter?

MATE: Let's see if you got any balls in them funny pants, boy.

SWABBIE: Watch out for the knife.

SAILOR: That's a real chango monkey suit he's got on.

MATE: I bet he's half monkey—just like the Filipinos and Niggers that wear them.

SWABBIE: You trying to outdo the white man in them glad rags, Mex? (*They fight now to the finish.* EL PACHUCO *is overpowered and stripped as* HENRY *watches helplessly from his position. The* PRESS *and* SERVICEMEN *exit with pieces of* EL PACHUCO's *zoot suit.* EL PACHUCO *stands. The only item of clothing on his body is a small loincloth.* HE *turns and looks at* HENRY, *with mystic intensity.* HE *opens his arms as an Aztec conch blows, and* HE *slowly exits backward with powerful calm into the shadows. Silence.* HENRY *comes downstage.* HE *absorbs the impact of what* HE *has seen and falls to his knees at center stage, spent and exhausted. Lights down.*)

........................ 7. ALICE ........................

*The* GUARD *and* ALICE *enter from opposite sides of the stage. The* GUARD *carries a handful of letters and is reading one of them.*

GUARD: July 2, 1943.

ALICE:

Dear Henry,

I hope this letter finds you in good health and good spirits—but I have to assume you've heard about the riots in Los Angeles. It was a nightmare, and it lasted for a week. The city is still in a state of shock.

GUARD: (*Folds letter back into envelope, then opens another.*) August 5, 1943.

ALICE:

Dear Henry,

The riots here in L.A. have touched off race riots all over the country—Chicago, Detroit, even little Beaumont, Texas, for Christ's sake. But the one in Harlem was the worst. Millions of dollars worth of property damage. 500 people were hospitalized, and five Negroes were killed.

GUARD: Things are rough all over.

ALICE: Please write to me and tell me how you feel.

GUARD: (*The* GUARD *folds up the second letter, stuffs it back into its envelope and opens a third.*) August 20, 1943.

ALICE:

Dear Henry,

Although I am disappointed not to have heard from you, I thought I would send you some good news for a change. Did you know we had a gala fund-raiser at the Mocambo?

GUARD: The Mocambo ... Hotcha!

ALICE:

... and Rita Hayworth lent your sister Lupe a ball gown for the occasion. She got dressed at Cecil B. DeMille's house, and she looked terrific. Her escort was Anthony Quinn, and Orson Welles said ...

GUARD: Orson Welles! Well! Sounds like Louella Parsons. (HE *folds up the letter.*) September 1, 1943.

ALICE: Henry, why aren't you answering my letters?

GUARD: He's busy. (HE *continues to stuff the envelope.*)

ALICE: Henry, if there's something I've said or done ... ? (*The* GUARD *shuffles the envelopes.*) Henry ... (*Lights change.* GUARD *crosses to center stage, where* HENRY *is still doubled up on the floor.*)

GUARD: Welcome back to the living, Reyna. It's been a long hot summer. Here's your mail. (*The* GUARD *tosses the letters to the floor directly in front of* HENRY's *head.* HENRY *looks up slowly and grabs one of the letters.* HE *opens it, trying to focus. The* GUARD *exits.*)

ALICE: Henry, I just found out you did ninety days in solitary. I'm furious at the rest of the guys for keeping it from me. I talked to Warden Duffy, and he said you struck a guard. Did something happen I should know about? I wouldn't ask if it wasn't so important, but a clean record ... (HENRY *rips up the letter he has been reading and scatters the others. Alarmed.*) Henry? (HENRY *pauses, his instant fury spent and under control.* HE *sounds almost weary, but the anger is still there.*)

HENRY: You still don't understand, Alice.

ALICE: (*Softly, compassionate.*) But I do! I'm not accusing you of anything. I don't care what happened or why they sent you there. I'm sure you had your reasons. But you know the public is watching you.

HENRY: (*Frustrated, a deep question.*) Why do you do this, Alice?

ALICE: What?

HENRY: The appeal, the case, all the shit you do. You think the public gives a goddamn?

ALICE: (*With conviction.*) Yes! We are going to get you out of here, Henry Reyna. We are going to win!

HENRY: (*Probing.*) What if we lose?

ALICE: (*Surprised but moving on.*) We're not going to lose.

HENRY: (*Forcefully, insistent, meaning more than* HE *is saying.*) What if we do? What if we get another crooked judge, and he nixes the appeal?

ALICE: Then we'll appeal again. We'll take it to the Supreme Court. (*A forced laugh.*) Hell, we'll take it all the way to President Roosevelt!

HENRY: (*Backing her up—emotionally.*) What if we still lose?

ALICE: (*Bracing herself against his aggression.*) We can't.

HENRY: Why can't we?

ALICE: (*Giving a political response in spite of herself.*) Because we've got too much support. You should see the kinds of people responding to us. Unions, Mexicans, Negroes, Oakies. It's fantastic.

HENRY: (*Driving harder.*) Why can't we lose, Alice?

ALICE: I'm telling you.

HENRY: No, you're not.

ALICE: (*Starting to feel vulnerable.*) I don't know what to tell you.

HENRY: Yes, you do!

ALICE: (*Frightened.*) Henry ... ?

HENRY: Tell me why we can't lose, Alice!

ALICE: (*Forced to fight back, with characteristic passion.*) Stop it, Henry! Please stop it! I won't have you treat me this way. I never have been able to accept one person pushing another around ... pushing me around! Can't you see that's why I'm here? Because I can't stand it happening to you. Because I'm a Jew, goddammit! I have been there ... I have been there! If you lose, I lose. (*Pause. The emotional tension is immense.* ALICE *fights to hold back tears.* SHE *turns away.*)

HENRY: I'm sorry ...

ALICE: (*Pause.*) It's stupid for us to fight like this. I look forward to coming here for weeks. Just to talk to you, to be with you, to see your eyes.

HENRY: (*Pause.*) I thought a lot about you when I was in the hole. Sometimes ... sometimes I'd even see you walk in, in the dark, and talk to me. Just like you are right now. Same look, same smile, same perfume ... (HE *pauses.*) Only the other one never gave me so much lip. She just listened. She did say one thing. She said ...

ALICE: (*Trying to make light of it. Then more gently.*) I can't say that to you, Henry. Not the way you want it.

HENRY: Why not?

ALICE: (SHE *means it.*) Because I can't allow myself to be used to fill in for all the love you've always felt and always received from all your women.

HENRY: (*With no self-pity.*) Give it a chance, Alice.

ALICE: (*Beside herself.*) Give it a chance? You crazy idiot. If I thought making love to you would solve all your problems, I'd do it in a second. Don't you know that? But it won't. It'll only complicate things. I'm trying to help you, goddammit. And to do that, I have to be your friend, not your white woman.

HENRY: (*Getting angry.*) What makes you think I want to go to bed with you. Because you're white? I've had more white pieces of ass than you can count, ¿sabes? Who do you think you are? God's gift to us brown animals.

ALICE: (ALICE *slaps him and stops, horrified. A whirlpool of emotions.*) Oh, Hank. All the love and hate it's taken to get us together in this lousy prison room. Do you realize only Hitler and the Second World War could have accomplished that? I don't know whether to laugh or cry. (ALICE *folds into her emotional spin, her body shaking. Suddenly she turns, whipping herself out of it with a cry, both laughing and weeping. They come to each other and embrace. Then they kiss—passionately. The* GUARD *enters. HE frowns.*)

GUARD: Time, Miss.

ALICE: (*Turning.*) Already? Oh, my God, Henry, there's so many messages I was going to give you. Your mother and father send their love, of course. And Lupe and ... Della. And ... oh, yes. They want you to know Rudy's in the Marines.

HENRY: The Marines?

ALICE: I'll write you all about it. Will you write me?

HENRY: (*A glance at the* GUARD.) Yes.

GUARD: (*His tone getting harsher.*) Let's go, lady.

HENRY: Goodbye, Licha.

ALICE: I'll see you on the outside ... Hank. (ALICE *gives* HENRY *a thumb up gesture, and the* GUARD *escorts her out.* HENRY *turns downstage, full of thoughts. HE addresses* EL PACHUCO, *who is nowhere to be seen.*)

HENRY: You were wrong, ese ... There's is something to hope for. I know now we're going to win the appeal. Do you hear me, ese? Ese! (*Pause.*) Are you even there any more? (*The* GUARD *re-enters at a clip.*)

GUARD: Okay, Reyna, come on.

HENRY: Where to?

GUARD: We're letting you go ... (HENRY *looks at him incredulously. The* GUARD *smiles.*) ... to Folsom Prison with all the rest of the hardcore cons. You really didn't expect to walk out of here a free man, did you? Listen, kid, your appeal stands about as much chance as the Japs and Krauts of winning the war. Personally, I don't see what that broad sees in you. I wouldn't give you the sweat off my balls. Come on! (HENRY *and the* GUARD *turn upstage to leave. Lights change.* EL PACHUCO *appears halfway up the backdrop, fully dressed again and clearly visible.* HENRY *stops with a jolt as HE sees him.* EL PACHUCO *lifts his arms. Lights go down as we hear the high sound of a bomb falling to earth.*)

············ 8. THE WINNING OF THE WAR ············

*The aerial bomb explodes with a reverberating sound and a*

*white flash that illuminates the form of pachuco images in the black
backdrop. Other bombs fall and all hell breaks loose. Red flashes,
artillery, gunfire, ack-ack.* HENRY *and the* GUARD *exit. The*
FOUR SERVICEMEN *enter as an honor guard. Music: Glen
Miller's "Saint Louis Blues March." As the* SERVICEMEN *march
on we see* RUDY *down left in his marine uniform, belt undone.*
ENRIQUE, DOLORES *and* LUPE *join him.* DOLORES *has his
hat,* LUPE *her camera.* ENRIQUE *fastens two buttons on the uniform as* RUDY *does up his belt.* DOLORES *inspects his collar and
gives him his hat.* RUDY *puts on his hat and all pose for* LUPE. *She
snaps the picture and* RUDY *kisses them all and is off.* HE *picks up
the giant switchblade from behind a newspaper bundle and joins the*
SERVICEMEN *as they march down in drill formation. The family
marches off, looking back sadly. The drill ends and* RUDY *and the*
SHORE PATROL *move to one side. As* RUDY*'s interrogation goes
on,* PEOPLE *in the barrio come on with newspapers to mime daily
tasks. The* PRESS *enters.*

PRESS: The Los Angeles Examiner, July 1, 1943.  Headline:
WORLD WAR II REACHES TURNING POINT. If the
late summer of 1942 was the low point, a year later the
war for the Allies is pounding its way to certain victory.

SHORE PATROL: July 10!

RUDY: U.S., British and Canadian troops invade Sicily, Sir!

SHORE PATROL: August 6!

RUDY: U.S. troops occupy Solomon Island, Sir!

SHORE PATROL: September 5!

RUDY: MacArthur's forces land on New Guinea, Sir!

SHORE PATROL: October 1!

RUDY: U.S. Fifth Army enters Naples, Sir!

PRESS: On and on it goes.  From Corsica to Kiev, from Tarawa
to Anzio.  The relentless advance of the Allied armies
cannot be checked. (*One by one,* HENRY*'s family and
friends enter, carrying newspapers. They tear the papers
into small pieces.*) The Los Angeles Times, June 6, 1944.
Headline: Allied forces under General Eisenhower land
in Normandy.

SHORE PATROL: August 19!

RUDY: American First Army reaches Germany, Sir!

SHORE PATROL: October 17!

RUDY: MacArthur returns to the Philippines, Sir!

PRESS: On the homefront, Americans go on with their daily lives
with growing confidence and relief, as the war pushes on

toward inevitable triumph. (*Pause.*)  The Los Angeles
Daily News, Wednesday, November 8, 1944. Headline:
District Court of Appeals decides in Sleepy Lagoon murder case ... boys in pachuco murder given ...
PEOPLE: FREEDOM!!! (*Music bursts forth as the joyous crowd
tosses the shredded newspaper into the air like confetti. The
BOYS enter upstage center, and the crowd rushes to them,
weeping and cheering. There are kisses and hugs and tears
of joy. HENRY is swept forward by the triumphal proces-
sion.*)

............... 9. RETURN TO THE BARRIO ...............

*The music builds and people start dancing.  Others just em-
brace.  The tune is "Soldado Razo" played to a lively corrido beat.
It ends with joyous applause, laughter and tears.*

RUDY: ¡Ese carnal!
HENRY: Rudy!!
DOLORES: ¡Bendito sea Dios! Who would believe this day would
    ever come? Look at you—you're all home!
LUPE: I still can't believe it.  We won!  We won the appeal!
    (*Cheers.*)
ENRIQUE: I haven't felt like this since Villa took Zacatecas.
    (*Laughter, cheers.*) ¡Pero mira! Look who's here. Mis
    hijos. (*Puts his arm around HENRY and RUDY.*) It isn't
    every day a man has two grown sons come home from so
    far away—one from the war, the other from ... bueno,
    who cares? The Sleepy Lagoon is history, hombre. For a
    change, los Mexicanos have won! (*Cheers.*)
GEORGE: Well, Henry. I don't want to say I told you so, but we
    sure taught Judge Charles a lesson in misconduct, didn't
    we? (*More cheers.*)  Do you realize this is the greatest
    victory the Mexican-American community has ever had
    in the history of this whole blasted country?
DOLORES: Yes, but if it wasn't for the unselfish thoughtfulness of
    people like you and this beautiful lady—and all the people
    who helped out, Mexicanos, Negros, all Americanos—our
    boys would not be home today.
GEORGE: I only hope you boys realize how important you are
    now.
JOEY: Pos, I realize it, ese. (*Laughter.*)

RUDY: I came all the way from Hawaii just to get here, carnal. I
　　only got a few days, but I'm going to get you drunk.
HENRY: Pos, we'll see who gets who drunk, ese. (*Laughter and
　　hoots.* HENRY *spots* EL PACHUCO *entering from stage
　　right.*)
DOLORES: Jorge, Licha, todos. Let's go into the house, eh? I've
　　made a big pot of menudo, and it's for everybody.
ENRIQUE: There's ice-cold beer too. Vénganse, vamos todos.
GEORGE: (*To* ALICE.) Alice ... Menudo, that's Mexican chicken
　　soup? (*Everybody exits, leaving* HENRY *behind with* EL
　　PACHUCO.)
HENRY: It's good to see you again, ese. I thought I'd lost you.
PACHUCO: H'm pues, it'd take more than the U.S. Navy to wipe
　　me out.
HENRY: Where you been?
PACHUCO: Pos, here in the barrio. Welcome back.
HENRY: It's good to be home.
PACHUCO: No hard feelings?
HENRY: Chale—we won, didn't we?
PACHUCO: Simón.
HENRY: Me and the batos have been in a lot of fights together,
　　ese. But we won this one, because we learned to fight in
　　a new way.
PACHUCO: And that's the perfect way to end of this play—happy
　　ending y todo. (PACHUCO *makes a sweeping gesture.
　　Lights come down.* HE *looks up at the lights, realizing
　　something is wrong.* HE *flicks his wrist, and the lights go
　　back up again.*)

　　But life ain't that way, Hank.
　　The barrio's still out there, waiting and wanting.
　　The cops are still tracking us down like dogs.
　　The gangs are still killing each other,
　　Families are barely surviving,
　　And there in your own backyard ... life goes on.

　　(*Soft music.* DELLA *enters.*)
DELLA: Hank? (HENRY *goes to her and they embrace.*)
HENRY: Where were you? Why didn't you come to the Hall of
　　Justice to see us get out?
DELLA: I guess I was a little afraid things had changed. So much
　　has happened to both of us.
PACHUCO: Simón. She's living in your house.

DELLA: After I got back from Ventura, my parents gave me a choice. Forget about you or get out.

HENRY: Why didn't you write to me?

DELLA: You had your own problems. Your jefitos took care of me. Hey, you know what, Hank, I think they expect us to get married.

PACHUCO: How about it, ese? You still going to give her that big pachuco wedding you promised?

HENRY: I have to think about it.

ALICE: (*Off-stage.*) Henry?

PACHUCO: (*Snaps fingers.*) Wish you had the time. But here comes Licha.

ALICE: (*Entering.*) Henry, I've just come to say good night. (DELLA *freezes and* HENRY *turns to* ALICE.)

HENRY: Good night? Why are you leaving so soon?

ALICE: Soon? I've been here all afternoon. There'll be other times, Henry. You're home now, with your family, that's what matters.

HENRY: Don't patronize me, Alice.

ALICE: (*Surprised.*) Patronize you?

HENRY: Yeah. I learned a few words in the joint.

ALICE: Yo también, Hank. Te quiero. (PACHUCO *snaps.* ALICE *freezes, and* RUDY *enters.*)

RUDY: Ese, carnal, congratulations, the jefita just told me about you and Della. That's great, ese. But if you want me to be best man, you better do it in the next three days.

HENRY: Wait a minute, Rudy, don't push me.

RUDY: Qué pues, getting cold feet already? (HENRY *is beginning to be surrounded by separate conversations.*)

DELLA: If you don't want me here, I can move out.

RUDY: Watcha. I'll let you and Della have our room tonight, bato. I'll sleep on the couch.

ALICE: You aren't expecting me to sleep here, are you?

HENRY: I'm not asking you to.

PACHUCO/ALICE/RUDY/DELLA: Why not?

RUDY: The jefitos will never know, ese.

ALICE: Be honest, Henry.

DELLA: What do you want me to do?

HENRY: Give me a chance to think about it. Give me a second!

PACHUCO: One second! (PACHUCO *snaps.* ENRIQUE *enters.*)

ENRIQUE: Bueno, bueno, pues, what are you doing out here, hijo? Aren't you coming in for menudo?

HENRY: I'm just thinking, jefito.

ENRIQUE: ¿De qué, hombre? Didn't you do enough of that in prison? Andale, this is your house. Come in and live again.

HENRY: 'Apá, did you tell Della I was going to marry her?

ENRIQUE: Yes, but only after you did.

RUDY: ¿Qué traes, carnal? Don't you care about Della anymore?

ALICE: If it was just me and you, Henry, it might be different. But you have to think of your family.

HENRY: I don't need you to tell me my responsibilities.

ALICE: I'm sorry.

RUDY: Sorry, carnal.

DELLA: I don't need anybody to feel sorry for me. I did what I did because I wanted to. All I want to know is what's going to happen now. If you still want me, órale, suave. If you don't, that's okay, too. But I'm not going to hang around like a pendeja all my life.

RUDY: Your huisa's looking finer than ever, carnal.

ALICE: You're acting as if nothing has happened.

ENRIQUE: You have your whole life ahead of you.

ALICE: You belong here, Henry. I'm the one that's out of place.

RUDY: If you don't pick up on her, I'm going to have to step in.

HENRY: That's bullshit. What about what we shared in prison? I've never been that close to anybody.

ALICE: That was in prison.

HENRY: What the hell do you think the barrio is?

RUDY: It's not bullshit!

HENRY: Shut up, carnalillo!

RUDY: Carnalillo? How can you still call me that? I'm not your pinche little brother no more.

GEORGE: (*Entering.*) You guys have got to stop fighting, Henry, or the barrio will never change. Don't you realize you men represent the hope of your people?

ALICE: Della was in prison too. You know you had thousands of people clamoring for your release, but you were Della's only hope.

HENRY: Look, esa, I know you did a year in Ventura. I know you stood up for me when it counted. I wish I could make it up to you.

DELLA: Don't give me your bullshit, Henry. Give it to Alice.

ALICE: I think it's time for Alice Bloomfield to go home.

HENRY: Don't be jealous, esa.

DELLA: Jealous? Mira, cabrón, I know I'm not the only one you ever took to the Sleepy Lagoon.

RUDY: The Sleepy Lagoon ain't shit. I saw real lagoons in those islands, ese—killing Japs! I saw some pachucos go out there that are never coming back.

DELLA: But I was always there when you came back, was'nt I?

DOLORES: (*Entering.*) Henry? Come back inside, hijo. Everybody's waiting for you.

RUDY: Why didn't you tell them I was there, carnal? I was at the Sleepy Lagoon. Throwing chingazos with everybody!

HENRY: Don't you understand, Rudy? I was trying to keep you from getting a record. Those bastard cops are never going to leave us alone.

GEORGE: You've got to forget what happened, Henry.

HENRY: What can I give you, Della? I'm an ex-con.

DELLA: So am I!

SMILEY: (*Entering.*) Let's face it, Hank. There's no future for us in this town. I'm taking my wife and kid and moving to Arizona.

DOLORES: (*Simultaneously.*) I know what you are feeling, hijo, it's home again. I know inside you are afraid that nothing has changed. That the police will never leave you in peace. Pero no le hace. Everything is going to be fine now. Marry Della and fill this house with children. Just do one thing for me—forget the zoot suit clothes.

ENRIQUE: If there's one thing that will keep a man off the streets is his own familia.

GEORGE: Don't let this thing eat your heart out for the rest of your ...

ALICE: Sometimes the best thing you can do for someone you love is walk away.

DELLA: What do you want, Hank?

RUDY: It cost me more than it did you.

SMILEY: We started the 38th and I'll never forget you, carnal. But I got to think about my family.

HENRY: Wait a minute! I don't know if I'll be back in prison tomorrow or not! I have nothing to give you, Della. Not even a piece of myself.

DELLA: I have my life to live, too, Hank. I love you. I would even die for you. Pero me chingan la madre if I'm going to throw away my life for nothing.

HENRY: But I love you ... (*Both* GIRLS *turn.* HENRY *looks at* ALICE, *then to the whole group upstage of him. Still turning,* HE *looks at* DELLA *and goes to embrace her. The freeze ends and other people enter.*)

LUPE: ¡Órale, Hank! Watcha Joey. The crazy bato went all the way to his house and put on his drapes.

JOEY: ¡Esos, batoooooosss! ¡Esas, huisaaaaaass!

TOMMY: Look at this cat! He looks all reet.

LUPE: Yeah, like a parakeet!

HENRY: ¿Y tú, ese? How come you put on your tacuche? Where's the party?

JOEY: Pos, ain't the party here?

RUDY: Yeah, ese, but this ain't the Avalon Ballroom. The zoot suit died under fire here in Los. Don't you know that, cabrón?

ENRIQUE: Rudolfo!

LUPE: And he was supposed to get Henry drunk.

RUDY: Shut up, esa!

ENRIQUE: ¡Ya pues! Didn't you have any menudo? Vieja, fix him a great big bowl of menudo and put plenty of chile in it. We're going to sweat it out of him.

RUDY: I don't need no pinche menudo.

HENRY: Watch your language, carnal.

RUDY: And I don't need you! I'm a man. I can take care of myself!

JOEY: Muy marine el bato ...

ENRIQUE: Rudy, hijo. Are you going to walk into the kitchen or do I have to drag you.

RUDY: Whatever you say, jefito.

GEORGE: Well, Alice. This looks like the place where we came in. I think it's about time we left.

ALICE: Say the word, George, just say the word.

DOLORES: No, no. You can't leave so soon.

JOEY: Chale, chale, chale. You can't take our Grandma. ¿Qué se trae, carnal? Póngase más abusado, ese. No se haga tan square.

GEORGE: Okay, square I got. What was the rest of it?

JOEY: Pos, le estoy hablando en chicas patas, ese. Es puro chicano.

RUDY: ¿Qué chicano? Ni que madre, cabrón. Why don't you grow up?

JOEY: Grow up, ese?

RUDY: Try walking downtown looking like that. See if the sailors don't skin your ass alive.

JOEY: So what? It's no skin off your ass. Come on, Bertha.

RUDY: She's staying with me.

JOEY: She's mine.

RUDY: Prove it, punk. (RUDY *attacks* JOEY *and they fight. The* BATOS *and* RUCAS *take out* JOEY. HENRY *pacifies* RUDY, *who bursts out crying.* ENRIQUE, DELLA, DO-LORES, ALICE, LUPE *and* GEORGE *are the only ones left.* RUDY *in a flush of emotion.*) Cabrones, se amon-tonaron. They ganged up on me, carnal. You left me and they ganged up on me. You shouldn't have done it, car-nal. Why didn't you take me with you. For the jefitos? The jefitos lost me anyway.

HENRY: Come on in the house, Rudy ...

RUDY: No! I joined the Marines. I didn't have to join, but I went. ¿Sabes por qué? Because they got me, carnal. Me chin-garon, ese. (*Sobs.*) I went to the pinche show with Bertha, all chingón in your tachuche, ese. I was wearing your zoot suit, and they got me. Twenty sailors, Marines. We were up in the balcony. They came down from behind. They grabbed me by the neck and dragged me down the stairs, kicking and punching and pulling my greña. They dragged me out into the streets ... and all the people watched while they stripped me. (*Sobs.*) They stripped me, carnal. Bertha saw them strip me. Hijos de la chingada, they stripped me. (HENRY *goes to* RUDY *and embraces him with fierce love and desperation. Pause.* TOMMY *comes running in.*)

TOMMY: ¡Órale! There's cops outside. They're trying to arrest Joey. (GEORGE *crosses to* TOMMY.)

GEORGE: (*Bursting out.*) Joey?

TOMMY: They got him up against your car. They're trying to say he stole it!

GEORGE: Oh, God. I'll take care of this.

ALICE: I'll go with you. (GEORGE, TOMMY *and* ALICE *exit.*)

HENRY: Those fucking bastards! (HE *starts to exit.*)

DELLA: Henry, no!

HENRY: What the hell do you mean no? Don't you see what's going on outside?

DELLA: They'll get you again! That's what they want.

HENRY: Get out of my way! (HE *pushes her out of the way, toward* DOLORES.)

ENRIQUE: (*Stands up before Henry.*) ¡Hijo!

HENRY: Get out of my way, jefe!

ENRIQUE: You will stay here!

HENRY: Get out of my way! (ENRIQUE *powerfully pushes him back and throws* HENRY *to the floor and holds.*)

ENRIQUE: ¡TE DIGO QUE NO! (*Silent moment,* HENRY *stands up and offers to strike* ENRIQUE. *But something stops him. The realization that if* HE *strikes back or even if* HE *walks out the door, the family bond is irreparably broken.* HENRY *tenses for a moment, then relaxes and embraces his father.* DELLA *goes to them and joins the embrace. Then* DOLORES, *then* LUPE, *then* RUDY. *All embrace in a tight little group.* PRESS *enters right and comes down.*)

PRESS: Henry Reyna went back to prison in 1947 for robbery and assault with a deadly weapon. While incarcerated, he killed another inmate and he wasn't released until 1955, when he got into hard drugs. He died of the trauma of his life in 1972.

PACHUCO: That's the way you see it, ese. But there's other way to end this story.

RUDY: Henry Reyna went to Korea in 1950. He was shipped across in a destroyer and defended the 38th Parallel until he was killed at Inchon in 1952, being posthumously awarded the Congressional Medal of Honor.

ALICE: Henry Reyna married Della in 1948 and they have five kids, three of them now going to the University, speaking calo and calling themselves Chicanos.

GEORGE: Henry Reyna, the born leader ...

JUDGE: Henry Reyna, the social victim ...

BERTHA: Henry Reyna, the street corner warrior ...

SMILEY: Henry Reyna, el carnal de aquellas ...

JOEY: Henry Reyna, the zoot suiter ...

TOMMY: Henry Reyna, my friend ...

LUPE: Henry Reyna, my brother ...

ENRIQUE: Henry Reyna ...

DOLORES: Our son ...

DELLA: Henry Reyna, my love ...

PACHUCO: Henry Reyna ... El Pachuco ... The man ... the myth ... still lives. (*Lights down and fade out.*)

# BANDIDO !

**TIBURCIO VASQUEZ**

# BANDIDO!
## AN ANTI-MELODRAMA

After almost two hundred years of incessant dramatization in dime novels, creaky melodramas and movie westerns, the history of the Old West is such a blend of fiction, fact, conjecture and sheer poppycock that it amounts to a flawed American mythology *under constant revision.* Manifest Destiny and White racial superiority, the Old West's sacred cows in the nineteenth century, no longer roam the range quite so freely as we near the end of the twentieth century. Yet the cliches are still out there, like sacred cow chips.

The fact is most of what Americans called the Old West occupied a vast landscape which was once half the national territory of Mexico, and before that, open Indian land. The Gold Rush in California was enough to evoke desperadoes of every race and description, but it was the aftermath of the U.S. War with Mexico, which ceded the Golden State to the *gringos,* that gave birth to *bandidos* such as Joaquín Murrieta and Tiburcio Vásquez.

Although hailed as *resistance fighters* by their own people, both men are unquestionably part of the American mythology of the Old West, for they share the rare distinction of having had their lives staged professionally on the melodrama stages of Los Angeles and San Francisco. Yet their claim to fame was based on their notoriety, and their enduring memory owes much to their incorporation into Western conquest fiction as *stereotypes.*

Joaquín Murrieta, identified with the Gold Rush—1849–53—occupies the place of a legendary icon, even among Anglo-Americans. Tiburcio Vásquez, whose career spanned from 1853–1873, holds no such honor. He was the last man to be legally, publically executed in California, hanged in San Jose in 1875. Yet he lived close enough to the modern era to be regally photographed in captivity, in the celebrity of his infamous life and death before the wide-eyed daguerreotype cameras of his day.

This contrast between photographic portrait and melodramatic stereotype is all that survives of Vásquez in history books. Therefore, finding it almost impossible to avoid stepping into "gringo" cliches, this Chicano playwright has resorted to slinging sacred cow chips for the sake of satire.

*BANDIDO!* is thus a play within a play.  As the latest revision of the History of the Old West, I call it: THE AMERICAN MELODRAMA OF TIBURCIO VÁSQUEZ, NOTORIOUS CALIFORNIA BANDIT.

Luis Valdez

# BANDIDO!

## The American Melodrama of Tiburcio Vásquez Notorious California Bandit

# CHARACTERS

## THE JAIL

TIBURCIO VÁSQUEZ, notorious California bandit.
SHERIFF J.H. ADAMS, Sheriff of Santa Clara County.
SAMUEL P. GILLETTE, an Impresario.
JIMMY, a young deputy.
PETTIGREW, an older deputy.
LADY IN BLACK, a French journalist.
MRS. GILETTE, an actress.
ASSORTED LADIES, visitors.
PHOTOGRAPHER.

## THE MELODRAMA

TIBURCIO VÁSQUEZ, the Capitán.
CALIFORNIA KATE, a madam.
DAISY DOLITTLE, a soiled dove.
OTHER SOILED DOVES, singers and dancers.

ABDÓN LEIVA, Chilean miner.
ROSARIO LEIVA, his wife.
CLEODOVIO CHÁVEZ, a sheepherder.
RITA MADRID, Fandango dancer.
FIDDLER FELIZ, a blind fiddler.
GONZALES, a Mexican.
MORENO, an ex-aristocrat.

A. SNYDER, Tres Pinos storekeeper.
MRS. SNYDER, his wife.
LEWIS, a young customer.
BASQUE SHEEPHERDER, a murder victim.

ANDRÉS PICO, Californio general.
OLD GABRIEL, indio servant.
SOLEDAD, a midwife.

*The cast calls for a bare minimum of fifteen actors—ten men
and five women. As the play moves from the JAIL to the MELO-
DRAMA STAGE, some multiple roles should cover several characters.*

# TIME AND PLACE

*San Jose, California, 1875.*

# SETTING

*The Courthouse Jail and The American Melodrama Stage.*

The design of the set must support a play within a play. Downstage, in the foreground, we see the flat realistic interior of a tall brick jailhouse, lit with gas lamps. This realistic framework of the jail, featuring TIBURCIO's cell downstage right, and an area up left separated from the rear corridor by a wall of bars, serves as the infrastructure for the gilded melodrama stage into which it transforms.

The action of the play thus alternates from the jail to the stage.

The contrast of theatrical styles between the realism of the jail, and the *trompe l'oeil* of the melodrama is purely intentional and part of the theme of the play. Their subtle interaction is a matter of interpretation, but their combined reality must be a metaphor—and not a facile cliché—of the Old West.

# BEFORE THE RISE: The Overture

*The San Jose Jail setting is empty, its gas lamps flickering in the shadows of night. After the orchestral musical introduction, the lamps fade to black, and through a series of falling painted drops and light changes in the public eye, the jail is magically transformed into the American Melodrama Stage.*

*The play begins.*

# ACT ONE

...................... SCENE ONE ......................

CALIFORNIA KATE, *a buxom madam, appears before the footlights of the melodrama stage and sashays in front of the grand drapes.*

KATE: Howdy folks, I'm California Kate. Welcome to my palace of pleasure where everyman gets the royal treatment. I'm

gonna tell you about my favorite bandit, who stole even
my heart.

*Music.* KATE *begins to sing "The Ballad of Tiburcio Vásquez:"*

JOAQUÍN MURRIETA WAS KILLED AND BEHEADED
THREE-FINGERED JACK HIS COMPANION IS DEAD
JACK'S BLOODY HAND'S IN A STOCKTON MU-
    SEUM
A JAR OF WHISKEY HOLDS MURRIETA'S HEAD

THE GOLD RUSH FEVER THAT SCORCHED CAL-
    IFORNIA
BROUGHT OUT THE UGLIEST WORST TRAITS
    IN MEN
BUT THINGS WERE DEAD AS THE HEAD OF
    MURRIETA
TILL VÁSQUEZ STARTED IT OVER AGAIN!

*The curtain opens to reveal an oleo drop curtain, depicting:*
California Kate's Palace of Pleasure on the Barbary Coast, San
Francisco. August 1873.
*Sitting on a plush vermillion settee,* TIBURCIO VÁSQUEZ,
*a thirty-seven-year-old elegant dandy, is surrounded by a chorus of
prostitutes caressing and fondling the desperado.*

LADIES: (*Singing.*)

TIBURCIO VÁSQUEZ, THE BANDIT NOTORIOUS
WON FAME AND FORTUNE BY ROBBING THE
    STAGE
AND STOLE THE HEARTS OF ALL THE LUCK-
    LESS
WOMEN WHO GAVE HIM SUCCOR IN HIS ES-
    CAPADES.

VÁSQUEZ *cavorts and dances with the whores.*

LADIES: (*Singing.*)

THE CURR IS WANTONLY WANTED ALL OVER
FOR CRIMES COMMITTED WITH SCOUNDRELS
    AND THIEVES,
TIBURCIO VÁSQUEZ, UN HOMBRE MUCHO MALO
IS WANTED MOST BY THE LADIES HE LEAVES!

*The musical number ends with a flourish, and* KATE *steps up into the scene, clapping her hands.*

KATE: Awright, girls, back on the line. This ain't no goddamn boarding house! Move that merchandise and make it snappy. I want to hear them bedsprings working. (*The whores exit quickly.* DAISY DOLITTLE *hangs back.*)

DAISY: Bye, Tiburcio.

TIBURCIO: (*Kissing her hand.*) Adiós, mi querida flor.

KATE: Flor? If that don't beat hell. Her name is Daisy. Daisy Dolittle, the gentlemen's spittoon. Now go on, girlie, git your brassy tail in there. (DAISY *goes.*) Testy little slut.

TIBURCIO: (*Sardonic.*) From a flower to a spittoon. It's a pity. (TIBURCIO *turns his attentions to* KATE.)

KATE: Pity ain't the word for it. It's business. Harlots, trollops, strumpets, harridans—it don't matter what you call 'em. A soiled dove is a bird of prey or she's a dead bird. And you, you sloe-eyed pigeon plucker, you know exactly what I'm talking about.

TIBURCIO: (*Smiling slyly.*) Good to see you again, Kate. (*He turns and goes to the window.*)

KATE: What the hell did you come back for, anyway? You barely escaped to Mexico with your hide. Wasn't that enough?

TIBURCIO: San Francisco de Asís. I remember this town as a peaceful little pueblo by the bay. Now, look at it. Hotels, restaurants, theaters, saloons—a delicate swamp of carnal delights.

KATE: Scurrilous libertine. The vigilantes are going to stretch your greasy neck until your lying Spanish tongue hangs down like a cravat. Then what? Just another Mexican horse thief dancin' on air.

TIBURCIO: Long live the dance, Katarina, and the ladies! (*Music.*)

DAISY: (DAISY *re-enters at a clip.*) Ma'm?

KATE: You again?

DAISY: Sorry to bother you, but ...

KATE: I do not want to be disturbed. And you have a guest, I believe?

DAISY: But ...

KATE: Out!

DAISY: Sheriff Rowland is coming!

TIBURCIO: Rowland?

DAISY: I saw him from my window!

TIBURCIO: (*Amused.*) The Sheriff of Los Angeles?

KATE: A regular customer.

TIBURCIO: (TIBURCIO *urgently turns, looking for a place to hide.*) ¡Carajo! I've got to hide! (*He gets an idea.*) Ahh, of course.

KATE: Daisy, go to the front door and stall him until I figure out what to do!

TIBURCIO: Sorry, Kate. (TIBURCIO *ducks under* KATE's *ample skirt, hiding under her bustle. She starts to react, but* SHERIFF ROWLAND *enters.* DAISY *leaves.*)

KATE: John! What a surprise!

SHERIFF: My sweet Kate, good to see you again.

KATE: What brings you to San Francisco?

SHERIFF: (*Sheepish.*) Business my dear, Business ... and pleasure. Do you have any time for an old friend?

KATE: For you, Johnny. I've got the best in the house. Go on ahead to the Roman Emperor Suite, room six. I'll be there ... as usual.

SHERIFF: I'll be waiting for you. (SHERIFF ROWLAND *exits.* TIBURCIO *peeks out.*)

KATE: God almighty, this is professionally embarrassing.

TIBURCIO: Is he gone?

KATE: Yeah!

TIBURCIO: (*Sighs.*) Ah, the act of love! The only antidote to death known to man.

SHERIFF: (ROWLAND *suddenly re-enters.*) Kate, was that room six? (*Spotting* TIBURCIO.) Who are you?

TIBURCIO: (*Bowing foppishly.*) Señor, I am a cavalier with the heart of a cavalier. Soy caballero con el corazón de caballero.

SHERIFF: (*Suspicious.*) The hell you say. Mexican, Chilean or Peruvian?

TIBURCIO: (*Smiling through his teeth.*) A native born Californio, señor. Now a citizen of this great country of the United States. I'm from San Juan Bautista.

SHERIFF: Mister, has anyone ever told you, you're a dead ringer for Tiburcio Vásquez?

TIBURCIO: (*Pause. He laughs.*) Sheriff, I know we all look alike, but is this noble countenance the twisted visage of a convicted stage robber? Señor, I am Don Mariano Alejandro Cojones, a sus órdenes. Call me Alex.

SHERIFF: (*Glancing at* KATE.) State your business. What are you doin' in San Francisco?

TIBURCIO: An indelicate question, my friend, seeing how you and I share the same appreciation for the finer things in life.

KATE: Keep it under your hat, John. We prefer to be discreet about our Spanish clientele.

TIBURCIO: Discretion is the better part of valor, Sheriff. Relax. If you are really looking for Tiburcio Vásquez, try the San Gabriel Mountains. My rancho servants tell me he's planning a series of robberies that's going to terrorize the whole of California.

SHERIFF: Let him try it. He'll have the railroad and the telegraph to contend with. Progress is going to hang the horse thief, mister, sooner or later.

TIBURCIO: The evil that men do lives after them, Sheriff. The good is oft interred with their bones. So let it be with Vásquez.

SHERIFF: I'll drink to that.

KATE: How 'bout some whiskey, gents?

SHERIFF: What was your name again?

TIBURCIO: Don Mariano Alejandro Cabrón, at your service.

SHERIFF: It's a relief to meet a civilized Mexican for a change. Of course, if you were Vásquez, you'd be a dead man.

TIBURCIO: I doubt it, Sheriff. You see, like yourself, I'm the kind of gentleman who wouldn't be caught dead in a whorehouse. Salud! (KATE *rings a bell.*)

SHERIFF: Room six, you said, Kate?

KATE: That's right, John. Straight ahead, the one with the big brass spittoon. I'll join you in a minute. (DAISY *re-enters.*) Daisy, would you escort the Sheriff to his room and make him comfortable until I get there?

DAISY: Certainly, ma'm.

SHERIFF: See you down in San Juan sometime, Cabrón.

TIBURCIO: Any time, Harry. Mi casa es su casa. (ROWLAND *exits with* DAISY. TIBURCIO *drops his foppish pose.*) Your house was my house.

KATE: (*Bristling.*) Godawmighty, five years of hiding you out in the lap of luxury, giving you every comfort a warm American bed provides, and still I can't figure you out. Mister, you are some kind of lying, crazy coyote. You dumb son of a ...

TIBURCIO: (*Playful.*) Ah! Coyote, yes. Dumb, no.

KATE: What do you mean you wouldn't get caught dead in a whorehouse? Is that all this place is to you?

TIBURCIO: That depends. When did you start taking the law into
    your own hands?

KATE: Are you jealous?

TIBURCIO: (TIBURCIO *smiles, getting down to business.*) Did
    you get the guns I ordered?

KATE: (KATE *glances down the hall and then goes to a closet. She
    pulls out a stack of rifles.*) I dunno. Something tells me
    you've got a powerful itch somewhere in your hide, and
    you're about to scratch it. Do me a favor, will you? Don't
    draw blood. It'll be yours.

TIBURCIO: (TIBURCIO *lovingly examines the weapons.*) Ca-
    ramba, these are beautiful! (*Pause.*) Thank you, mi que-
    rida. I must go.

KATE: Go ahead! Get yourself killed! See if I care.

TIBURCIO: You sound like you mean that.

KATE: A twenty dollar gold piece says you don't make it across
    the Santa Clara valley.

TIBURCIO: Make it a hundred!

KATE: Heads or tails?

TIBURCIO: Tails, what else? (KATE *flips.*) What's the verdict?

KATE: Maidenheads ... You always were unlucky at gambling.

TIBURCIO: Ah! But I'm lucky at love. I'll pay you next time.
    Adiós mi querida Kate. May you and your lovely ladies
    prosper and live forever. (TIBURCIO *kisses her and then
    goes out with a flourish.*)

KATE: Just don't let them hang your ass, you hear me? Stay alive!
    You splendid scoundrel.

ROWLAND: (*Offstage.*) Kate!

KATE: Coming, Sheriff! Keep your britches on. Or better yet—
    take them off. (KATE *exits to her rendezvous with* ROW-
    LAND, *as the curtain falls.*)

*Musical interlude: set transformation.*

*Lights change: the oleo drops of the melodrama stage fly again
to reveal the barred iron framework of the San Jose Jail, complete
with its flickering gas lamps. The brick wall slides into position,
and the transformation is accomplished.*

...................... SCENE TWO ......................

*The Courthouse Jail, San Jose, California, 1875. It is morning.*
VÁSQUEZ, *age thirty-nine, is in his cell, holding a small hand*

*mirror and fastidiously finishing a trim on his goatee. A basin sits on a wash stand next to his bunk with cologne water, towel, books, etc. Presently,* J.H. ADAMS, *Sheriff of Santa Clara County, enters up center.*

ADAMS: Morning, Vásquez.

TIBURCIO: Buenos días, Harry.

ADAMS: You sound cheerful. Had breakfast?

TIBURCIO: Ate like a horse. A full belly, a happy heart, as the saying goes. Any more coffee?

ADAMS: Certainly. (*Calls off.*) Jimmy! More coffee for Vásquez.

TIBURCIO: (VÁSQUEZ *splashes cologne water on his face.*) What's the day like outside? ¿Mucho sol?

ADAMS: Fair to middlin'. Spring's upon us.

TIBURCIO: I've been quite comfortable in your modern jail, Sher-iff. Sure beats the dank dungeons of San Quentin prison. But the sun barely squeezes in through those squint-eyed holes up there. A man can barely read and write in this light, which, for a poet such as yours truly, amounts to cruel and unusual punishment.

ADAMS: Maximum security, Vásquez. That's why we brought you here from Salinas in the first place.

TIBURCIO: (VÁSQUEZ *puts on his gentleman's coat.*) I've got to hand it to you, Harry. You're a good man at eating humble pie. You chase me all over the state for months, but it's the Sheriff of Los Angeles that finally bags me. If I were you, I'd be grievously pissed.

ADAMS: If I were you, Tiburcio, I'd be grievously worried about my upcoming trial for murder. I've seen grown men break down and cry on the gallows.

TIBURCIO: Damned if I don't put on a bravura performance, Harry ... when the time comes. In fact, I'll wager you ten bucks, a bottle of wine and a Havana cigar, I'll hang.

ADAMS: You've got a bet, mister. (ADAMS *exits.* JIMMY, *a young deputy, enters with a coffee pot.*)

JIMMY: Fresh coffee, Mr. Vásquez.

TIBURCIO: Pour. (*He sticks his cup through the bars.* JIMMY *refills it.*) Hot as hell—perfecto. You're getting to be quite expert at this. Don't forget to brew another pot.

JIMMY: Jesus. I don't know how you sleep at night. All the coffee you drink all day.

TIBURCIO: No rest for the wicked, boy ... As for me, I'm sleeping fit as a well-fed dog. How's the roster today? Lots of lady visitors?

JIMMY: A mess of 'em. As usual.

TIBURCIO: (VÁSQUEZ *checks on his cards.*) Caramba, I'm almost out of photographs. Again. Another thousand ought to do it. Maybe two, three ... ¿quién sabe? Would you like one of these?

JIMMY: Sure.

TIBURCIO: Let me autograph it for you. (VÁSQUEZ *sits down and arranges his cards, pen and ink with a sense of self-importance.*)

JIMMY: Real fine hand ... your penmanship? Most folks don't expect it from a greas—greenhorn. (VÁSQUEZ *signs the card and blows on the ink, ignoring the gaff.*)

TIBURCIO: Tiburcio Vásquez, presente ... Simpático. The ladies say: he doesn't seem like such a bad fellow. Then they buy my pictures at fifty cents a shot. Here. On the house.

JIMMY: Thanks, Mr. Vásquez. (*Points at the basin.*) You done with that?

TIBURCIO: She's all yours ... But watch it. The water's a little greasy. (ADAMS *returns with* SAMUEL P. GILLETTE, *a theatrical impresario.* JIMMY *exits quickly.*) That's a fine muchacho, Harry. Won't make much of a Mexican-killer, though. Better send that one to law school ... Like the old Indian, he doesn't kill but he makes the arrows. (VÁSQUEZ *pulls a lean cigar from his coat, staring at* GILLETTE.)

SHERIFF: Tiburcio, you have a visitor.

TIBURCIO: Well, well. Samuel P. Gillette. What brings you to San Jose?

IMPRESARIO: Show business, sir. The lure of the footlights.

TIBURCIO: Have a chair—partner. (*The* IMPRESARIO *sits outside the cell.*)

SHERIFF: Gentlemen, you have five minutes. You may smoke, if you wish, but no drinking or profanity is allowed. I'll be back shortly. (SHERIFF ADAMS *exits.*)

IMPRESARIO: Can you believe I've turned that pasty-faced sheriff into a genuine western hero? Almost played him myself. You're looking damn good, Vásquez. How are you?

TIBURCIO: (VÁSQUEZ *smiles ironically: subdued, calm, realistic.*) Awaiting trial without a proper defense, Gillette. I need money for lawyers.

IMPRESARIO: You're a cause célèbre, sir. Catnip to the ladies. You ought to charge them admission.

TIBURCIO: How's the theater business?

IMPRESARIO: Risky, as always.

TIBURCIO: I hear the play was a great success.

IMPRESARIO: Rip-roaring-turn-away business for a fortnight, then nothing. You stole all the magic, sir, when they transfered you from Los Angeles. The public lost interest.

TIBURCIO: The business is all up here now, Gillette. People are hot to see the notorious Tiburcio before the hanging.

IMPRESARIO: Never fear, Vásquez. You'll get due process in court first. Then they'll hang you.

TIBURCIO: (*Pause.*) You violated the terms of our agreement, Gillette. Friends who saw your melodrama tell me you made me look like an ass.

IMPRESARIO: An ass?

TIBURCIO: I don't hide under women's skirts, mister. I'm not a coward. I thought we were partners.

IMPRESARIO: Partners in business, sir, not in crime.

TIBURCIO: Where's my money?

IMPRESARIO: Here. Your share of the profits from Los Angeles. (*The* IMPRESARIO *pulls out a leather sack and tosses it to* VÁSQUEZ, *who catches and weighs it with a knowing hand.*)

TIBURCIO: This is only two hundred dollars.

IMPRESARIO: It is indeed.

TIBURCIO: The deal was a thousand.

IMPRESARIO: Or forty percent of the profits. That's it.

TIBURCIO: (*Smiling cynically.*) Gillette, you cheap swindler.

IMPRESARIO: Are you questioning my honesty?

TIBURCIO: You have the nerve to try to rob me?

IMPRESARIO: You and I can still do a lot of business together, Vásquez. What would you say to a San Francisco production of the play? The public is attracted to your villainy, sir.

TIBURCIO: Get your thespian ass out of here, Gillette.

IMPRESARIO: Think of the money we could make, Vásquez. Between now and the trial? We ran for two solid weeks to packed houses in Los Angeles. But San Francisco? Think of it ... the populace is eager to slake their thirst, sir, drinking at the dark well of your notoriety. We'd make a fortune!

TIBURCIO: Am I really so notorious?

IMPRESARIO: You vain popinjay, you know you are!

TIBURCIO: A hundred years ago, my great grandfather founded San Francisco with De Anza. Fifty years ago José Tiburcio Vásquez was the law in San José. But today I, his namesake and grandson, cannot even walk the wooden side-walks of either city without a leash.

IMPRESARIO: Oh, come on, Vásquez. You're an outlaw, man. A bad man. The history of the West is replete with villains of your type. You're in every dime novel.

TIBURCIO: My life is not a cheap dime novel.

IMPRESARIO: Your criminal life is public domain, sir. I can always do the production without you.

TIBURCIO: Then, why come to me?

IMPRESARIO: As you so aptly reminded me in L.A., theaters have been known to burn down. I assume the warning is still in effect?

TIBURCIO: I'd find a way to kill you, if I had to.

IMPRESARIO: (*Pause.*) You know, that's the first honest thing you've said to me. Rather in character, wouldn't you say?

TIBURCIO: I'll agree to the deal on two conditions, Gillette. I want fifty percent of the profits ...

IMPRESARIO: Fifty percent!

TIBURCIO: ... before the trial. And I want it in cash. Moreover ...

IMPRESARIO: Moreover?

TIBURCIO: If I'm to be hanged for murder, I want the public to know I'm not guilty. (*He picks up a hand-written manuscript from his bedstand.*) Here's a few scenes I jotted down from memory. I want you to use them in your melodrama.

IMPRESARIO: That's preposterous.

TIBURCIO: How can you know until you read them?

IMPRESARIO: They're lies, and you know it. You're only trying to save your own neck.

TIBURCIO: Do you expect me to hang myself?

IMPRESARIO: Twenty years as a vicious desperado and never a single, solitary slaying? It won't wash Vásquez. You're entire career is full of too many dubious moral questions. We're talking about melodrama here. What's right is right, what's wrong is wrong. The public will only buy tickets to savour the evil in your soul.

TIBURCIO: (VÁSQUEZ *suddenly grabs the* IMPRESARIO *menacingly by the collar.*) Don't make me prove I'm a murderer, as well, Gillette. (SHERIFF ADAMS *enters, over-*

*hearing this last remark.* VÁSQUEZ *stuffs his manuscript into the* IMPRESARIO*'s pocket and releases him.*)

SHERIFF: Time is up, gentlemen.

TIBURCIO: The Impresario was just leaving.

IMPRESARIO: Good luck at your trial, Vásquez. May the best liar win. Adieu! (*The* IMPRESARIO *leaves, trying to regain his dignity.*)

TIBURCIO: Sheriff, I hope you weren't deceived by my little melo-dramatic aside to Gillette? It was just an act.

SHERIFF: Save your act for the court, Tiburcio. It's the jury you have to convince. Not me.

TIBURCIO: The bad weed never dies, Harry. I'll give them the performance of my life.

*Lights down. The set is transformed to the melodrama stage.*

......................... SCENE THREE .........................

*The Pinnacles.* VÁSQUEZ *caves. August, 1973.*

*A large dark cavern with an underground stream is slashed by shafts of light from above, cutting between giant boulders. Blind* FIDDLER FELIZ *is sitting on a rocky ledge, playing a lively song on the violin.* RITA MADRID, *the feisty camp follower, is singing and dancing. She is dressing* CLEODOVIO CHÁVEZ *with the various accoutrements of banditry.* MORENO *and* GONZALES *sit on the ground, cleaning their guns and enjoying the merriment.*

RITA: (*Singing.*)

YOU TAKE A MEXICAN, GIVE HIM A BIG SIX
    GUN
A PAIR OF SPURS AND A BIG SOMBRERO
A BIG MUSTACHE, A KNIFE WITH FLASH
A GRINNING LEER FROM EAR TO EAR THAT
    MEANS
DINERO ...

GRINGO, MESS IF YOU CAN WITH SUCH A MES-
    SICAN
THOSE CRAZY LAZY PISTOLEROS
THEY'LL TAKE YOUR LIFE AND RAPE YOUR
    WIFE
SO DON'T BE RASH GIVE THEM YOUR CASH
AND KEEP YOUR EARS!

MORENO *and* GONZALES *pop up, joining in on the singing. They instruct* CHÁVEZ *on their bandit technique.*

RITA:

UP WITH YOUR HANDS, SEÑOR!

GONZALES:

YOU, MEESTER, HEET THE FLOOR!

RITA:

EMPTY YOUR WALLETS AND YOUR POCKETS

MORENO:

WATCHES AND ALL THE REST ...

GONZALES:

WHAT'S THAT INSIDE YOUR VEST?

CHÁVEZ: (CHÁVEZ *tries out command, getting the hang of it.*)

WE WANT ALL RINGS AND SILVER THINGS

MORENO:

AND GOLDEN LOCKETS!

BANDIDOS: (*Together.*)

DREAMS OF REVENGE UNFOLD FOR CALIFOR-
    NIOS
RIDING THE NIGHT AS BOLD BANDIDOS
WE ROB THE WHITES AND KNOW WE'RE RIGHT
CAUSE IT'S NO CRIME AT ANY TIME
TO STEAL FROM THIEVES!

ROSARIO: (ROSARIO *enters: she is a tragic, aristocratic beauty.*)
        For the love of dignity, señores. Enough! Capitán Vásquez
        told you to lay low. Not to sing and dance like buffoons.
        (*The bandits are cowed, but* RITA *huffs with fury.*)
FELIZ: My child, don't be so ill-bred.
RITA: ¡Caramba! Who does this vieja think she is? The Capitán's
        lieutenant?
GONZALES: I give the orders here. I'm second in command.
ROSARIO: Not anymore. That job now belongs to my husband.

GONZALES: Since when?

ROSARIO: Since this morning. Ask the Capitán.

GONZALES: What?

RITA: (*Sarcastic.*) Well, what do you know. The old Chilean miner. He just joined, and now he's Vásquez's right hand man. I wonder why.

GONZALES: We'll see about that.

RITA: Chiquita, why don't you give your old man a break? He doesn't belong with these pack rats. Look at 'em. Your husband's not cut from the same rag. He just ain't bandido material. Now Chávez here, he's going to make a great bandit. It won't take much for this Mexican to look dangerous. Tell 'em what you used to do, corazón. (CHÁVEZ *shrugs his big shoulders, shy and humble.*)

CHÁVEZ: Up until now I've been a sheepherder all my life.

MORENO: Sheepherder? Where?

CHÁVEZ: Spent the last five years on the burnt hills of the Quién Sabe Ranch. I don't know much, and I ain't seen much. Except sheep.

GONZALES: Moreno knows about sheep. That's why he never got married. Too many wooly girlfriends!

FELIZ: Gonzales, there is a lady present!

RITA: (RITA *looks at* ROSARIO, *throwing knives with her eyes.*) Only one? Gracias, but what about your aristocratic daughter? Oh, that's right. She only married a peasant miner.

ROSARIO: (*Icily.*) ¿Oh, sí? Well, I think I know my husband better than a ... better than you.

RITA: You can have him ... if you want him.

ROSARIO: What's that supposed to mean?

RITA: Nothing. But I got eyes. Big eyes. (*She looks off.*) Tiburcio, sweetheart!

TIBURCIO: (TIBURCIO *makes his entrance in a cape.*) Is everybody ready?

BANDIDOS: ¡Sí, Capitán!

TIBURCIO: Good, where is Leiva?

RITA: Not here yet. What's the hurry? Shake a leg, hombre! Old man, música!

TIBURCIO: (*Firmly.*) No, Rita. If we delay another hour, my whole plan will go haywire.

FELIZ: He's right. The stage arrives in Tres Pinos at sundown.

MORENO: Let's ride, Capitán.

TIBURCIO: The plan calls for five men. We need Leiva.

GONZALES: Leiva's a chicken liver.

ROSARIO: (*Passionately.*) That's not true! Abdón said he'd meet us here, and he will. It's just that he had to sell the ranch.

TIBURCIO: Señora Leiva has a point. Abdón is sacrificing a lot to come with us.

GONZALES: Is that why you made him second in command?

TIBURCIO: Who told you that?

GONZALES: La Señora Leiva ... Is that true?

TIBURCIO: (*Without missing a beat.*) Yes, Gonzales. Because a second lieutenant has sense enough not to be drinking in the middle of a raid, as you were at Firebaugh's Ferry. Abdón Leiva follows my orders implicitly. It's the kind of dedication I need from my men. Men of quality and distinction.

RITA: With a high-class wife and a blind father-in-law?

TIBURCIO: (*Ironic, smooth.*) Quality is a rare commodity, Rita. This blind man and his family used to own half of northern California. Yes, we will wait for Leiva. Now to our melodrama. I have the guns. Let me see your get-ups. And I want to see some tough, mean looking hombres. (MORENO *steps up for inspection, followed by the others.*) Cousin, good to have you with us. Our noble ancestors would be proud of you, but that gray suit, señor, dirty it up. You're a bandido now. Look sloppy and more desperate. (MORENO *dirties his suit.*) Good, you get the Henry rifle. Gonzales, you look like a natural born greaser.

GONZALES: Gracias, jefe ... I think.

TIBURCIO: We've ridden together before. You're more experienced than the others. You get the shotgun. But control yourself, hombre. You'd scare your own mother. Chávez as the new recruit, welcome. But do me a favor. Pull that sombrero down a little ... No, that's too much ... That's better. Good! That's it. You get a dragoon revolver.

RITA: Tiburcio, mi amor. I bet you don't even recognize the big hearted cholo, do you?

TIBURCIO: Should I?

RITA: Your mother's tamale parlor in San Juan ...

CHÁVEZ: You always used to send me out for your cigars ...

TIBURCIO: ... and you always brought back the change?

CHÁVEZ: (*A kid again.*) I told you I was going to join you someday, Capitán!

TIBURCIO: So you did, Chávez, so you did! On second thought, a rifle is more your style. You'll be terrifying just like

Murrieta.

CHÁVEZ: Murrieta ...

RITA: Speaking of Joaquín Murrieta, you've been a hero to our people for a long time, mi amor. Don't let anything—or anyone—lead you astray. Know what I mean, hombre? You are the last of our warriors.

LEIVA: (*Offstage.*) Helloooo?

ROSARIO: It's Abdón!

LEIVA: Helloooo! Vásquez where are you?

TIBURCIO: (*Calling off.*) Straight ahead, Leiva. Keep coming. (LEIVA *enters.* ROSARIO *goes to him.*)

LEIVA: These infernal caverns ... like the depths of hell.

ROSARIO: How did it go, Abdón? Did you sell the ranch?

LEIVA: (*Depressed.*) Everything. It went for nothing. Twenty-three years in this alien Yankee land, and I'm back where I started.

TIBURCIO: My friend, you came all the way back from Chile in hope of riches? Remember the Gold Rush? Did they let you mine?

LEIVA: Only quicksilver, for them.

TIBURCIO: So you ended up with an acre of land, two cows and three chickens. No more chicken feed, Abdón. This time, you'll get the gold you came for.

RITA: If he's lucky ...

LEIVA: (*Blindly.*) What do you mean?

TIBURCIO: Stay out of it, Rita.

RITA: I mean, señor, that you don't belong in this crowd of locos. You're a family man. Forget Tres Pinos. Go to the San Joaquín Valley and take your wife and father-in-law.

ROSARIO: The señora's wrong.

RITA: Señorita!

ROSARIO: (*Caustically.*) Oh. I'm sorry. I keep forgetting you're not married.

RITA: And you keep forgetting you are.

TIBURCIO: (*Starting to anger.*) Rita, ya basta. You've said enough. Now leave them alone, like a lady.

RITA: Huy. You and your Monterey upbringing, Capitán. You really think every woman is your oyster, don't you? Just eat the meat and throw the shells away.

TIBURCIO: (*Handing* LEIVA *a cape.*) My friend, here. A cape for the lieutenant, just like mine. Once in this land, there were many Joaquíns. Perhaps now, everywhere they turn they will see Tiburcios.

RITA: Yes. Little Tiburcios

LEIVA: Vásquez, you know, after eight years my wife is expecting our first child.

TIBURCIO: No. I didn't know that. Congratulations. I'm going to let you use one of my guns. But be careful, it's got a hair trigger.

RITA: As every woman knows.

TIBURCIO: All right, Rita. I warned you. Now get out of here. Go back to San Juan.

RITA: I live in Los Angeles now.

TIBURCIO: (*Fiercely.*) Then go! Just get out of my sight. Don't ever let me see you close to my men again.

RITA: You know, if you weren't Tiburcio Vásquez, I'd make you eat those words, Capitán. But who knows? Perhaps you are just another bastardo. ¡Adiós, señores! (RITA *storms out.*)

TIBURCIO: (TIBURCIO *turns to his men, all business.*) Paisanos, a final word before we go. First cardinal rule: as long as you ride with me, no killing. If there's any shooting to be done, I'll do it. The purpose is to steal, not to kill. It always hurts the gringo more to lose his money than his life. (*He draws on the sand.*) Second, to review our plan: here we are, here's Tres Pinos. We'll split up into two groups. Leiva, you will be in charge of the first group. You, Moreno and Gonzales will ride slowly into Tres Pinos. You will go directly to Snyder's store, check out the place and wait. Chávez and I will be outside of town holding up the stage. When we have the payroll for the mine, we will ride into town and join you. Together we'll rob the store, hotel, livery stable and any customers in the street. All able bodied men will be tied up and left face down on the ground.

GONZALES: And all the women face up!

TIBURCIO: The women are not to be harmed, and no one—I repeat—no one is to be killed. Theft with dignity, gentlemen. Just the site of Tiburcio Vásquez and his band of cut-throats ought to do the trick. Understood? Remember, I didn't return from Mexico last winter to go back to stealing horses. If they intend to strangle California with railroads, fine. We'll rob the trains. If they insist on building in the wilderness, we'll sack their towns.

FELIZ: Tres Pinos!

TIBURCIO: Today Tres Pinos, and tomorrow Kingston and Millerton Lake and Coyote Holes. And then with enough men and ammunition ...
FELIZ: A Revolution! We'll take Los Angeles!
TIBURCIO: (*Sardonically.*) Take it where, Don Casimiro? We're just a bunch of flea-bitten bandidos. To Tres Pinos!
GONZALES: ¡A los caballos!
MORENO: ¡Vámonos!
CHÁVEZ: ¡A Tres Pinos!
TIBURCIO: (TIBURCIO *waits and turns to* LEIVA.) Make your goodbyes quickly and join us by the horses.
ROSARIO: Tiburcio? Good luck. (TIBURCIO *pauses a beat, then exits.*)
LEIVA: (LEIVA *is extremely nervous.*) I don't like this, Rosario. I feel like our whole life is ripping apart.
FELIZ: Abdón, my daughter and I will be waiting at Elizabeth Lake. After that, we'll all rendezvous at Little Rock Creek. And we'll be rich—let's think of that.
LEIVA: Why did you call Vasquez by his first name just now?
ROSARIO: I did? Abdón, I didn't even notice.
LEIVA: Woman, are you certain you want me to do this thing? I have just enough money to book our passage to Chile, before it's too late.
ROSARIO: (*Determined.*) It's already too late, hombre. The Capitán's counting on you. He needs you.
LEIVA: Don Casimiro, I respect your opinion. Am I doing the right thing?
FELIZ: Yes, son-in-law. For the land that belongs to us.
ROSARIO: Remember, Abdón, you're the Capitán's trusted lieutenant.
LEIVA: I've become a vengeful man, Rosario. I'm afraid of what I might do.
FELIZ: At least be as good a man as Rosario.
LEIVA: (LEIVA *pulls out an ordinary brown shawl.*) I bought you this. Will you wear it?
ROSARIO: Yes! (*Puts it on.*) And God go with you my husband. (ROSARIO *kisses* LEIVA *on the cheek, and he exits. After a beat,* TIBURCIO *returns silently and grabs* ROSARIO. *They kiss passionately.*)
FELIZ: (FIDDLER FELIZ *sits up blindly. Sniffing the air.*) Rosario, who's here? I smell horse sweat and tobacco smoke. Vásquez! Has the Capitán returned?

*Curtain.*


...................... SCENE FOUR ......................

*Before the grand curtain. Banjo music.* A. SNYDER, *a store keeper, enters with a broom.*

SNYDER: (*Singing.*)

> THERE'S MEN WHO LABOR HARD FOR LOVE
> FOR GLORY, GOLD AND RICHES
> BUT I MAKE MORE AT THE GENERAL STORE
> WITH WHISKEY, CHEESE AND BRITCHES.
>
> SAY HI, HO THE OHIO
> WE'VE CROSSED THE WIDE MISSOURI
> IN COVERED WAGONS 'CROSS THE PLAINS
> WE LEFT BEHIND ST. LOUIS.

MRS. SNYDER: (MRS. SNYDER *enters, with a Winchester rifle.*)

> WE'RE COMMOM CLAY, GOD FEARING FOLK

SNYDER:

> WE DEAL IN CASH AND CREDIT

TOGETHER:

> THE LAND IS OURS BY DESTINY
> IT TOOK A LOT TO GET IT.
>
> SAY HI, HO THE OHIO
> WE'VE CROSSED THE WIDE MISSOURI
> IN COVERED WAGONS 'CROSS THE PLAINS
> WE LEFT BEHIND ST. LOUIS.

MRS. SNYDER:

> MOLASSES, YARN AND CALICO
> GUNPOWDER, FLOUR AND NOTIONS

SNYDER:

> WE'RE HERE TO SERVE THE PIONEER
> TO SOW THE SEEDS OF FORTUNE.

TOGETHER: (*Speaking.*)

>That's it, Mother ...
>Just like old times, Andrew ...
>Back in St. Louis!

>(*Singing.*)

>WE BUILT OUR TOWN OUT IN THE WILDS
>WHERE THERE'S NO ONE TO WARN YA
>BUT WE'VE NO FEAR, OUR HOME IS HERE
>TRES PINOS, CALIFORNIA.

>SAY HI, HO THE OHIO
>WE CROSSED THE WIDE MISSOURI
>IN COVERED WAGONS 'CROSS THE PLAINS
>WE LEFT BEHIND ST. LOUIS.

*The curtain opens to reveal the interior of* SNYDER*'s store in Tres Pinos, California. August 26, 1873. A.* SNYDER *walks to the counter in his store as* MRS. SNYDER *exits.* LEWIS PIERCE, *age eighteen, enters, running.*

LEWIS: Evening, Mr. Snyder! Stage from Hollister pass through yet?

SNYDER: Whoa, Lewis! Slow down. It's barely 5:30 pm.

LEWIS: Whew! I guess I just ran the fastest mile in the history of the county. Seven minutes flat.

SNYDER: Get a horse, son. And run for office.

LEWIS: Funny you should mention that. I got youth, health, ambition. Pa says folks are talking about splitting Monterey County in half. The whole territory east of the Gabilans on down to New Idria. (*We hear the sound of horses riding up to the store outside.* SNYDER *looks out.*) The new county seat's got to be right smack dab in the heart of the area too. Right here, Mr. Snyder, in Tres Pinos! Just watch us grow.

SNYDER: Hope you're right, boy. The city's already got pert' near fifty inhabitants, but there's plenty of room for growth for workin' people.

LEWIS: Could you post this letter, sir?

SNYDER: Another application to law school? Sure thing, Lewis.

LEWIS: Is this the new Sears and Roebuck catalogue? Swell!

SNYDER: Hold on there, son. Don't let me catch you looking at pictures of ladies wearin' corsets.

MRS. SNYDER: (*Comes out carrying a bowl of soup.*) Andrew? I'm going across the street to the hotel. Hattie tells me Mr. Davidson's been ailing. Poor soul. Maybe he can keep down some of my soup.

SNYDER: Go right ahead, mother. Then maybe you can get around to feeding your hungry spouse.

LEWIS: Evening, ma'm.

MRS. SNYDER: What 'je readin' Lewis?

LEWIS: The good book ma'm.

MRS. SNYDER: (GONZALES *and* LEIVA *make their entrance at the front door.* MRS. SNYDER *does not disguise her racist disgust. She fearfully skirts around them exiting.*) Excuse me.

GONZALES: Buenas noches.

SNYDER: That'll be two cents for the letter, Lewis. Can I help you, señor, with something? Clothes, vittles, whiskey?

GONZALES: Two whiskey's.

LEIVA: Gonzales ...

GONZALES: Both for me. Mi amigo don't drink. (GONZALES *laughs.*)

SNYDER: (*Pours, studying* LEIVA.) Say, don't I know you, mister? You got a place up New Idria way, ain't you? Sure, you're one of the miners. You've stopped here with your wife, askin' me for credit. What's your name again?

LEIVA: (*Nervously.*) Leiva ... Abdón Leiva.

GONZALES: Another whiskey!

LEIVA: Maybe I will have drink.

GONZALES: Same here! Gimme another shot. In fact, ¿sabes qué? Leave the bottle ...

LEIVA: NO! (LEIVA *slams on the counter.*)

GONZALES: (GONZALES *slams back.*) ¡SÍ! And how about handing over some of them sardines in a can? And crackers. And oysters.

SNYDER: Looks like you fellows are going to have quite a repast.

GONZALES: We've got to build up our strength for the long ride ahead. You got any Tabasco sauce?

SNYDER: (*Suspiciously.*) Just how far you planning to go?

LEIVA: (*Quickly.*) Hollister.

LEWIS: (*Eavesdropping.*) Hollister? That's only eleven miles.

SNYDER: (*Starting to get nervous.*) You boys seem to be mighty well armed and dressed for a casual business trip. What's going on in Hollister?

GONZALES: A Fandango!

LEIVA: A baptism ... my wife just had our first child ... a fine boy ... we're going to celebrate.

GONZALES: That's right. He's the father and I'm the god-father. Right, compadre? (*Gaffaws.*) Here's to the child with two fathers. ¡Salud! (*Outside we hear the sound of an approaching stage coach.*)

LEWIS: The stage coach! The stage coach. Here it comes.

SNYDER: You fellows help yourself to all the food and whiskey you want. Just leave two bits on the counter on your way out. (SNYDER *follows* LEWIS *outside to greet the stage.*)

LEIVA: Gonzales! Don't joke about my child. You mention my son again and I'll horsewhip you!

GONZALES: Son? Don't count your huevos before they hatch! Sardines in a can. What will those gringos think of next? They're smart ... You know, sardines always remind me of a woman I knew down in San Gabriel. Maybe I'll look her up when we get down there. With a bottle of whiskey, to kill the taste. (*He guffaws.* LEIVA *yanks the whiskey bottle out of his hands.*) Hey!

LEIVA: Vásquez said no drinking.

GONZALES: Come on, son of a whore.

LEIVA: No more, Gonzales! I mean it ... and don't call me a son of a whore, you son of a whore.

GONZALES: ¡Chihuahua, hombre! Thou art taking all this second lieutenant bullshit too seriously, compadre.

LEIVA: I'm not your compadre and never will be.

GONZALES: (*Pointedly.*) I know. (GONZALES *ducks behind the counter.*)

MORENO: (MORENO *enters, carrying a Henry rifle.*) Leiva ... I came to warn you. Tom Williams, your old boss, is on the New Idria stage.

LEIVA: The Mine Superintendent?

MORENO: Don't let him see you.

LEIVA: Don't tell me what to do!

MORENO: I saw the strongbox! And it smells of money! (*Pops up with a half cake of cheese.*)

GONZALES: Fuchi! Look at this—somebody cut the cheese. (*Gaffaws.*)

LEIVA: Gonzales, you idiot, get out there.

GONZALES: The gringo said we could get anything we wanted.

LEIVA: I gave you a command. Do as I say!

GONZALES: (*Steps out from behind the counter.*) Some lieutenant. You know what this stupid idiot did, Moreno? He

gave Snyder his full name. Just like that. Then he has the
nerve to call me an idiot. Chileno goat! Don't you know
why Vásquez made you second in command? In honor of
your kid.

MORENO: Gonzales! You have the sense of a javelin pig. Watch
your tongue.

GONZALES: My tongue has no hair on it, Moreno. It speaks
too loosely perhaps. But Leiva's woman is no concern of
mine. What she does is his business.

LEIVA: What do you mean?

GONZALES: Ask the Capitán, cabrón!

LEIVA: Animal!

MORENO: Por favor, señores. This quarrel is insane! The stage
is leaving, they're coming in. (LEIVA *stares at* GONZA-
LES. SNYDER *enters with the mail bag, followed by* MRS.
SNYDER *and* LEWIS. *They stop.*)

SNYDER: So, you fellows are still here, eh? Hope you got enough
to eat and drink. (MORENO *shrugs and exits.*)

MRS. SNYDER: (*Nervous.*) Won't you stay for supper, Lewis?

LEWIS: Thanks, ma'm, but I think I gotta run.

SNYDER: Whoa, hold on there, son. Let me just sort through
this mail, Mother. Young Pierce wants to know if any law
school has fished or cut bait. Go ahead and set the table.
I'll be in shortly ... Well, go on.

MRS. SNYDER: (*Hesitating fearfully.*) Andrew, shouldn't you
ought to tell these Mexicans we're closing up? Lord knows,
they can't hang around here all night. This is a working
community. People are up at the crack of dawn. (*She
exits.* LEIVA *and* GONZALES *start to feel awkward.*)

SNYDER: I see you boys found the cheese and the rope? Well,
four bits ought to pay for everything. That's two bits a
piece. Here's your letter, Lewis.

LEWIS: Gee, swell, thanks. (LEIVA *pays, but he doesn't move.*)

SNYDER: Fifty cents it is. Mucho gusto, señores. Have a safe
journey. (*Pause.*) Yes? Is there something else?

LEIVA: A letter ... in Spanish ... from my mother in Chile. It
should be addressed to me.

GONZALES: Abdón Sánchez ...

SNYDER: (*Losing his patience.*) From Chile, you say? Well,
Mr. Leiva, I don't recall seeing any letter ... and I would
appreciate it if you and your amigos would leave this es-
tablishment as I am closed!

LEIVA: (*In desperation.*) Please look! (SNYDER *turns to look in the mail boxes behind him.*)

LEWIS: (*Reads something in his letter and suddenly exclaims.*) Holy cow! (GONZALES *pulls his gun.*) Mr. Snyder, I'm in law school. I've been accepted in San Francis ... (*Looks up.*) ... ooOOH SHIT!

GONZALES: Lay down.

LEWIS: (*Blanching.*) Huh?

GONZALES: Hit the floor! (LEWIS *falls to the floor on his stomach.* SNYDER *turns and finds himself staring into* ABDÓN LEIVA*'s pistol.*)

MORENO: (MORENO *comes to the door with his rifle. He aims at* SNYDER*'s head.*) Lay down, Snyder ... Down!

SNYDER: All right, all right! Just don't shoot.

MORENO: Mister, if you don't get down, I'm going to shoot the top of your GODDAMN HEAD!!!

SNYDER: I'm down! Please don't kill me! I have a family.

LEWIS: (*Cowering on the floor.*) Jesus! Oh, holy Jesus, please have mercy!

GONZALES: Shut up!

SNYDER: Go ahead and take whatever you like. Help yourselves! Just spare our lives, that's all I ask of you. For pity's sake!

LEWIS: (*Being tied.*) Oh m'god! Oh m'god!

SNYDER: (LEIVA *ties up* SNYDER.) Mr. Leiva, I beseech you, sir. You have a family. For God's sake, don't hurt my wife! (LEIVA *tightens the rope.*) Oww! That's too tight! I can't breath.

MORENO: (*Horses ride up outside.* MORENO *runs to the door.*) It's the Capitán! (*He runs out.*) We couldn't wait, Tiburcio. It's underway.

TIBURCIO: (*Offstage.*) It's all right. Cousin, you and Chávez go over to the livery stable and round up the horses. ¡Pronto! (TIBURCIO *comes in. He faces* LEIVA.) What happened, Leiva? Why didn't you wait?

LEIVA: This is madness ... madness!

TIBURCIO: It seems that way, the first time ... stay calm and nobody will get hurt. Check behind the counter and in the mail boxes. Take all the valuables you can find. Move, hombre, pronto! (LEIVA *obeys.*) Hello, Snyder. ˙Enjoying our little melodrama?

SNYDER: (*On the floor.*) Vásquez! I had a powerful suspicion it was you all along. Oh, God in Heaven.

TIBURCIO: Stop shivering. Nobody's going to harm you.

SNYDER: I'm cold! And tired and hungry. And these ropes are cutting my wrists.

TIBURCIO: (*Grabs some blankets, and throws one to* LEIVA.) Here, Leiva, throw a blanket on that kid. Looks like he's cold too. Gonzales, check who's in the back.

SNYDER: My wife! Aw, shit! (GONZALES *goes.* VÁSQUEZ *covers* SNYDER *with a blanket.*)

TIBURCIO: She won't be harmed, I give you my word. I have the utmost respect for married ladies. Sorry to have to treat you this way, Mr. Snyder, but it's the only way I can make money. I'll loosen your ropes ... What's this? This is a fine watch, Señor. (GONZALES *escorts* MRS. SNYDER *in.*)

MRS. SNYDER: It's a family heirloom, sir. In the family for generations. I beg you not to steal it. Take this one instead, please. (MRS. SNYDER *grabs a watch off the counter and tosses it to* VÁSQUEZ.)

TIBURCIO: You misjudge me, madam. I was merely admiring the craftsmanship of your husband's time piece. He may keep it, with my compliments. As for this other. This is a cheap watch, but I have never been known to refuse a gift from a lady. Thank you. (*Pockets the watch.*) Now to business. Obviously, we didn't stage all of this to merely pilfer your store. Where is the safe and who's going to open it? (*Pause.*) Come now. It's only money. Not your lives. Don't be foolish.

SNYDER: Go ahead, Mother. Show him where it's at.

MRS. SNYDER You are a villain, sir. And a pusillanimous coward.

TIBURCIO: Perhaps. Yet so many people are going to come to see the scene of this dastardly crime, you'll make your profit back in no time. You might even think of me as your hero ... (VÁSQUEZ *examines a pretty red shawl on a counter and takes it.*) Leiva. Gonzales. Go across the street to the hotel and round up the guests. I'll meet you there.

GONZALES: Sí, Capitán. (GONZALES *exits.* LEIVA *hangs back, looking unnerved.*)

TIBURCIO: What's the matter with you, Leiva? Snap out of it.

LEIVA: Vásquez, how can you be so cold-blooded?

TIBURCIO: You're coming unglued, hombre. Don't be such a bloodless coward. Now go! (*Turns to* MRS. SYNDER.) My lady?

GONZALES: (*Offstage.*) Leiva, come on! (*Suddenly there are gun-shots outside. Yelling and running.* LEIVA *unholsters his gun and turns to go.*)

LEIVA: (*Exiting.*) No killing! No killing! No killing! No killing!

MORENO: (*Offstage.*) Watch out! He's got a gun! Get him!

CHÁVEZ: (*Offstage.*) Leiva, look out! He's heading your way! (*A* BASQUE SHEEPHERDER *comes running up to the porch of the store. A shot is fired, and the* SHEEPHERDER *is hit in the back. He falls into the store, gasping and dying.* LEIVA *re-appears at the door.*)

TIBURCIO: Go to the hotel and join the others!

LEIVA: (*Horrified.*) Oh my God! Oh my God! (LEIVA *exits. More shots are heard from offstage as lights go out. Curtain.*)

*Before the grand curtain: THE PUBLIC OUTCRY.*

CALIFORNIA KATE *appears in front of the oleo curtain with* DAISY *and* JENNY. *They carry a newspaper gazette and sing.*

KATE AND THE LADIES: (*Singing.*)

> OH! THE STATE OF CALIFORNIA'S IN A STATE
> OF SHOCK
> THREE MEN WERE SHOT AND MURDERED ON
> THE SPOT
> THE TOWN OF TRES PINOS HAS BEEN SACKED
> AND ROBBED
> BY VÁSQUEZ THE BANDIT AND HIS MEN
>
> HORRORS! HORRORS! WHAT A DREADFUL SCENE.
> OH!
> WOE TO THE WIDOWS, DAMN THE MURDER-
> OUS FIENDS
> WANTED! WANTED! CAUGHT ALIVE OR DEAD
> ONE THOUSAND DOLLARS ON TIBURCIO'S BLOODY
> HEAD ...

KATE: You've done it now, Vásquez

> HEAR THE PUBLIC OUTCRY, JUSTICE LIFT THY
> SWORD
> SMITE DOWN, O LORD, THE BANDIT HOARD
> GET THE GALLOWS READY, THERE'S A GOOD
> REWARD
> FOR VÁSQUEZ THE BANDIT AND HIS MEN!

*The curtain falls.*

# ACT TWO

...................... SCENE ONE ......................

*The Courthouse Jail. San Jose, California, 1875.*

DEPUTY PETTIGREW *unlocks* TIBURCIO's *cell, while a* PHOTOGRAPHER *sets up outside the bars. The* DEPUTY *escorts* VÁSQUEZ *to a chair downstage, where he cuffs one of his ankles to a ball and chain. As this happens,* SHERIFF ADAMS *escorts in some* LADIES, *excitedly agog at seeing* VÁSQUEZ *in person.*

LADIES: Oh, my ... Oh, Lord ... There he is. (VÁSQUEZ *sits before the* PHOTOGRAPHER's *daguerreotype camera, watched by the armed* DEPUTY. *The* LADIES *sit behind the barred wall.*)

SHERIFF ADAMS: Ladies, may I remind you that Vásquez is a convicted felon, legally tried in a court of law, found guilty of murder, and sentenced to be executed on March 16, which, of course, is just two weeks away. You may observe the prisoner, but please refrain from speaking to him ... unless he speaks to you. You have five minutes. (ADAMS *exits.*)

TIBURCIO: (*Studies his female observers.*) Ladies. Thank you for coming to see me. It takes a strong stomach to meet thieves, cut-throats and libertines—but as I am none of the sort—welcome and be at ease. Tiburcio Vásquez is at your eternal loving service. (*The deputy snorts and chuckles.*)

LADY IN BLACK: Monsieur Vásquez?

TIBURCIO: Caramba. A lady in black? (THE LADY IN BLACK, *wearing a veil, steps up to the bars.*)

LADY IN BLACK: Parlez vous français?

TIBURCIO: (*Mystified.*) Desgraciadamente, madame, ni un *peu.* ¿Habla usted español?

FRENCH LADY: Con toda seguridad, mon Capitain.

PETTIGREW: Speak English, you two! That's the rules.

TIBURCIO: Some men achieve English, madame, and some have it thrust upon them. You are French?

LADY IN BLACK: Quebecois, monsieur. I am a journalist from Montreal, Quebec, Canada.

TIBURCIO: Have we met? Yes, you were in the courtroom during the trial. Weren't you?

LADY BLACK: Señor Vásquez, I am curious as to the motives for your way of life. Could you explain, please?

TIBURCIO: You mean my career?

LADY BLACK: Your crimes, yes.

TIBURCIO: The roots of banditry in California run deep, madame. God made us all alike, and some even worse. However, I continue to protest my innocence of the killings at Tres Pinos. I have never spilled the blood of another human being, and that's the God's truth.

PHOTOGRAPHER: Freeze! (VÁSQUEZ *turns toward the camera and freezes in heroic position. Flash! Then he turns toward the* LADIES *again, charmingly sincere.*)

TIBURCIO: In fact, my case is on appeal before the State Supreme Court ... and as I am so regrettably short of funds ... (VÁSQUEZ *stands and reaches into his coat pocket to extract some of his photographic cards.*) If any of you ladies are interested, I am offering this professionally printed photo card, with a complete chronological listing of my exploits, from my escape from San Quentin prison to the raid on Firebaugh's Ferry. And as an added bonus, on the opposite side, you will find a personally autographed photographic portrait of your humble servant. Yours, for only fifty cents. Two bits. A half dollar for my defense.

LADIES: I'll take one ... Me too! ... I want one ... etc.

TIBURCIO: (*Picks up his ball and chain, and begins to hustle his cards.*) Ladies, I cannot tell you what this support means to me. I do not deny my twenty years as a horse thief and stage robber, but my career grew out of the circumstances by which I was surrounded. I was thirteen when gold was discovered. As I grew to manhood, a spirit of hatred and revenge took possession of me. I had many fights in defense of what I believed to be my rights and those of my countrymen ...

LADY IN BLACK: Pardon, monsieur, but I heard all that during the trial. That is not what I was asking about.

TIBURCIO: (*Puzzled.*) So sorry ... What was the question again?

LADY IN BLACK: To be blunt ... is free love your philosophy of life?

TIBURCIO: (*Surprised but maintaining.*) Hardly, my lady ... but a life without love is like a wheel without axle grease.

PETTIGREW: And you've greased many a wheel in your day, no, Vásquez?

TIBURCIO: There are ladies here, Pettigrew. Don't be impertinent. (*The* DEPUTY *snorts angrily.*)

LADY IN BLACK: (*The* LADY *presses on.*) And don't you be a hypocrite, monsieur. Did you not seduce a true lady in Abdón Leiva's wife?

TIBURCIO: (*Pause.*) The perfect wife never marries, madame.

LADY IN BLACK: Why did she testify against you in the trial, monsieur? Did you really steal her from her husband, then leave her to die, pregnant, in the wilderness?

TIBURCIO: That ... is a pair of pregnant questions.

LADY IN BLACK: Could you answer please? (*Pause.*) Or is your silence an admission of guilt?

TIBURCIO: I was tried and convicted for the murder of three men in the Tres Pinos hold-up, madame. But my only guilt was the love of a beautiful woman. (*There is a sorrowful pause.*)

PETTIGREW: (*The* DEPUTY *smirks cynically.*) Nasty brutish business, Vásquez—leaving a pregnant woman out in the wilderness to die. You've got a streak of evil in you that's beyond comprehension. No wonder Leiva wants to hang you.

TIBURCIO: Leiva lost his sanity in a place called Little Rock Creek. That was the second act of my melodrama.

*Lights change. As the jail set transforms to the melodrama stage,* VÁSQUEZ *faces the* LADY IN BLACK *and sings a love ballad to her before the grand curtain.*

TIBURCIO:

CON UN SINCERO AMOR TE IDOLATRABA
CUANDO, HERMOSA, A TU LADO TE TENÍA
CON UN SINCERO AMOR, PRENDA ADORADA
TE IDOLATRA, TE ADORA, EL ALMA MÍA

*The* LADY IN BLACK *lifts her veil. It is* ROSARIO.

TIBURCIO / ROSARIO:

AUNQUE LEJOS LOS DOS NOS ENCONTRAMOS
SIEMPRE MI CORAZÓN POR TI PALPITA,

TIBURCIO:

Y UN APRETÓN LE MANDO AUNQUE DE MA-
NOS
EL ÁNGEL DE MI AMOR QUE ES FULANITA.

*The lovers separate. The oleo curtain rises.*

...................... SCENE TWO ......................

*San Bernardino Mountains. Rock Creek Canyon. Night.*

*A jackrabbit is roasting on a spit over a small campfire.* CHÁ-
VEZ *is eating, sitting on a log.* FIDDLER FELIZ *is asleep in a
blanket, and* ROSARIO, *feeling lonely, is pulling a pretty red shawl
from her belongings. Suddenly there is a sound of rapid hoofbeats.*
CHÁVEZ *leaps to his feet and grabs the shotgun.*

CHÁVEZ: Somebody's coming!

ROSARIO: Don't shoot. It might be Tiburcio. (*The horse comes
to a stop offstage.* ROSARIO *puts her red shawl away. She
puts on the one* LEIVA *gave her.*)

CHÁVEZ: 'S that you, jefe?

TIBURCIO: (*Enters, bristling from the hard ride.*) Riding on the
wind, Chávez. Is there any water? (CHÁVEZ *hands him
a water canteen.* TIBURCIO *starts to drink, pauses and
offers some to* ROSARIO.)

ROSARIO: (*Smiling.*) No, thank you, Capitán. Please.

CHÁVEZ: Did you catch up with Leiva?

TIBURCIO: (*Drinks long and hard, then shakes his head.*) I rode
all the way to the mouth of Little Rock Canyon. He must
have been driving like a madman. I shouldn't have let
him go alone.

ROSARIO: He's probably just in a hurry to get back, Capitán. Like
you were.

TIBURCIO: Something's up. The hairs on the back of my neck
can sense a posse within a hundred miles. But we're safe
for a couple of days. After that we'd better make a run
for it.

CHÁVEZ: To Mexico?

ROSARIO: Beyond the Colorado River!

CHÁVEZ: That's where Moreno and Gonzales said they were going. I always wanted to go south of the border.

TIBURCIO: We'll go west, north of Los Angeles. I only hope
Abdón doesn't pull anything crazy in San Gabriel.

CHÁVEZ: He's going to pay for the supplies. What could go
wrong?

ROSARIO: In this old buckboard, nobody will recognize him.

CHÁVEZ: He's harmless ... looking.

TIBURCIO: (*Disturbed.*) He hasn't been right since Tres Pinos.
The whole experience unnerved him. Three men dead ...
and for what? Two hundred lousy dollars in gold, some
cheap groceries and a dozen swayback horses. Now, the
whole state is up at arms.

ROSARIO: Tiburcio, it's not your fault. I convinced Abdón to go
with you.

TIBURCIO: I should have known he'd go berserk and start killing.

ROSARIO: (*Ironically.*) They were only gringos. You're too much
a gentleman, Capitán. Like my uncles. That's how we lost
our lands ... by playing host to the pie-eating Yankees,
while they slit our throats.

CHÁVEZ: That's right, jefe!

ROSARIO: What's so funny?

TIBURCIO: (*Laughing.*) The blood in your eyes. Why does your
hatred always inspire such love in me? (TIBURCIO *stares
at her lovingly for a moment.* CHÁVEZ *squirms.*)

ROSARIO: Perhaps I remind you of who you are, Capitán. And
what you must do.

TIBURCIO: Chávez, you'd better go stand the watch. And like a
hawk—in the other direction.

CHÁVEZ: What about Leiva?

TIBURCIO: He shouldn't be back before midnight. Now, do as
your captain asks you. ¡Pronto! (CHÁVEZ *exits with his
shotgun.*)

ROSARIO: Do you realize this is the first moment we've been
together in close to seven weeks?

TIBURCIO: How's your father?

ROSARIO: Asleep. My poor Papá—I hope he isn't taken with
consumption. The things I've put him through just to be
with you. Oh, Tiburcio! All the little games I've played
just to catch a glimpse of your eyes. The secret glances in
a hundred stolen moments just to say I love you, I love
you, I love you!

TIBURCIO: And Abdón glancing at us, wondering what's going on, what's going on, what's going on? (TIBURCIO *lustily pulls her to him; she pulls back.*)

ROSARIO: Are you making fun of me?

TIBURCIO: Your eyes betray you, mi vida. That deep haunting look of yours ... as haunting as the moon.

ROSARIO: (*Peeved.*) Tiburcio, my God, what do you expect me to do? Not even look at you? I feel the baby growing like a wildflower day by day. It's your son.

TIBURCIO: My son? Are you so powerfully certain that you want it to be mine? (ROSARIO *shoots him a hurtful look.*) I only mean that we must separate soon.

ROSARIO: Take me with you, Tiburcio. I'll die if you leave me behind.

TIBURCIO: I'm a hunted animal, Rosario. As long as you're with me, you and the child will be in greater danger. The proud line of Tiburcio Vásquez ends in a noose at the end of a rope. That's no place to cradle a son.

ROSARIO: Then I don't want to live either. If you leave me, I'll kill myself and take your son with me.

TIBURCIO: My little Capitana, you drive a hard bargain.

ROSARIO: (*Deadly serious.*) Don't treat me like one of your cantina women, Tiburcio. I have my pride, too. I don't want to hate you.

TIBURCIO: There's that flame in your eyes again ... I'd hate to think what you would do, if you didn't love me. (VÁSQUEZ *passionately kisses* ROSARIO *and she relents. Then she pulls out the bright red shawl and wraps it around her shoulders.*)

ROSARIO: There's a sandy place down by the creek bed, Capitán. Come with me. (VÁSQUEZ *exits with* ROSARIO. BLIND FIDDLER FELIZ *sits up. There is a pause. A rustling in the bushes.* ABDÓN LEIVA *steps into the campfire.*)

FELIZ: Who's there? Chávez is that you? Answer me. Is it man or beast stalking the night?

LEIVA: It's me, old man.

FELIZ: (*Surprised.*) Abdón! What are you doing back so soon?

LEIVA (*Looking like a mad man.*) Where's my wife, señor? Have you seen Rosario?

FELIZ: (*Alarmed.*) I haven't seen anything.

LEIVA (*Hoarse.*) Rosario? Where are you, niña? Rosario!

FELIZ: (*Shouting.*) Rosario!

LEIVA: Rosario!

FELIZ: Calm yourself, hombre. She's probably in the dark, taking care of her natural needs.

LEIVA: Where's Vásquez?

FELIZ: (*Dissembling.*) He's standing watch, ¿que no?

LEIVA: No, señor. Chávez is standing guard alone! I passed within twenty feet of him on foot in the brush. The young fool didn't even notice.

FELIZ: On foot? Where's your wagon? What are you up to, hombre? Crawling through the underbrush like a skunk?

LEIVA: (*Obsessed.*) So it is true ... Mother of God, my nightmare is real. Rosario!

FELIZ: (*Echoing.*) Rosario! What are you saying, hombre?

LEIVA: Don't act blind, old man. You know what I'm talking about. But if I find them together, I'll kill them! (ROSARIO *steps out of the shadows, carrying some herbs.*)

ROSARIO: (*Feigning.*) Abdón, what's the matter? Is everything all right?

LEIVA: Where's Tiburcio?

ROSARIO: How should I know? I've been gathering medicinal herbs for my father.

LEIVA: In the dark?

ROSARIO: In the moonlight, the way my mother taught me. Papá's been very ill. (FELIZ *starts coughing.*) He may even be taken with consumption. I've got to make some tea. (LEIVA *is momentarily confused.*)

TIBURCIO: (*Enters coolly from the other side, carrying a load of firewood.*) Abdón, my friend, back so soon? Good. I was afraid the posse might have gotten you. Where's the supplies? The jackrabbit needs salt. (VÁSQUEZ *goes to the campfire.* ROSARIO *is busy making tea.* LEIVA *studies them incredulously.*)

LEIVA: (*Slowly.*) Wait a minute ... what's going on here? Do you take me for some kind of jackass? It won't work, Vásquez. You thought I'd be away until tomorrow, and you'd be free to ... to ... !

TIBURCIO: To do what? (*Pause.*) Abdón, tsk, tsk, tsk. You ought to apologize to your wife.

LEIVA: No, señor! Are you saying she means nothing to you? That you find her repulsive?

TIBURCIO: I didn't say that.

LEIVA: Then what did you say? That you're a coward, a liar and a thief? And you? What are you doing wearing that shawl?

ROSARIO: It's for the chill in the night air.

LEIVA: Where did you get it? He gave it to you, didn't he? Why didn't you use the one I bought you?

ROSARIO: I just grabbed this one.

LEIVA: Liar! ¡Puta! (LEIVA *starts to slap her.* VÁSQUEZ *catches his hand.*)

TIBURCIO: That's enough, Leiva! (*Pause.*) All right. You caught us en flagrante delicto. What do you want, blood? Have you lost your senses?

LEIVA: (*Grievously.*) No, Vásquez, it appears I have lost my wife. And now you will die for it. Or you will kill me.

TIBURCIO: Hombre, stop this peasant melodrama.

LEIVA: You refuse to defend yourself?

TIBURCIO: That's not the point. I never meant to do you any harm.

LEIVA: (*Drawing his pistol.*) Liar! Fornicator!

ROSARIO: Abdón!

CHÁVEZ: (*Enters running with his shotgun.*) Leiva, you pull that trigger and I'll blow your brains out!

TIBURCIO: (*Bemused.*) Cleodovio. Put down your shotgun.

CHÁVEZ: Not before this stinkbug hands over his gun. You may not care if you live or die, Capitán, but I do. Leiva?

LEIVA: (*Gives* CHÁVEZ *his gun.*) Why are you being so loyal? For this maggot who will devour your heart, if you let him? Ask him why he kept the money from the stage hold-up. Ask him!

TIBURCIO: (*Firmly.*) We never robbed the stage coach.

LEIVA: ¡Mierda! I saw the stage leave Tres Pinos. The strong box was on it.

TIBURCIO: So was Tom Williams, the Mine Superintendent from New Idria. Remember him? Live and let live. As long as he was on that stage, there was no way I could stop it. On my word as a gentlemen. Ask Chávez.

CHÁVEZ: He's telling the truth.

LEIVA: What did he buy you off with, the horses?

TIBURCIO: (*Angered,*) You want the horses, Leiva? Take them. Go on, take them! Just remember, I've never said a word about the two men you killed at Tres Pinos.

LEIVA: Chávez killed the other one! (*Swept with remorse.*) What difference does it make? You've turned us all into murderers. You've ruined the decency of my marriage ... What kind of animal are you? Isn't any woman safe from you? You pretend to defend California from the gringos, but California needs to be defended from you. There are

ways, Vásquez, for an honest man to pay his debts to society. But you ... I hope to see you hanged. Rosario,
get your father, and gather our belongings. We're leaving. (ROSARIO *looks at* TIBURCIO *for a long desperate
moment.*)

ROSARIO: Tiburcio?

TIBURCIO: Do as your husband says.

ROSARIO: (*Breathless, in shock,* ROSARIO *goes to her father.
There are no tears.*) Vámonos, Papá. (*She helps* FID-
DLER FELIZ *to his feet.*)

FELIZ: (*Coughing.*) Dios mío, this is crazy. Where are we going
in the middle of the night? Vásquez, Leiva, Rosario ...
forget this madness. Don't we have enemies enough in
the world? For the love of God, I'm sick. I need some
tea. (LEIVA *comes and lifts* FELIZ, *helping him.*)

LEIVA: I'll help you to the wagon, Don Casimiro. Let's go. (RO-
SARIO *looks at* TIBURCIO *one more time. So does*
CHÁVEZ, *who is acutely aware of the Capitán's inner
torment.*) ¿Niña? (ROSARIO *starts to follow* LEIVA.
TIBURCIO *takes a step after her, undecided.*)

CHÁVEZ: (*Cautiously.*) Let her go, jefe. It's for the best. She'll
only slow us down. She's only a woman. (TIBURCIO
*stares at* CHÁVEZ.)

ROSARIO: (*Stops and takes control of her own destiny. She turns
to* LEIVA *with aristocratic defiance.*) You can't hate me
any more than you already do, Abdón, but I want you to
know ... I'm carrying Tiburcio's son. (ROSARIO *turns
and runs to* VÁSQUEZ.)

LEIVA: (*Practically speechless.*) His son? His son!! (VÁSQUEZ
*is embarrassed.* LEIVA *doesn't know whether to laugh or
cry. The life drains out of his eyes.*) Vásquez, I don't know
when or where or how, but I swear to God, I will kill you
the first chance I get.

TIBURCIO: I admit I have wronged you, Leiva. But I warn you
too. Be careful. The next time I shall defend myself.

ROSARIO: Papá, we're staying.

FELIZ: No, my child, not I. If it's not to much to ask, Abdon
will leave me in Los Angeles ... where we have family.
As for you, the Capitán and Chávez, may God be with
you in the wilderness. I no longer can. (LEIVA *exits with*
FELIZ. *There is a long pause.*)

TIBURCIO: Okay, Chávez, you're next. Get on your horse.

CHÁVEZ: What did I do?

TIBURCIO: Rosario's only a woman. She'll slow us down. Go on, save your hide! Join Moreno and Gonzales in Mexico.

CHÁVEZ: (*Stubbornly.*) No, Capitán, I'm not going.

TIBURCIO: You're going to disobey my orders?

CHÁVEZ: (*Helpless.*) Jefe, I ain't such a coyote to stay out here all by myself. You're all I got ... All I ever wanted in life was to be like you ... to ride with you.

ROSARIO: Tiburcio, he loves you too. Please forgive him. (*Pause.*)

VÁSQUEZ: (*Throws his arms around the both of them.*) All right, the three of us shall ride together like a vengeful wind ... sweeping the landscape of California! (*They freeze in a heroic pose.* CHÁVEZ *lifts his rifle. Music. Curtain.*)


...................... SCENE THREE ......................

*Mission San Fernando. A thunder storm. Two months later. Night. Interior fireplace. The home quarters of* DON ANDRÉS PICO *at his estate on the grounds of the old mission. There is a steady persistent knocking.* OLD GABRIEL, *an Indian servant, enters with a candle.*

GABRIEL: ¡Santo Niño Jesús! Who can that be waking the very muertos in the dead of night? (*More knocking. A flash of lightning and thunder. He hesitates.*) A godless soul perhaps ... only the Diablo himself could be out in the middle of this storm. (*Knocking.*)

PICO: (*Enters from within.*) Who is it, Gabriel?

GABRIEL: At this hour, Don Andrés, only Satan knows. Maybe just the wind, ripping the old wooden gate off it's leather hinges ... Wait, while I see, eh? (GABRIEL *exits.* PICO *lights a candle. There is another flash of lightning, then a clap of thunder, as* TIBURCIO *enters carrying* ROSARIO *in his arms. She is in labor.*)

TIBURCIO: Don Andrés, please forgive this regrettable intrusion. I've come to impose on your hospitality.

PICO: Is that you, Vásquez? You must be mad!

TIBURCIO: Only desperate, señor. My wife is about to have a baby. (OLD GABRIEL *re-enters.*)

PICO: Your ... wife? Gabriel, summon Soledad.

GABRIEL: (*Calling.*) Soledad? Soledad, the master wants you!

PICO: (*Turns, with a master's patience.*) No, Old Gabriel, go to
   her chamber. You'll wake the whole house. (GABRIEL
   *exits.* TIBURCIO *looks worn and haggard.*)
PICO: Hombre. You look terrible. Exhausted.
TIBURCIO: (*Sitting down.*) She's the one that's exhausted. I had
   to bring her down from the mountains ... Rosario? How
   are you feeling, mi amor?
ROSARIO: Tiburcio ... where are we?
TIBURCIO: San Fernando Mission. The house of Don Andrés
   Pico, my old friend. You'll be safe here. (*Another light-
   ning flash and clap of thunder.* ROSARIO *has a contrac-
   tion and starts moaning in pain.*)
PICO: Soledad! Soledad, come quickly.
SOLEDAD: (*Enters in a hurry. She is another Indian servant.*) ¿Sí,
   señor?
PICO: This woman is about to have a child.
SOLEDAD: ¡Santo Niño! This way, señor, bring her in here. I
   will do what I can. (ROSARIO *screams with pain.* OLD
   GABRIEL *re-enters.*)
ROSARIO: ¡Ay, Tiburcio!
TIBURCIO: Only a moment more, Rosario. It's almost over.
   (TIBURCIO *exits with* ROSARIO.)
GABRIEL: Rosario? Isn't that the woman they say Vásquez stole
   ...
PICO: Old Gabriel ... gossip doesn't suit your antiquity. Did you
   see who else came with Don Tiburcio?
GABRIEL: Only one other man I could see. He's standing out by
   the gate ... in the rain.
PICO: That would be Chávez. Watching the road to Los Angeles,
   no doubt. (*Pause.*) Go to the kitchen and bring dried
   meat, cheese and bread. And a bottle of good wine.
GABRIEL: Wine?
PICO: Yes, Old Gabriel, in spite of the hour, we must be hos-
   pitable to our guests. (OLD GABRIEL *goes out, just as*
   TIBURCIO *re-enters.* ROSARIO *groans with pain in another room.*) Relax, Vásquez. There's nothing you can do.
   No one is more useless at a birth than the father. Don't
   worry she'll deliver—Leiva's woman. (TIBURCIO *turns
   sharply.*) The word's out, Tiburcio. Even the Indian servants talk about it. Frankly, I think it's a disgrace. This
   time, your womanizing ...
TIBURCIO: I didn't come to talk about my womanizing.

PICO: (*Concerned.*) You're taking too many risks, hombre. I hear Leiva's surrendered to the authorities, turned state's evidence in that Tres Pinos affair. They say he wants to see you hanged. Things couldn't be worse for you.

TIBURCIO: They could raise the price on my head.

PICO: They have. Two days ago in Sacramento. $8000, alive, $6000, dead! (TIBURCIO *laughs hysterically.*) Are you going out of your wits? What is there to laugh about?

TIBURCIO: The melodrama, my friend. The deadly melodrama of Tiburcio Vásquez.

PICO: (*Frustrated.*) ¡Caramba! Why haven't you escaped to Mexico like any sane, ordinary horse thief? I can't say I'm proud about your criminal exploits, Tiburcio, but I admit you've given all of us Californios twenty years of secret, vicarious revenge. Now save yourself. Or at least save the rest of us the grief and humiliation of watching them hang you.

OLD GABRIEL: (*Re-enters with a tray.*) Here comes your gentlemen's supper, señor. Meat, cheese, bread, wine ... and even a spring rose from the mission garden. Around here we're civilized at all hours ... May I go back to my warm bed now, Don Andrés? (ROSARIO *crys within.*) I forgot. My warm bed is occupied.

PICO: Go look, Gabriel. Soledad might need help.

GABRIEL: The Holy Virgen never made such a fuss ... and she gave birth to God. (GABRIEL *exits.*)

PICO: Please, Tiburcio. Help yourself to food and drink, while we wait.

TIBURCIO: (*Eats as he talks, but he is totally preoccupied with* ROSARIO's *condition.*) Don Andrés, your loyalty and hospitality have always been an inspiration to me. Even through all the years of horse thievery and petty hold-ups, you have always respected me as a fellow Californian ... which is why I now ask your help in executing the most daring scheme I've ever conceived.

PICO: No, señor. Stop there. I cannot help you in any way to commit robbery.

TIBURCIO: I'm talking about a revolution. With a hundred well armed men, I can start a rebellion that will crack the state of California in two, like an earthquake, leaving the Bear Republic in the north, and Spanish California Republic in the south!

PICO: My God, Vásquez, you're serious about this, aren't you?

TIBURCIO: My friend, the seam in the state is already there, like the San Andreas Fault, just waiting to be ripped apart. We must strike now while there is still time. In one year the Southern Pacific Railroad will cut through the San Bernardino Mountains, and it will be too late. We'll be finished.

PICO: No, Vásquez, you'll be finished. Aren't you over dramatizing your own predicament? We Californios may have lost ground, but we're not entirely powerless yet.

TIBURCIO: (*Pause.*) I had hoped for less compromise from the man who defeated the U.S. Cavalry at the Battle of San Pasquel.

PICO: Yes, Vásquez, I did lead my lanceros against the gringos; and we did win battles, but that was twenty-five years ago. We lost the war, remember? We're all Americans now. (*There is a slap in the adjoining room. A baby cries out.*) There! I think she's had the baby.

TIBURCIO: My son!

GABRIEL: (*Comes rushing in.*) It's a girl! The woman has given birth to a female.

TIBURCIO: My son?! (*He smiles sardonically.*) Forgive me. For a moment I thought the child might be Leiva's after all ... Nevermind. How's the mother?

GABRIEL: She's asking for you.

TIBURCIO: Tell her I'll be right there. (GABRIEL *goes out again. Pause.*) Don Andrés, my old friend, my back is against a brick Yankee wall, and I've got to stand firm or make a run for it. I've never relished the idea of spending the rest of my days in Mexico. This is where I belong. So who knows? Could you see that Rosario gets back to San Jose safely? She has sisters there who will care for her ... and the child.

PICO: Consider it done.

TIBURCIO: One more thing: the law will arrest and prosecute her as my accomplice, unless it's established otherwise. Spread the story that I stole her from Leiva, used her, then left her pregnant in the wilderness ... where she suffered so much she lost the baby.

PICO: Aren't you being overly cruel ... to yourself?

TIBURCIO: Don't you think they'll buy it?

PICO: (*Pause.*) I'm afraid so. But why deny the existence of the child?

TIBURCIO: The offspring of a raping, murderous bandit can only be looked upon as a freak. That's not going to happen to my child.

OLD GABRIEL: (*Re-enters.*) The woman wants you to see the baby.

TIBURCIO: (*Straightens his coat, then lifts the rose off the tray.*) The daughter of Don Tiburcio Vásquez, Liberator of California, has been born a lady. (TIBURCIO *goes with rose in hand.*)

*Thunder and lightening. Light change. The set transforms again*

...................... SCENE FOUR ......................

*The jail. Daytime. The* IMPRESARIO *enters with* SHERIFF ADAMS.

IMPRESARIO: Vásquez, I'll never understand all the maudlin sympathy lavished on you by hundreds of weak-headed women, but I must say I continue to admire your perspicacity.

TIBURCIO: It's the charm of the condemned man, Gillette.

IMPRESARIO: At fifty cents a shot, your photo cards must have turned quite a handsome little profit by now.

SHERIFF: You know the rule, gentlemen. Five minutes. (ADAMS *exits. The* IMPRESARIO *sits outside the cell.*)

IMPRESARIO: I got word you wanted to see me. What's on your reptilian mind?

TIBURCIO: The scales of blind justice, Gillette. A noose in one hand, a bag of gold in the other. I'm still prepared to sell you all the rights to my story for a small advance and a couple of minor conditions. Are you interested?

IMPRESARIO: Hell, no! They're going to hang you in two weeks. What kind of an offer is that? Goddamn your eyes, Vásquez, we could have had a deal months ago. You've squandered a fortune, sir. There's no time to launch a play now. Not in San Francisco.

TIBURCIO: Last time you opened in ten days.

IMPRESARIO: You'll be in your grave before opening night, Vásquez. Public interest will be deader than you are.

TIBURCIO: The State Supreme Court has yet to rule on my appeal, Gillette. All hope's not lost.

IMPRESARIO: Are you kidding me or yourself?

TIBURCIO: Do you really think I'll be forgotten so quickly?

IMPRESARIO: We're entering an industrial age, Vásquez. The persistence of public memory is rapidly being determined by the speed of machinery. Railroads, steam engines, the telegraph.

TIBURCIO: Have one of my signed daguerreotypes. The science of photography has already granted me immortality. (ABDÓN LEIVA *enters, behind the wall of bars.*) Hello, Abdón. How did you get out of your cell?

LEIVA: It's never locked.

TIBURCIO: What do you want?

LEIVA: Just to see you ... I have nothing to say.

TIBURCIO: I'm not surprised. You said it all in court. No matter what you do for the rest of your natural life, Abdón, you'll know the truth about Tres Pinos.

LEIVA: That's not true, Vásquez ... you killed my son. May your soul be damned in the fires of hell! (LEIVA *exits.*)

IMPRESARIO: What does that mean, you killed his son?

TIBURCIO: The death of an illusion, Gillette. Nothing more.

IMPRESARIO: (*Suddenly intrigued.*) How much more of an advance do you require?

TIBURCIO: One thousand, like before.

IMPRESARIO: I'll give you two hundred, like before.

TIBURCIO: Make it seven-fifty.

IMPRESARIO: Five hundred.

TIBURCIO: Sold!

IMPRESARIO: Not so fast, Vásquez. I'll only make the deal on one condition. I want the full story, warts and all, including the dirt on your illicit affair with Mrs. Leiva.

TIBURCIO: Don't worry. I'll set the record straight.

IMPRESARIO: And none of this Liberator of California horseshit either. I'd be laughed out of the state if I tried to stage that. That's the tallest story I've ever heard. Shame on you. It's not in character.

TIBURCIO: (*Sardonically.*) What do you know about my character? Did you ever read the manuscript I gave you?

IMPRESARIO: (*Scoffing.*) Poppycock, sir. Bunk! The dramaturgy was turgid, and your self-aggrandizement, more than even bad melodrama can sustain. Not worth a damn or a dime.

TIBURCIO: (*Angering.*) Like your dime-novel "History of the American West?"

IMPRESARIO: (*Bristling.*) You're a convicted killer, Vásquez. What good is it to white-wash the gallows? Nobody will buy it. The gringos are the victors of this land, sir. Mexicans and Indians are the vanquished. That's the only history that matters.

TIBURCIO: (*Laughs bitterly, as he takes control of his emotions again.*) A hundred years from now, my friend, people will still speak of Tiburcio Vásquez the bandit.

IMPRESARIO: We needn't waste any words extolling your modesty, I can see that.

TIBURCIO: What part of my story are you willing to believe?

IMPRESARIO: Your capture. Or are you going to deny that happened as well?

TIBURCIO: Why should I? Where would our story be without a fitting dramatic climax?

*Music. Light change. The set is transformed.* SHERIFF ROWLAND *and* POSSE COMITATUS *appear, singing before the grand curtain.*

POSSE: (*Singing.*)

> WE'VE GALLOPED O'ER THE PLAINS
> THROUGH MOUNTAIN GORGE AND RANGE
> WE'VE HUNTED VÁSQUEZ DAY AND NIGHT
> TO CAPTURE HIM DEAD OR ALIVE
>
> WE'VE GOT OUR WEAPONS READY
> WE'RE FEELING BRAVE AND STEADY
> WE'RE LOADED UP WITH SHOTGUN SHELLS
> WE'RE HORRIBLY HEELED WITH BOWIE KNIVES
>
> 'CAUSE WE'RE THE POSSE
> THE POSSE COMITATUS
> WE'RE COMING THROUGH FOR JUSTICE
> WE'RE THE LONG ARM OF THE LAW!

*The oleo lifts.*

........................ SCENE FIVE ........................

*Cahuenga Pass. Near Laurel Canyon. May 1874. Morning.*

SHERIFF ROWLAND *and his* POSSE *rendezvous in the hills north of Los Angeles. The* SHERIFF *addresses his men as they settle down.*

SHERIFF: Relax, men. We're going to wait here a spell while the morning mist burns away down below. But gather around, I've got some words to say: (*Singing.*)

> OUR LIVES ARE IN OUR HANDS
> TO DO OR DIE IS GRAND
> WE'RE ABLE BODIED HEROES ALL
> WITH NEVER A THOUGHT FOR REWARD!
>
> BUT FORTUNE FAVORS THE BRAVEST
> THERE'S A SCHEME THAT YET MAY SAVE US
> WE'RE GOING TO THE CULPRIT'S LAIR
> AND HE DOESN'T KNOW WE'RE COMING THERE.

(*Speaking.*) Why!

POSSE: (*Singing.*)

> 'CAUSE WE'RE THE POSSE
> THE POSSE COMITATUS
> WE'RE COMING THROUGH FOR JUSTICE
> WE'RE THE LONG ARM OF THE LAW!

SHERIFF: Nope, that ain't it. The real reason is that a "little bird" has sung and told us the exact location of Vásquez's hideout. Ain't that right, Señor Leiva? (SHERIFF ROWLAND *has some field glasses. He looks off into the distance.*) Now, I can see through these spy glasses the premises of Greek George's cabin down in Rancho La Brea ... I see a white horse picketed at the edge of a mustard patch which surrounds the house, and that must be Vásquez's mount ... waiting for the bandido to make his get away ... Well men, this time he's not going to escape, 'cause we're playing it smart. (*He calls over* THE MEXICAN.) Instead of chargin' down the mountain like a pack of Comanches, lettin' the bandit know we're comin', we're gonna crawl into this here Mexican's wagon and sneak up on the rascal ... little by little, till we're at his doorstep and on his throat! Right, amigo?

THE MEXICAN: ¡Sí, Señor!

SHERIFF: Damn right. Maybe it ain't brave, maybe it ain't grand, but it sure as hell means the end of Tiburcio Vásquez. You men with me?

POSSE: (*The* POSSE *cheers, then singings.*)

> WE'VE GALLOPED O'ER THE PLAINS
> THROUGH MOUNTAIN GORGE AND RANGE
> WE'VE HUNTED VÁSQUEZ DAY AND NIGHT
> TO CAPTURE HIM DEAD OR ALIVE!

SHERIFF: To the wagon!
POSSE: (*Singing.*)

> WE'VE GOT OUR WEAPONS READY
> WE'RE FEELING BRAVE AND STEADY
>
> WE'RE LOADED UP WITH SHOT GUN SHELLS
> WE'RE HORRIBLY HEELED WITH BOWIE KNIVES.

SHERIFF: We're coming to get you, Vásquez!
POSSE:

> 'CAUSE WE'RE THE POSSE
> THE POSSE COMITATUS
> WE'RE COMING THROUGH FOR JUSTICE
> WE'RE THE LONG ARM OF THE LAW!

*The* POSSE *exits. The oleo lifts to reveal* GREEK GEORGE's *cabin.*

.......................... SCENE SIX ..........................

GREEK GEORGE's *cabin. The mouth of Laurel Canyon. Afternoon.*

RITA MADRID *is in a happy mood, dancing around the room, while she sets the table.* CLEODOVIO CHÁVEZ, *dressed exactly like* VÁSQUEZ, *seems uneasy, sitting at the table cleaning his guns and watching* RITA *out of the corner of his eye.*

RITA: Cleodovio, hombre. Why the sour puss? Don't tell me you hate my cooking? Cheer up.
CHÁVEZ: There's nothing to be happy about.
RITA: I made nopalitos for lunch. Tender little cactus leaves in red chile sauce. You'll love 'em.
CHÁVEZ: Cactus gives me the runs.
RITA: (*Perturbed by his reluctant attitude.*) Not if you eat them with the thorns. Would you move your clumsy pistolas?

Whatever became of that innocent sheepherder I used to know?

CHÁVEZ: (*Moves his guns.*) He grew up and became a coyote.

RITA: With a taste for blood?

TIBURCIO: (*Enters from the outside.*) Caramba, that white palomino has got to be the most beautiful horse alive. Where in the world did you find him Chávez?

CHÁVEZ: Up in the Little Tujunga. I knew you'd like him.

TIBURCIO: I hope you left the rider with his boots.

CHÁVEZ: (*Cryptically.*) He didn't seem worried when I left him. (CHÁVEZ *looks down at his new boots.* RITA *shivers.*)

RITA: Capitán, please sit down and eat. I made your favorite delicacy—nopalitos.

TIBURCIO: Nopalitos—from Rita Madrid? Now that's a twist. This marriage to Greek George has turned you into a new woman, virgin as a new born cactus leaf ... George told me it was your idea to hide us out here. I owe you for that.

RITA: (*Meaningfully.*) You'll pay me back one way or another. (TIBURCIO *smiles at her insinuation;* CHÁVEZ *understands it differently.*)

TIBURCIO: Where's George?

RITA: Gone to Los Angeles to spy on Sheriff Rowland, like you said. He won't be back until dark.

CHÁVEZ: All this waiting around. We've got to do something, jefe. Sooner or later, somebody's bound to sell us out. Rowland is offering money for information. I'm not even sure we can trust Greek George anymore.

RITA: (*With an edge.*) Chiquito, why don't you check the seat of your pants? That Syrian camel driver has risked his neck to hide your dirty rear end.

TIBURCIO: Rita's right, Chávez. George is above suspicion.

CHÁVEZ: I say we ought to plug the Sheriff.

RITA: That's your answer for everything these days, isn't it, Cleodovio? An ear for a tooth and a head for an eye! You might dress like the Capitán, but you're not fit to walk in his shadow.

CHÁVEZ: Are you?

RITA: What do you think?

CHÁVEZ: I think you're a whore.

RITA: (*In a rage.*) Get out! Get out of my house, cabrón!

TIBURCIO: All right, you two! Chávez, I believe you owe this lady an apology.

RITA: Get him out of my house, Tiburcio.

CHÁVEZ: Yeah, that's what you want, huh? So you can be alone with the jefe. Well I ain't going. I saw what happened with Leiva and his woman, and I ain't gonna let it happen to Greek George. Not while our lives depend on it ... I'm sorry now I never said nothing about Leiva.

TIBURCIO: (*Angrily.*) Leiva? That dog of a turn-coat just testified at my cousin's trial in Salinas, and sent him to San Quentin for life! Is that what you're feeling sorry about? He wants to hang you.

CHÁVEZ: No, jefe, it's you he wants ... for what you did to him.

TIBURCIO: (*Pause.*) Is my right hand pointing a finger in judgement?

CHÁVEZ: You're not living up to what you are, jefe! You're the Capitán ... our revenge against the gringos ... like Joaquín Murrieta ... only he was never afraid to spill their blood.

TIBURCIO: Murrieta was a myth. I'm the reality.

CHÁVEZ: How you gonna start a revolution without bloodshed? They call you a blood-thirsty killer, but for what? Three lousy murders in Tres Pinos you didn't commit? I say let's slaughter every gringo we meet! If they're gonna hang us, it might as well be for something good—not petty thievery.

TIBURCIO: (*Pause.*) I just noticed your new boots, Cleodovio. Where did you get them?

CHÁVEZ: I took them off that dead rider in Little Tujunga.

TIBURCIO: So you did kill him?

CHÁVEZ: (*Pause.*) Sure, why not? I wanted that white horse for you, so people could look up and see Capitán Tiburcio Vásquez sitting on that silver palomino like the sun!

TIBURCIO: (*Long pause.* TIBURCIO *visibly saddens.*) Cleodovio, my young paisano, you still don't know me, do you? I want you to take that white horse and go.

CHÁVEZ: Go? But ... who's going to ride with you, and protect your back?

TIBURCIO: That's not your concern anymore.

CHÁVEZ: (*Shaking his head.*) No, jefe, I ain't leaving you.

TIBURCIO: (*Fiercely.*) Chávez! I mean it. You and I are finished. Your not fit to ride with Tiburcio Vásquez.

CHÁVEZ: But ... ?

TIBURCIO: Go, I said! Please ... this is the last command I shall ever give you, you're on your own.

CHÁVEZ: (*Gathers his pistols, with tears in his eyes.*) That woman will betray you, jefe ... watch your back ... from now on, don't trust nobody. (CHÁVEZ *leaves.*)

RITA: (*Goes to* TIBURCIO, *wheedling up to him.*) Who would have guessed that funny little kid would turn out so cold-blooded?

TIBURCIO: Looks like I'm back where I started.

RITA: Just me and you.

TIBURCIO: (*Pause.*) No dice, Rita. Chávez was dead right about that. Greek George isn't going to be another Leiva, and you certainly aren't Rosario.

RITA: (*Furious.*) You were mine years before you even met that high class bitch! I knew back in New Idria she couldn't hack being your woman. Where is she now? Back in San Jose, accusing you of kidnapping and rape.

TIBURCIO: (*Looks out the door.*) Hold it ... who's that coming down the road in that wagon?

RITA: (*Looking.*) A neighbor from the next rancho. He's okay. He's a friend of George's.

TIBURCIO: (*Relaxes, but he cannot shake a feeling of nervousness.*) Caray ... I'm going to have to find some new men I can trust, men of quality and distinction. Or at least, some poor dog to watch the road while I eat. (TIBURCIO *wearily takes off his guns.*)

RITA: (*Pause.*) I'm the woman you need, Tiburcio. I'll ride with you, until the day we die, even if they hang us, so long as it's together! You ought to get some sleep.

TIBURCIO: (*Sits down to eat.*) Sleep, eat and make love ... that's all there is to this mortal fandango. That's what all the killing is about. Fulano wants to sleep better than Mengano; Mengano wants to eat better than Zutano; and each one wants to steal the other's woman and make love to her ... It's not a melodrama after all; it's a farce.

RITA: (*Looks out the door and screams.*) Tiburcio ... the wagon, look out! It's a posse! (*We hear the* POSSE *outside, yelling and shouting.*)

SHERIFF: (*Offstage.*) You men, cover all the windows and doors! We're going in!

TIBURCIO: ¡Carajo! I'm trapped. (TIBURCIO *makes a dive for the window, just as* SHERIFF ROWLAND *bursts through with his men.*)

SHERIFF: Stop or we'll shoot! (*One of the men fires a shotgun blast.* TIBURCIO *is hit, and slams against the wall, spurt-*

*ing blood all over the window. He remains on his feet.*)

SHERIFF: He's still alive! Easy now, take it easy with him. Get that chair over here!

TIBURCIO: Well, well ... Sheriff Rowland, we meet again. Remember me? I'm Alejandro Cojones.

SHERIFF: It's no use, Tiburcio. I know you too well. I've been after you for years.

TIBURCIO: How did you find me?

SHERIFF: A little bird told us ... pointed out the exact location.

TIBURCIO: Little bird? (TIBURCIO *turns toward* RITA.)

RITA: (*Hysterical.*) It wasn't me, Tiburcio! I swear to God it wasn't me, Tiburcio!

TIBURCIO: You're a good man, Sheriff, a kind man. You dress my wounds, nurse me carefully, and you boys will get $8000 dollars. If you let me die, you only get $6000. So you get $2000 for being kind!

DEPUTY: Sheriff, that other man on the white horse ... he got away.

SHERIFF: Well, we got what we came for. Good work. Get that wagon here, back it up to the door!

TIBURCIO: You're all brave boys, congratulations, Sheriff, but I'm afraid I won't make it to your necktie party. I'm done in ... Tiburcio Vásquez is about to ... escape! (TIBURCIO *blacks out.*)

SHERIFF: Don't let him die, you men. Don't let him die!

*The* POSSE *panics, hovering over* TIBURCIO *as the curtain falls.*

*Lights change. The set transforms back to the jail.*

*Dressed in black,* CALIFORNIA KATE *enters and comes downstage, singing the ballad of a whore: "Cut Down in My Prime."*

KATE: (*Singing.*)

> WHEN I WAS A YOUNG GIRL
> I USED TO SEEK PLEASURE
> WHEN I WAS A YOUNG GIRL
> I USED TO DRINK ALE
> RIGHT OUT OF THE ALEHOUSE AND INTO THE
>     JAILHOUSE
> RIGHT OUT OF THE BARROOM AND INTO MY
>     GRAVE

SEND FOR THE PREACHER TO COME AND PRAY
  O'ER ME
SEND FOR THE DOCTOR TO BIND UP MY WOUNDS
MY POOR HEAD IS ACHING
LORD MY SAD HEART IS BREAKING
MY BODY'S SALVATED AND HELL IS MY TOMB

IF HE HAD JUST TOLD ME BEFORE HE DISHON-
  ORED ME
IF HE HAD JUST TOLD ME I'D'VE HAD IT IN
  TIME
I MIGHT HAVE GOT SALTS THEN OR PILLS OF
  WHITE
MERCURY, BUT NOW I'M A YOUNG GIRL
CUT DOWN IN MY PRIME

SEND SIX PRETTY GIRLIES TO CARRY MY COF-
  FIN
I WANT SIX, SIX SOCIAL LADIES
LET'EM BEAR UP MY PALL
AND I WANT EACH OF THEM TO CARRY—GODDAMMIT!
A BUNCH OF WHITE LILIES
TO LAY ON MY COFFIN AS I PASS ALONG.

KATE *puts on a black veil and exits.*


...................... SCENE SEVEN ......................

*The jail. Night.* SHERIFF ADAMS *enters and goes to* VÁS-
QUEZ's *cell.* TIBURCIO *sits up, waiting for the news.*

ADAMS: Tiburcio, it is my sad duty to inform you that the Gov-
       ernor has denied to grant a stay of execution. He upheld
       the decision of the State Supreme Court to execute your
       sentence tomorrow.
TIBURCIO: So ... looks like I win the bet, doesn't it?
ADAMS: I'm sorry.
TIBURCIO: Better luck next time, Harry. You owe me ten bucks,
       a bottle of wine and a Havana cigar. (ADAMS *hands him
       a stogie, then lights a match for him.*)
ADAMS: Lots of people are worried about tomorrow, Tiburcio.
       Chávez has threatened to attack Hollister.
TIBURCIO: So I hear.

SHERIFF: The whole town is running scared. Even San Jose is like an armed camp tonight. Many innocent lives could be lost.

TIBURCIO: Only one that I know of. Mind if I collect that bet? You know how it is. Here today, gone tomorrow. (SHERIFF ADAMS *pays him.*)

SHERIFF: Sam Gillette is here to pay his last respects.

IMPRESARIO: (*Enters.*) I'm here to settle our final accounts, sir. I've decided to stage your play in San Francisco.

TIBURCIO: Well, hallelujah. That calls for a drink. Sheriff?

ADAMS: My pleasure. (*Uncorks a bottle.*) Some wine, gentlemen?

IMPRESARIO: Well, I'll be damned.

ADAMS: We bend the rules occasionally. (ADAMS *pours the drinks.*)

TIBURCIO: Here's to love.The only antidote to death known to man. (*They toast and drink.*)

IMPRESARIO: Your thoughts must be on the hereafter, sir, on this your last night on earth.

TIBURCIO: Actually, I was counting the days since I last made love to a woman. Sages and wise men say there is an afterlife. For my part, I don't know.

ADAMS: Rest assured, Tiburcio. There is a Heaven and a Hell.

TIBURCIO: In that case, Harry, tomorrow I shall be dancing again with all my old sweethearts.

IMPRESARIO: What about Rosario Leiva, Vásquez? Has she been to see you? Seems to me that if that love story you told was true ...

TIBURCIO: It was as true as you make it, Gillette. Did you bring my five hundred dollars?

IMPRESARIO: (*Pulls out his billfold.*) Caveat emptor, sir. I want to be certain that I'm buying the right to portray you as I see fit. Can you guarantee your friends won't burn down my theater?

TIBURCIO: You have my word as a gentleman.

IMPRESARIO: How do I know I can trust you?

TIBURCIO: I could ask you the same question.

IMPRESARIO: And I still wouldn't know how to answer you. The moral vagaries of your life confound the melodrama, sir. Are you comic or tragic, a good man or a bad man?

TIBURCIO: All of them.

IMPRESARIO: Reality and theater don't mix, sir. That's your problem. You're too damned real, like those photographs

of your face. If you were less familiar, like that Murrieta fellow, I'd turn your life into a genuine California
romance. Your legend needs a little more grandeur.

TIBURCIO: You'll have it tomorrow, my friend.

IMPRESARIO: Tiburcio, my wife has been asking to meet you for
months. I would be honored if you would say hello to her.

TIBURCIO: The honor would be mine.

IMPRESARIO: (*Escorts in* MRS. GILLETTE. *She is* ROSARIO.)
In that case, may I present my lady, the lovely Spanish
actress, Carlota Montez de ... Gillette. My dear, this is
the notorious Tiburcio Vásquez.

MRS. GILLETTE: How do you do? Meeting you, I feel as though
I already know you.

TIBURCIO: Madame, you are as beautiful as someone I once
knew. (VÁSQUEZ *tenderly kisses her hand.*)

MRS. GILLETTE: (*With tears.*) We shall treasure your memory
forever, señor. May God bless you.

TIBURCIO: Hello and goodbye.

IMPRESARIO: Goodbye, my friend.

TIBURCIO: So long, Sam. Take care of my melodrama. (*The*
IMPRESARIO *exits with* MRS. GILLETTE. TIBURCIO
*is somber. Picking up letters.*) Do me a favor, will you,
Sheriff? See that Rosario gets this letter and this money.
There's a small fortune in here for her ... and my daughter. Give her this other letter and the gold watch, as well—
they're for Chávez.

SHERIFF: Chávez?

TIBURCIO: She'll know how to get in touch with him. He once
promised to give me his life, if I ever needed it. The
letter tells him that I accept—not to get himself and a
lot of innocent people killed—and that through this gold
watch I bequeath him the rest of my lifetime.

ADAMS: (*Takes the letters, money and watch.*) Listen, Tiburcio,
about tomorrow ... knowing you and Leiva after all these
months, well, I just want you to know I think his testimony in court was always suspect. I just wish there was
something more I could do.

TIBURCIO: (*Pause.*) How about letting me see my coffin?

SHERIFF: You want to see your coffin?

TIBURCIO: My pine box. Where is it?

SHERIFF: Right in there. You have one final visitor. (SHERIFF
ADAMS *opens the cell.* VÁSQUEZ *steps out. The* LADY
IN BLACK *emerges from the shadows.*)

TIBURCIO: ¡Caramba! The Lady in black again? This must be the end.

KATE: The end, my ass, you bounder. It's me! Parlez vous? (KATE *throws off her black veil.*)

TIBURCIO: (*Embraces her.*) Kate!

KATE: (*Wincing with pain.*) Careful with the love stuff, honey. I'm feeling a little fragile down there these days. I just came to pay my last respects, before we both rendezvous up at them pearly gates.

TIBURCIO: Both?

KATE: I told you they were gonna hang you, didn't I? Well, I should have been a mite more careful myself. The wages of sin, my dear. And the grim reaper is comin' to collect his due. I thought you might feel better knowin' you'll have my company up there in about six months.

TIBURCIO: How did it happen, Kate?

KATE: Hell, you know how it happened. He was such a gentleman, too. You know me, always a sucker for gentlemen. God almighty, somewhere's along the line there's gotta be a big payoff for all of us workin' girls. But it was worth it, wasn't it?

TIBURCIO: More than worth it, Kate. It was a glorious mortal fandango while it lasted.

KATE: I hear you've been askin' for your coffin? Well you flea-bitten bandit, I wasn't about to let you go out in a pine box, so I had one specially made for you. Compliments of the girls at the house. Bring it on in, Mister Daver. (*The* UNDERTAKER *enters with a coffin.*) Ain't it a beauty?

UNDERTAKER: Craftsmanship of the highest quality, Mister Vásquez. The pride of the undertaking art, all for you. (TIBURCIO *frowns.*)

KATE: What's the matter? You don't like it.

TIBURCIO: It's too short.

KATE: Too short? Vásquez, that's impossible. I gave Mr. Daver your exact measurements, and I oughta know'em. Measure it—go on. (TIBURCIO *steps into the coffin and brings himself to full height. It fits perfectly.*)

UNDERTAKER: Does everything meet with your satisfaction, sir?

TIBURCIO: (*Smiles.*) Perfectly.

UNDERTAKER: Of course.

TIBURCIO: I shall sleep well here ... forever. (*The* UNDERTAKER *starts to close coffin lid.* TIBURCIO *stops him.*) Hold it, amigo. I still have a bit of unfinished business.

Sheriff, would you please call a priest? I think I'm ready now.

KATE: Om'god! Vásquez calling for a priest? Now I know this is the end.

TIBURCIO: (*Heroically.*) On the contrary, mi querida Kate. The American Melodrama of Tiburcio Vásquez, Notorious California Bandit, could never be complete without it's climactic, obligatory finale. Thus ... let it be!

*Light change. Final transformation to the melodrama stage.*

...................... SCENE EIGHT ......................

*Music.* SHERIFF ADAMS *comes downstage and addresses the* audience, as the DEPUTY *ties* VÁSQUEZ's *hands behind his back. A priest enters.*

ADAMS: Ladies and gentlemen, pursuant to the statute in these affairs, you have been invited into the jail today to witness the public execution of Tiburcio Vásquez at one thirty P.M. exactly, March 19, 1875 A.D. And may God have mercy on his soul.

TIBURCIO: Let's get on with it, Harry.

*The entire* CAST *enters playing* SPECTATORS, *singing as they* gather at the foot of the gallows. VÁSQUEZ *is brought forward, led by the priest, as he slowly and nobly ascends the stairs.*

SPECTATORS: (*Singing.*)

JOAQUÍN MURRIETA WAS KILLED AND BEHEADED
THREE-FINGERED JACK HIS COMPANION IS DEAD
JACK'S BLOODY HAND'S IN A STOCKTON MU-
    SEUM
A JAR OF WHISKEY HOLDS MURRIETA'S HEAD

THE GOLD RUSH FEVER THAT SCORCHED CAL-
    IFORNIA
BROUGHT OUT THE UGLIEST WORST TRAITS
    IN MEN
BUT THINGS WERE DEAD AS THE HEAD OF
    MURRIETA
TILL VÁSQUEZ STARTED IT OVER AGAIN!

*At the top,* VÁSQUEZ *looks out at the crowd. Then* ADAMS *drops a black hood over his head and adjusts the noose.*

> TIBURCIO VÁSQUEZ, THE BANDIT NOTORIOUS
> WON FAME AND FORTUNE BY ROBBING THE
>    STAGE
> AND STOLE THE HEARTS OF ALL THE LUCK-
>    LESS WOMEN
> WHO GAVE HIM SUCCOR IN HIS ESCAPADES
>
> THE CURR IS WANTONLY WANTED ALL OVER
> FOR CRIMES COMMITTED WITH SCOUNDRELS
>    AND THIEVES
> TIBURCIO VÁSQUEZ, UN HOMBRE MUCHO MALO
> IS WANTED MOST BY THE LADIES HE LEAVES!

TIBURCIO: (*On the scaffold.*) ¡Pronto!

*The trap door opens.* VÁSQUEZ *slams through on his way to eternity. The final curtain.*

# CHARACTERS

BUDDY VILLA
CONNIE, his wife
SONNY, their son
ANITA, Sonny's friend

# SCENE

*The den of a comfortable, middle-class, suburban tract home in Southern California. Built some twenty years ago, the large den has all the features one might expect: black leather couches, bookshelves, trophies (bowling, golf, football, baseball, basketball), family photographs, liquor cabinet, fireplace, 25" console TV, stereo, VCR, etc. Upstage left, overlooking the sunken den, is the breakfast bar with stools, plus all the standard appliances beyond. A long hallway juts off diagonally, upstage right, toward the front of the house. Downstage right, through a large portico is the formal dining and living room, rarely used and largely unseen. Another door, down left of the breakfast bar, opens onto a two-car garage. Extreme doors open onto a worn wooden deck, supposedly overlooking a huge, neglected, imaginary swimming pool.*

*The entire scene has a comfortable, lived-in quality, particularly the den which is certainly the most lived-in room in the house. It is the family cockpit. Perhaps the only sign of the family's ancestral heritage is the familiar, round Aztec calendar stone, cast in plaster and painted gold, hanging above the fireplace. An old framed poster of Humphrey Bogart's 1948 classic "The Treasure of Sierra Madre" hangs on another wall, and one of those electrical plastic signs hawking Asahi Beer stands in the corner.*

# TIME

*The Reagan years, early in 1985.*

# PLACE

*Monterey Park—a suburb of Greater Los Angeles, on the distant fringe of Hollywood, USA.*

# NOTE

*The entire set sits within the confines of a TV studio. The scenery flats and their supports are entirely visible, as they might be to a live studio audience at a taping. Huge TV lamps hang above the set, and assorted equipment looms here and there above and beyond the limits of the set. A studio boom is poised above one of the flats, as if waiting to come on. Two studio monitors sit at extreme upstage right and upstage left, unobtrusive but activated from time to time with shots of the play picked up by two live video cameras in the house, and with shots on video tape.*

*The video-taped inserts must be pre-recorded, showing the family pool, cars coming and going, the front door, etc. The presence and participation of television equipment in this play must remain in the background until the final scene, but it is an integral part of the theatrical reality at hand in our story.*

*The use of music in this play approximates the sort of underscoring found in television and on film. Buddy must definitely have a "theme," but it is also appropriate for each of the four characters to have their own lietmotif.*

# PROLOGUE

*Darkness. A single clear note from a clarinet pierces the dark and plays the opening to Gershwin's "Rhapsody in Blue" slowly and hauntingly.*

DIRECTOR: (*Voice over. On the studio speakers.*) Lights . . .

*In the den: A lamp slowly comes on, revealing* BUDDY VILLA, *54, sitting asleep late at night in front of the TV (Unseen and invisible.) at extreme downstage right.*

DIRECTOR: (*Voice over.*) Video . . . Action!

*Behind* BUDDY VILLA, *the VCR on, a rack comes on, playing a scene from "The Treasure of Sierra Madre." On the studio monitors: A wily Mexican bandit is confronting a scruffy Humphrey Bogart with toothy disdain, somewhere in the wilds of Mexico.*

BANDIDO: (*Affronted.*) Badges? We don't have no badges. I don't have to show you any stinkin' badges!

*Gunfire. Action. In a mist,* SONNY *appears in the patio, dressed as a Hollywood Director. The french doors open automatically, and* SONNY *enters in slow motion, as in a dream, riding in on a dolly behind a phosphorescent camera.* BUDDY *stirs from his sleep and walks over to him, also in slow motion, moving his lips silently as if to say "Sonny what are you doing here?"* SONNY *commands him to sit down and sleep, and* BUDDY *does as he is told.* SONNY *then turns off the TV, affectionately kisses his father on the forehead, and exits out the french doors which close automatically behind him.*

*Slow fade to black*


# ACT ONE


........................ SCENE ONE ........................

*Early morning.*

*At rise: Coffee is perking in the kitchen. We hear the up-beat sounds of a 50's Rock'n'Roll classic. In the den,* CONNIE VILLA, *an attractive 48-year-old Chicana, is dancing. Dressed in a fluffy pink nightgown, she ambles over to the phone and makes a call, while the music on the stereo tape deck plays. Sitting on a wooden stool at the breakfast bar,* CONNIE *dials carefully, dangling a fluffy pink bedroom slipper from her foot. As the music ends, she is talking into the phone with a laid-back, brassy tone and worldly air.*

CONNIE: (*On phone.*) Hello, Betty? This is Constance D'Ville— Connie Villa! How ya doin' today? ... Great. Listen, any word on that Jack Nicholson picture? ... Well, when was I supposed to go back for that interview? I know we talked about it yesterday, but ... well, I was wondering ... Did you get a chance to ask the casting director about Buddy? ... Nothing? Nothing at all? Please, Betty. Without him I'm sunk! Central America's out of the question ... Yeah ... yeah. I'll hold, sure. (*The back door, down the hall, opens and closes. The sound of heavy breathing and footsteps.*) Buddy? ... Is that you, viejo?

BUDDY: (*Enters, jogging in place.*) *Viejo* my ass. Look at me— I'm an animal! (BUDDY *is a hefty, well-preserved Chicano, hungover but dressed in a jogging suit and running shoes, with the balding hair and body weight of an aging prizefighter. He jogs up to* CONNIE, *tosses her the morning paper and then picks her up and spins her around while she is still talking to her agent.*)

CONNIE: Wait a minute, Betty. There's an animal in the house! No, it's only Buddy. (BUDDY *drops to the floor and does ten, grunting and counting vociferously.*) What? ... Oh. What about Buddy? ... Nothing, huh? A part in what? ... "The Hairy Ape"?

BUDDY: (*Puffing.*) All right! ¿No *que* no?

CONNIE: No, Betty, I don't think so. We don't do waiver theatre. Screw the exposure. We don't work for free.

BUDDY: Twenty minutes flat, old lady! (CONNIE *makes a face and stands, still on the phone. She wipes his sweat off the floor.* BUDDY *hops on the exercise bike.*)

CONNIE: He's right here, dripping sweat all over my floor ... Yeah, he was out jogging. Or as we say in Spanish— "hogging." (BUDDY *playfully grunts like a hog, heading for the kitchen.*) Which reminds me: the residuals for the AT&T commercial, when do they start? ... Well okay, keep me posted. See you at the banquet tonight. Ciao (*Hangs up.*) Betty says there might be something in a couple of days. (BUDDY *opens the refrigerator door, we hear a beer pop open.*) Beer, hombre? It's still morning.

BUDDY: Gotta replace my body fluids. Would you believe I just ran five miles?

CONNIE: No.

BUDDY: Okay. Would you believe three miles?

CONNIE: I believe you ran around the house, slowly.

BUDDY: Honest. *Hice jog hasta la* freeway and back. Ran like an Apache ... (CONNIE *reaches up to the cabinet for vitamins; Buddy eyes her over.*) What's for breakfast?

CONNIE: What would you like?

BUDDY: How about a little *chorizo con huevos* ... in bed?

CONNIE: Don't start, *señor.*

BUDDY: (*Sidling up to her.*) Jogging always makes me horny.

CONNIE: Breathing makes you horny.

BUDDY: At my age I hate to let a good erection go to waste.

CONNIE: Down, boy. (*Flicks at his feigned erection.*) How about some butterless toast?

BUDDY: I'll stay on my liquid diet. (*He takes a long swig on his beer, and straddles one of the breakfast stools, noticing a letter on the counter. He picks it up as* CONNIE *pours orange juice and sets out the vitamins for* BUDDY.) What's this?

CONNIE: (*Exchanges* BUDDY's *beer for a glass of juice.*) It's from Lucy. She says Bob and her are doing just fine. Bob just got tenure in the Economics Department at Arizona State, and she's about to open her own practice in pediatrics in downtown Phoenix, which is why they've decided to wait to have a baby of their own. Go ahead, read it.

BUDDY: What the hell for? You just told me all that's in it.

CONNIE: Pick up your beer cans. (*He tosses the letter back on the counter; then he crosses down into the den, taking his beer, and starts picking up other empty beer cans.*) At least your daughter writes. Sonny, on the other hand, forget it. Not one written word since he got back East. We're lucky if he even calls once a month to ask for money. Do you think he's okay?

BUDDY: Sixteen years old and studying pre-law at Harvard? What could go wrong? A bad case of zits? The kid's a prodigy. He'll own his own law firm by the time he's twenty-five.

CONNIE: God knows, the last thing I want to be is one of those clinging *madrecitas* that won't let their kids grow up or they lose their purpose in life. *Chale*, man, not me, boy.

I hung up my uterus a long time ago. I like my freedom, and I'm ready to go places. (BUDDY *crosses up into the kitchen, carrying several empty beer cans.*) How late did you stay up last night?

BUDDY: Late. I was listening to a little Gershwin and I fell asleep watching my favorite picture. (*He deposits the can into a garbage bag under the sink.*)

CONNIE: (*Archly.*) What's that, a whole twelve pack? I thought you looked a little hung over this morning!

BUDDY: I always look hung-over in the morning.

CONNIE: After twenty-five years, you think I don't ... ?

BUDDY: (*Laughs defensively.*) It was just a few beers, *chingao.* Can't I have a few lousy beers—alone, by myself, in my own *pinche* den, in my own *pinche* house?

CONNIE: Not when you had a *pinche* drinking problem, just a few *pinche* years ago ...

BUDDY: (*Drops cans into a trash bag.*) That's ancient history.

CONNIE: Especially if you drink alone.

BUDDY: Actually, I had a weird dream Sonny was here in the house, right here in the den. I was there in my chair, there was someone outside and he came in, setting up shots, like he was directing a new Twilight Zone or something, can you beat that?

CONNIE: Mm, hmm, Harvard School of Law, Class of '92.

BUDDY: Anyway, this morning I woke up with a new movie idea.

CONNIE: Finish taking out the garbage.

BUDDY: This one's real hot. You wanna hear it? It'll only take a second. (BUDDY *crosses to the stereo, and turns on the Star Wars theme, on cassette.*)

CONNIE: (*Patiently tolerating him.*) Go on.

BUDDY: Well, the first shot shows him speeding across the giant screen in his space ship, blasting all rockets. Right? And his little ship sorta resembles a chopped down '56 Chevy, with fuzzy dice hanging over the dashboard, while the hero sits in the cockpit, down low, see? His head barely visible. *Órale, mamacita.*

CONNIE: (*Dully.*) Like a lowrider.

BUDDY: You got it. Well, suddenly there's these laser beams shooting at his tail, see? And the screen fills up with this giant space battle cruiser in hot pursuit.

CONNIE: Sounds familiar.

BUDDY: Except that the giant battle cruiser looks like a huge sombrero! A sombrero flying saucer! (*Laughs, enthused.*) And it's chasing the Chicano spaceman, 'cause they're the Interplanetary Border Patrol, the Space Migra, and he's trying to escape across the border to Earth! You get it?

CONNIE: (*Crosses to the stereo and turns it off.*) Take out the garbage.

BUDDY: It's a satire.

CONNIE: It won't sell, Buddy.

BUDDY: (*Angered.*) How the hell do you know? You're trying to tell me I don't know the *pinche* business? Shit, I was personal friends with Humphrey Bogart when you were still in grammar school, lady. Bogey and me were like that! (BUDDY *takes the garbage to service patio.*) Won't sell, my ass. I could pick up that *pinche* phone right now and peddle this *pinche* idea to a dozen *pinche* big time directors. (*Offstage. Exits to garage.*) Spielberg, Redford, Brian de Palma—they all know me! (*We hear the trash can lid slammed on. Pause. Buddy re-enters.*)

CONNIE: (*Concerned.*) What's with all the *pinches*? What's eating you?

BUDDY: The García's German shepherd chased me down the *pinche* block this morning.

CONNIE: (*Crosses to hall closet for cleaning equipment.*) Again, *hombre*?

BUDDY: Fifth time. And he's not the only one. The new Oriental families on the other block have pit bulls. *¡Pinches perros!* Why is it all the rich *gabachos* over in Beverly Hills have all these lousy little Chihuahuas, and all the Mexicans and Chinks on this side of town have these big Nazi killers?

CONNIE: (*Carpet sweeping.*) We could use a guard dog ourselves, for when we go out of town. It's been years since we went to Mexico. Wouldn't it be nice to travel now that the kids are out of the house?

BUDDY: (*Looks out toward the backyard, with a darkening mood.*) Dogtown ... Here we are in Monterey Park, and all these people still live in Dogtown. Know what I mean? In their minds, they never left.

CONNIE: And you did?

BUDDY: Lock, stock and *perros*. I was drafted.

CONNIE: Well, personally, I like "this side of town." I'm glad we left the barrio, but I wouldn't live in Beverly Hills if they paid me. Too many Latina maids at the bus stops.

BUDDY: In Korea I even ate some *perro* once.

CONNIE: East is east, and west is west, especially in L.A. Of course, there is always north and south, south of the border—way south? Honduras would be nice. Or Belize. Or Costa Rica.

BUDDY: (*Puts his arms around her.*) We never use the goddamn pool anymore ... Remember when we first put it in? Sonny and Lucy went crazy out there. We had some great times together.

CONNIE: (*Squirts armpits, getting away.*) That was ten, fifteen years ago, *señor.* that pool hasn't been cleaned in so long, there's something slimy growing at the bottom.

BUDDY: (*Tongue in cheek.*) I'm growing some class 'A' Colombian seaweed.

CONNIE: Be serious. (*He turns and faces her tensely, in a showdown of sorts.*)

BUDDY: Okay. Then let's talk about the Nicholson movie.

CONNIE: So that's what's eating you!

BUDDY: I know damn well you really want to do it.

CONNIE: (*Cautiously.*) Betty says I still have a good chance at the part of the madam.

BUDDY: (*Scoffing, spreads legs into the air.*) Another Mexican whore?

CONNIE: (*Trying to joke, sliding up to him.*) Of course not, she's Costa Rican! Come on, at least I own the house! Buddy, it's a great part. A speaking part. I'd only be on location for three weeks. A month's shoot at the most.

BUDDY: (*Tightening.*) I got news for you. They're already shooting down there.

CONNIE: Where?

BUDDY: Everywhere! Nicaragua, El Salvador, Miami.

CONNIE: The location's in Costa Rica.

BUDDY: (*Blowing up.*) People are KILLING each other down there! Don't you understand? You'd be all alone. You wanna get killed, or even worse, raped to death?

CONNIE: (*Cleaning trophies.*) Then come with me.

BUDDY: I've got a business to run.

CONNIE: Betty can talk to them. Get you some kind of small role.

BUDDY: Small role? I read for those people, same as you. If they don't want me, I ain't gonna beg them. Fuck 'em. Who needs their two-bit TV movies, anyway? Cecile B. DeMille once ate at my restaurant.

CONNIE: (*Pleading.*) It's a feature, Buddy ...

BUDDY: (*Goes to fridge for beer.*) Outta town we work as a team or no dice! Remember? Nobody goes anywhere alone. (CONNIE*'s face takes on an undaunted look.*)

CONNIE: What about the Stallone picture last year in Mexico? You went alone.

BUDDY: On restaurant business. I brought back Pedro Wong, didn't I? Where else was I to find a Chinese-Mexican cook?

CONNIE: But you acted.

BUDDY: (*Goes to the phone and dials.*) For Pedro's sake, I saved our business! Fried rice and refried beans, our chile relleno runneth over now. In this case, Wong was right. (CONNIE *groans, returns stuff to hall closet.* BUDDY*'s call connects with his restaurant; he talks to his cook. On the phone.*) Pedro, joe san! ... *Frijoles* ju ho mee-ah? *Menudo* ju ho mee-ah? *Tortillas* gow mee-ah? Ngaw dee you jew-ng mole? Gup gaee chicken chow yuk? Ngaw, chee dee lai gwaw. *¡Hay te watcho!* (*Hangs up.*) Besides, Sly cut my scene out of the picture, so it didn't count, sweetheart.

CONNIE: Well, maybe Jack will cut my scene out of the picture and it won't count either, sweetheart.

BUDDY: *¿Sabes qué?* Before you start getting on a first name basis with stars, you better make damn sure you've even got a job.

CONNIE: Oh, that's cruel, Buddy. That's really cruel.

BUDDY: It's a cruel business.

CONNIE: I'm only asking for a little support and encouragement. Is that such a big deal?

BUDDY: I knew it was a mistake to let you start acting.

CONNIE: All I want is a little harmless fun in my life! Who knows, maybe I've got a talent or two I never had a chance to develop before. Is that so bad?

BUDDY: (*Like Jackie Gleason.*) Put 'em in a couple of pictures, way in the background, and suddenly everybody wants to be a star!

CONNIE: Why do you have to be such a fat ass *cabezudo*?

BUDDY: (*Pause.*) Okay ... now you're hitting below the belt, see? Enough's enough. Get this whole crazy scheme outta your head. Get dressed and get on the phone and work on your little real estate sideline. *¡Ya estuvo!* No more show business today. I'm gonna drain the pool. (BUDDY *heads for the backyard.* CONNIE *follows him.*

CONNIE: If it weren't for my little real estate sideline, we wouldn't even have the goddamn pool! (*The phone rings.* CONNIE *and* BUDDY *look at each other, then race to the phone.* CONNIE *answers.*)

CONNIE: Hello? Oh, hi, Betty ... Yeah? (*Brightening.*) Really?

BUDDY: (*Hanging on her shoulder.*) I'm serious, Connie. Don't take it.

CONNIE: (*On phone.*) I'll take it! ... When? That soon? ... Right ... MGM, sound stage eighteen. Great! Got it ... Thanks, Betty. Ciao. (*Hangs up.*)

BUDDY: (*Frustrated.*) What? What?

CONNIE: "DALLAS!" over at MGM. They want both of us.

BUDDY: (*Impressed.*) Both of us? (BUDDY *turns to tuck shirt into pants.*)

CONNIE: (*With a caustic edge.*) Work for a whole two days, *mi amor*. Both of us—right here in town, just the way you like it. A maid and a gardener. Are you happy now?

BUDDY: (*With gardener accent.*) Well, you could have consulted me before you agreed to do it.

CONNIE: (*Blowing up, furious, hits* BUDDY *in the stomach.*) Look, Buddy, if you don't want the goddamn job, you call Betty! I'm taking it. Interview's on the lot in fifty minutes. (CONNIE *starts to storm out;* BUDDY *chases her, looking like the cat who ate the canary.*)

BUDDY: (*Holding* CONNIE.) Heh, heh, wait a minute. How much is the Nicholson picture worth? You know the score. We haven't gotten this far by fooling ourselves, right? I'm the Silent Bit King and you're my Queen! No more, no less. Right?

CONNIE: (*Deadly serious, pushes* BUDDY *away.*) Buddy, I'm tired of being silent. (CONNIE *walks out without another word.* BUDDY *holds back for a beat, then glances at the Bogart poster.*)

BUDDY: So, who am I, Charlie Chaplin? (BUDDY *exits, walking like "The Little Tramp."*)

*Fade to black.*

......................... SCENE TWO .........................

*Early evening. Mozart's "Rondo in C" plays sprightly, as the lights come up to half, simulating dusk.* SONNY *enters the house, coming down the hallway, carrying a suitcase. He is a tall, slim seventeen-year-old law student, looking quite Anglo in his casual winter wear, despite his classic handsome Latin features. He enters tentatively, apprehensively calling out "Mom" and then "Dad?" as he checks the garage. Confident no one is home, he tosses his suitcase on the couch, and looks about the den with an ironic haughty demeanor. He then steps out onto the wooden deck and looks out towards the pool. Shuddering suddenly, he spins around and heads for his suitcase. Opening it up, he extracts a portable cassette recorder, and presses PLAY and draws an anxious breath, before he speaks.*

SONNY: Greater East Los Angeles. February 20th. 6:30 p.m. Home away from home away from home. Concept for possible "Twilight Zone." i.e.—"Sonny, the Harvard Homeboy Comes Home." So what's on your mind, homes? (*Pause.*) Sonny's mind is on my mind, homes. Little Son, *mamacita's* little *m'ijo*, daddy's little chicken. Chicken Little. The sky is falling! (*Paces, growing agitated.*) Fuck. The whole inside of your refried skull is falling, Sonny boy! Raining cats and dogs. A veritable *chubasco* of cranial slime, drowning your brain in your own biological soup, the primordial chicken broth of your own egg, your *huevo*, one egg instead of two. With two *huevos* you might have been born a human. Add a polish sausage and you might have been born a man. A Lech Walesa in solidarity with your Polish balls! (*As SONNY pours out his anxieties, ANITA SAKAI, gorgeous but frazzled twenty-eight-year-old Asian-American brunette, enters from the rear and pauses, crossing her arms and leaning against the corner of the hallway, pops a Valium.*) What are you doing here, Sonny? Your *mamá* and *papá* have great expectations. Are you real or are you Memorex? Reach out, reach out and touch someone, asshole!

ANITA: Sonny?

SONNY: (*Startled.*) What?

ANITA: Remember me? (SONNY *stares at her with embarrassment, suddenly tongue tied.* ANITA *comes down and examines her surroundings, toting her baggy purse.*)

ANITA: (*On edge but playful.*) Hello, hello? Is this the Villa household? Does Sonny Villa live here?

SONNY: Sorry. I'm still in rapid transit between realities.

ANITA: Your folks are out, huh?

SONNY: (SONNY *and* ANITA *kiss and hug.*) Uh ... yeah. Right.

The place is all ours, baby. (SONNY *regains his com-posure, superficially putting on the sophisticated airs of a "Harvard Man." He nuzzles into her neck and kisses her.*)

ANITA: Nice place. At least one of us is home.

SONNY: Just your standard Southern California suburban tract home. Nothing special. (ANITA *notices the Aztec calendar clock above the fireplace.*)

ANITA: What's that?

SONNY: An Aztec Timex, I think. Same category as Tijuana tin-can sculptures and paintings on black felt. My parent's taste—not mine.

ANITA: Listen to you. Where did the Ivy League snob come from?

SONNY: Harvard, where else? (ANITA *looks out into the back-yard, affecting a snobbish accent.*)

ANITA: Oh. We have a pool!

SONNY: (*Playing back.*) Doesn't everybody? That's where I first learned all about sex.

ANITA: (*Knowingly.*) Skinny dipping with the girls?

SONNY: Playing squirrel with the boys.

ANITA: Squirrel?

SONNY: Grab nuts and run. (ANITA *laughs playfully, sits on the rug and begins to stretch.*)

ANITA: I keep forgetting you still remember puberty. (SONNY'*s sophistication melts in a sudden flush of adolescent cha-grin.*)

SONNY: (*Looking at a picture of* LUCY.) Actually, it was fat dip-ping my big sister, who tried to drown me more than once. She knew all the medical terms by the time she was eleven. I was an embryo. I was born believing *genitalia* was the name of an opera star. (ANITA *groans as* SUNNY *holds her from behind.*) Tired? (*As he rubs her inner thighs and midriff.*)

ANITA: (*Stretching.*) Wired, actually. I'm just quietly going out of my fucking mind. The Peugeot finally wheezed and crapped out on me. It won't even turn over. It's just sitting out there, sagging on its last tires, waiting for the final bullet.

SONNY: Maybe it just needs another rest? I mean, it worked in Las Vegas. Didn't it? Overnight?

ANITA: (*Jumping out of* SONNY'*s arms.*) Nevermind last night. Everything I own is sitting out there in that car. Poor baby. We've been through a lot together. I can't believe this is the end of the road, but then, the way my life has been going lately, I feel Peugeot'd out myself.

SONNY: (*Solicitously, pulls her to him.*) How about some coke? Pepsi, milk or anything? Tea! How about some hot tea?

ANITA: Okay. Red Zinger, (*Grabs his butt.*) if you have it.

SONNY: (*Pausing.*) Red Zinger? I can't promise that. This is more of a Lipton Tea house.

ANITA: (*Bending over, looking in bag.*) Mind if I use your phone? It's a local call. Pacific Palisades.

SONNY: Who do you know in Palisades? (SONNY *comes up behind* ANITA *and holds her by the waist and presses himself up to her butt.*)

ANITA: My brother. I was going to call him last night, when we got to Vegas, except, well, you know. Somebody distracted me. I thought all you Latino dudes knew about sex and cars. I was half right. (SONNY *looks for the tea in the kitchen cabinet;* ANITA *crosses to her purse on the couch, extracting her phone book.*)

SONNY: (*Looking for tea.*) Sorry. I'm a mechanical idiot. Auto shop just wasn't my thing in high school. Fact is, I was never a Latino dude, per se. My mom insisted on my taking college prep. My Dad's a Chicano tho'. He fixes cars. Maybe he can fix yours. (ANITA *pauses before the "Treasure of Sierra Madre" poster.*)

ANITA: I can't ask him to do that, especially since he was in "Treasure of Sierra Madre," and I've never even seen it. My old boyfriend and I never owned a TV. (*Pops a valium.*)

SONNY: (*Serves himself wine.*) I'll be damned. They do have Red Zinger! What was that?

ANITA: (*Crossing up.*) The Bogart movie . . . in the poster. Didn't you say your folks were in it?

SONNY: My Dad.

ANITA: He was the head bandit, right?

SONNY: More like the tail. My Dad's brought up the rear in a lot of movies. I told you he's only an extra. Like my Mom. They've made a career of playing nothing but bit parts.

ANITA: Hey, I'd still put Humphrey Bogart on my resume.

SONNY: Wouldn't work. He's dead. Old Bogey cashed in his chips before we were born. (ANITA *dials the phone, sitting on one of the breakfast bar stools.* SONNY *fills a cup with water and puts it in the microwave to heat.*)

ANITA: Your folks have worked Hollywood a long time, huh? I'm beginning to understand you better. (SONNY *smirks bit-*

*terly.* ANITA*'s call connects on the other end.*) Hello? This
is Anita Sakai, Doctor Sakai's sister. May I speak to my
brother, please? You're his answering service? ... But ...
when do you expect him back? ... What! Did he leave
me a key or anything? I'm supposed to stay with him ...
I see ... No, no, there's no message ... Wait! Yes, there is
... Tell him: Thanks a lot for leaving me stranded, Kuso
Tare! K-U-S-O T-A-R-E. That's right. Sign it: Anita. Bye.
SONNY: (*Perking up.*) KUSO TARE—that's your brother's name?
ANITA: (*Devastated.*) It means shithead. He's out of town. Left
L.A. about the same time we left Cambridge and won't be
back for ten days. Gone to a conference in Hawaii, of all
places ... to push some of his grass.
SONNY: Your brother pushes pot?
ANITA: (*Laughing and crying.*) He sells lawn seed. He's a Turf
Doctor, retained by several professional football stadiums
around the country, including the Rose Bowl. I told him
I was coming, but he's always got fertilizer on the mind.
Anita, girl, you're on your own.
SONNY: So, what are you going to do?
ANITA: (*Clicking glass to cup.*) I don't know. Call up one of my
gypsy friends, I guess. It's as if my life just came to a
sudden halt, and it's sitting out there in that pooped-out
Peugeot, waiting to get towed someplace else.
SONNY: (*Serious pause.*) Wherever that is, I'll come with you.
ANITA: You're home, Sonny.
SONNY: Stay here then with me. At least for tonight.
ANITA: Sleep with you in your parent's house? Sorry. That would
be like making love in church.
SONNY: (*Holding* ANITA*'s hand.*) You'd have your privacy. My
sister's room hasn't been used since she moved out. It's
really huge—like my sister. How about it? I promise to
only indulge in the passions of the mind. (*Kisses* ANITA
*up the arm to forehead.*)
ANITA: That's no fun.
SONNY: (*Hugging* ANITA *from behind.*) In essence, my life didn't
make sense until I met you. Your my only reality now.
And my fantasy. Did we really make love last night at
the Bluebird Motel, or was I dreaming? The last few days
have been the most exhilarating period in my life! Is it
my fault I love you? (SONNY *approaches her tenderly.*)
ANITA: (*Not unkindly.*) I knew I shouldn't have jumped your
bones.

SONNY: Symbolically, you're the distillation of everything beautiful in my life.

ANITA: (*Tongue in cheek.*) Symbolically?

SONNY: The woman of my dreams.

ANITA: That's what scares me. How old are you really? Eighteen? Nineteen? I'm at least ten years older than you are.

SONNY: So? I've always preferred older women.

ANITA: Thanks. But I can't make love to you again, Sonny. Honestly now. I shouldn't have ever let you come on this trip ... it sure knocked the hell out of your studies. Your parents are going to love me for that.

SONNY: (*Angrily, forcefully.*) My parents don't have a damn thing to say about this! Okay? This is my life. Come on, stay one night and one night, only. Please?

ANITA: (*Sighing.*) I know I'll regret this, but what the hell, I'm too tired to think about it. Okay! I'm yours! (ANITA *hugs and kisses him passionately, rolling onto the floor with* SONNY. *The phone rings and the answering machine picks up.* ANITA *perks up when she hears* CONNIE's *voice. She stops the ensuing actions by gathering her things together.*)

ANITA: But first! I'd like a long hot shower. Think your folks would mind?

SONNY: First door on the right, upstairs ... I Love You!

ANITA: Passions of the mind, remember? (ANITA *smiles and exits, swinging her bag.* SONNY *picks up his suitcase and takes it to the couch. He opens and pulls out a tiny cassette recorder. Then he reaches over, turns on a lamp in the darkening room, clicks on the recorder and settles back. He pauses breathing deeply.*)

SONNY: So what's on your mind now, Sonny? Sex is on my mind, Sonny. Time to take the cosmic plunge into the orgasmic sea of your own creation, just to see what's there ... With all the sharks and crabs and little fishes. Are you a man or a sea urchin? Like the night in Harvard you thought you caught a glimpse of a white whale in there, deep down? Scared the piss out of you, didn't it? The friggin' whale was bigger than you! Is that possible? Do you suppose there might be an ocean inside of you, Sonny? A Moby Dick. Are you here to save the white whale? (*He laughs suddenly, self-mockingly talking "Chicano."*) ¡ÓRALE! Is that why you came back, *es-saaay*? To save Moby's WHITE DICK? (*We hear the sound of a car pulling into the driveway.* SONNY *snaps off the recorder and freezes. The garage door opens, and the car pulls in and parks.* SONNY *is galvanized into action at the sound of* CONNIE*'s voice.*)

CONNIE: (*Offstage.*) *Viejo,* don't forget to get the groceries outa the back. (*Car doors slam. Almost panicking,* SONNY *gathers his coat, cassette recorder and suitcase. Spinning around to see if he's forgotten anything, he bounds out of the den and down the hallway.* CONNIE *enters from the side door, followed by* BUDDY *carrying the groceries. They are completely transformed in appearance, wearing old shabby clothes.* BUDDY*'s slouch hat, worn flannel shirt, faded jeans and boots complete his "gardener look."* CONNIE, *dressed as a Mexican maid in a print dress and sweater, looks a generation older than she is.*) Am I glad to be home or what? I hope you're not starving. I'm gonna soak in the tub for a while. (BUDDY *enters singing "Born in East L.A." He crosses up into the kitchen where he unpacks groceries.* CONNIE *flops on the couch.*)

BUDDY: (*Putting stuff in fridge.*) Where's my beer? Store-bought *tortillas,* woman? What kind of 7–11 *groserías* did you buy? Some kinda Mexican maid you are.

CONNIE: Made in the USA, *cabrón.* Can you believe we still have the L.A. Latino Actors banquet tonight?

BUDDY: (*Pulling out a fryer.*) LALA? Forget it. Let's stay home and I'll fix dinner. Suchi Shicken. You like raw *gallina,* Mama San? (*Laughs.*) Beats the rubber chicken at the Hilton.

CONNIE: You're in an awfully good mood.

BUDDY: Hey, is it my fault they used me in a shot and not you? Speaking part *y todo*! How did you like the way I said: *Sí Señor ... No, Señor ... Pronto,* J.R.!

CONNIE: (*Peeved.*) Up yours, Buddy. The whole day was a complete waste of time.

BUDDY: Speak for yourself. Today between takes on the soundstage—I got another movie idea. This one's really hot!

CONNIE: No, Buddy, please, no more hot ideas! I need a hot bath. (BUDDY *snaps on a tape on his portable cassette recorder. The sound of the music holds* CONNIE *in the room. She falls back onto the couch and listens.* BUDDY *starts the tape with James Bond "Goldfinger" theme.*)

BUDDY: There's a Chicano James Bond type, see? It's one of those international spy thrillers—set in Guadalajara,

where an American narcotics agent has been kidnapped,
maybe snuffed. So who do they call?

CONNIE: (*Already bored.*) Ghostbusters.

BUDDY: (*Fanfare.*) Ta-raan! NIGEL LOPEZ—Agent Double-O
Eleven—the brilliant, suave, sophisticated Chicano Spy
and International Latin Lover! (CONNIE *turns to sneak
away, and suddenly notices that the lamp in the den is on.
She pauses, staring at it quizzically, as* BUDDY *rattles on,
self-absorbed.*)

CONNIE: Buddy? What's this lamp doing on?

BUDDY: Lighting up the room. Who cares? Son of an English
mother and a Mexican father, Nigel López is a black belt
in Karate. In fact, he's mastered Judo, Tae Kwan Do,
Jujitsu—all the *Chino* stuff.

CONNIE: Did you turn it on this morning?

BUDDY: (*Distracted.*) What?

CONNIE: The lamp.

BUDDY: (*Peeved.*) How should I know? Maybe. I dunno. I don't
think so. Aren't you listening? (CONNIE *crosses down
into the den, spotting something.*)

CONNIE: There's a glass of wine here! You weren't drinking wine
this morning.

BUDDY: (*Puzzled, turning off the tape player.*) Correct. You're
the *wina* in this family. (CONNIE *sniffs the glass, then
surveys the room, growing apprehensive.* BUDDY *starts
paying attention.*)

CONNIE: Somebody's been here.

BUDDY: (*Tongue in cheek.*) Maybe there's a little blonde asleep
on our bed upstairs? Little Goldifingers?

CONNIE This is no joke, *hombre*! No home in L.A. is safe anymore.

BUDDY: (*Checking around.*) The stereo's still here, the TV, VCR.
If it was burglars, why should they just go after our fine
Gallo wines? (*The same thought strikes them simultane-
ously.*)

CONNIE: Unless ... ? (*There is a sound upstairs.*)

TOGETHER: They're—still—here? (BUDDY *puts a finger to his
lips and signals* CONNIE *to back up. He grabs a big trophy
and sneaks to the hallway, then shouts.*)

BUDDY: OKAY, *CABRONES*! I HAVE A THIRTY EIGHT
HERE, IF YOU'RE STILL IN THE HOUSE ... (*He looks
to* CONNIE *for inspiration.*)

CONNIE: ... Get the fuck out ...

BUDDY: GET THE FUCK OUT!

SONNY: (SONNY *calls back from within.*) You don't have a thirty-eight! It's a twenty-two, and it's upstairs. (BUDDY *and* CONNIE *exchange surprised glances.*)

CONNIE: Sonny?

SONNY: (SONNY *comes out reading Shogun.*) Hi, Mom.

BUDDY: (*Shocked.*) Well, I'll be! It is him!

SONNY: Hi, Dad.

CONNIE: SONNY! (CONNIE *comes running up to* SONNY *and showers him with motherly hugs and kisses, as he stiffens and tries to shy away.*)

CONNIE: *M'ijo*, what a surprise! What's the idea of playing games? Why didn't you call and let us know you were coming?

BUDDY: (*Puts away the trophy and comes up to* SONNY, *as well, giving him fatherly backslaps. The questions come fast.*) Good to see you, *m'ijo*! Are you all right? This sure is one hellava surprise!

CONNIE: When did you arrive?

SONNY: Just a little while ago.

BUDDY: But how? When? Did you fly?

SONNY: Drove. (BUDDY *and* CONNIE *exchange a puzzled look.*)

CONNIE: You drove?

BUDDY: I thought I noticed? ... Who's over-stuffed Puegeot is that parked outside?

SONNY: Anita's. We drove out together. How's the 'Vette?

BUDDY: Who's Anita? Some French babe?

CONNIE: You drove all the way from the East coast? (SONNY *nods mysteriously, giving them a nervous smile. He strolls into the den, trying to sound casual, but sounding cocky.*)

SONNY: We ran into a couple of snowstorms in the Midwest, but aside from that, it was a breeze. I-80 to Salt Lake City, then down to San Berdoo. Made it in four and a half days with, uh, a brief pitstop in Vegas. The rites of passages, folks. No sweat.

BUDDY: (*Flabbergasted.*) No sweat? They're having blizzards back there! It was on the 11 O'clock News just last night. Worst winter on record.

SONNY: (*Superciliously.*) Really? Well, I haven't watched any TV since I left home. We made it okay.

CONNIE: (*Sighs.*) Thank God. Maybe it's good you didn't tell me you were coming, after all. I would've died from worrying.

SONNY: You sound like a Jewish mother.

CONNIE: (*Suddenly peeved.*) *Qué* Jewish mother *ni que madres,
  ¡cabrón!* First you don't call in months, and then you
  come breezing in here, driving through blizzards? Who
  do you think you are, Sergeant Preston of the Yukon?
SONNY: Sergeant Who?
BUDDY: Why aren't you in law school? Aren't you in the middle
  of the semester or something?
SONNY: (*Evasively.*) Spring break's coming up. What's this? "The
  Grapes of Wrath"—in Spanish? (*He indicates* BUDDY
  *and* CONNIE's *clothes.*)
CONNIE: We had an audition today.
SONNY: Get the job?
CONNIE: Don't we always?
BUDDY: Who's Anita?
SONNY: (*Shaking his head.*) You must be awfully tired of playing
  Mexican maids.
CONNIE: (*Archly.*) As Hattie McDaniel used to say: "I'd rather
  play a maid than be one."
SONNY: What's the difference? (CONNIE *is a little stunned
  by* SONNY's *flippant, slightly supercilious manner. She
  glances at* BUDDY.)
BUDDY: Don't look at me. I'm just the wetback gardener. Who's
  Anita?
SONNY: A friend.
CONNIE: Girl friend?
SONNY: (*Annoyed.*) A woman friend. A lovely human being, if
  you must know. She was coming out to the West Coast, so
  we shared the driving and gas expenses. She's from New
  York.
CONNIE: A Chicana from New York? *Oy Vey.*
SONNY: No, Mom.
CONNIE: (*Smiling wisely.*) Ah. A *Puertorriqueña*, then.
SONNY: (*Exasperated.*) What difference does it make? There's
  other people in the world besides Latins, you know!
BUDDY: (*Responds, insulted and angered.*) *Oye, oye*, watch the
  attitude, eh? *¡Pos, mira!* We're your parents, remember?
  The ones putting you through Harvard Law School? We
  don't deserve this!
SONNY: (*Pause.* SONNY *calms down and takes a deep breath.*)
  I'm sorry.
BUDDY: (*Perturbed.*) You still haven't told us what you're doing
  back here. (SONNY *looks at* BUDDY, *then at* CONNIE,

holding back his surging emotions. He begins to pace nervously.)

CONNIE: (*Concerned.*) What's the matter, Sonny? Did something
happen to you at Harvard?

BUDDY: (*Pause.*) You didn't ... flunk out ... did you, *m'ijo*?
(SONNY *looks at* BUDDY, *with a strangely sad smile,
and slowly shakes his head.* BUDDY *seems relieved.*)

CONNIE: Oh course, he didn't flunk out, *Señor*! How could he?
He's always been an honor student.

BUDDY: (*Paternally.*) ¿*Sabes qué?* We'd better sit down. Come
on. (SONNY *reluctantly sits between* BUDDY *and* CON-
NIE *on the couch.*)

SONNY: I'm not a kid, you know.

BUDDY: Now, you just tell your ol' *jefe* straight out. What's the
problem? It can't be money. (*Suddenly worried.*) Can it?

SONNY: No.

BUDDY: (*Cautiously.*) Drugs?

SONNY: Sure. I'm snorting $100 worth of flaked Peruvian coke a
day. Do you want a toot?

BUDDY: Toot, my ass! I'll rip your nose off.

SONNY: Why? You smoke majoon.

BUDDY: I smoke what?

SONNY: Hemp, bhang, ganja, cannabis, weed, boo, mota, maui
waui. In a word, *Shit*, daddy-O.

BUDDY: (*Guiltily.*) Since when?

SONNY: (*Cooly cynical.*) Since we lived in Boyle Heights. Lucy
and I used to smell it in the house all the time. At least
cocaine is more sophisticated—the drug of choice of the
upwardly mobile.

CONNIE: (*Mocking* SONNY.) The drug of choice of the upwardly
mobile!

BUDDY: Bullshit! You oughta see some of your "sophisticates"
in the studios. A Mack truck could park in one of their
nostrils.

SONNY It's not drugs, okay? My problem's a bit more personal
than that. (SONNY *unleases his pony tail, to reveal a
shock of long black hair.*)

CONNIE: It's a girl, isn't it, *m'ijo*? Are you having troubles with
your love life?

SONNY: (*Wincing.*) Come on, Mom.

BUDDY: (BUDDY *grimaces with uneasiness.*) When did you let
your hair grow out like that? You look like a fugitive from
a Cochise picture.

CONNIE: (*Playing with* SONNY*'s hair.*) He's a handsome *Indio,
   ¿qué quieres? Pero, ay m'ijo,* shouldn't you cut off your
   split ends at least?

SONNY: (SONNY *stands up impatiently.*) Look, both of you, give
   me a break, will you? Part of my problem is that you've
   always assumed certain things about me.

CONNIE: (*Pause.*) What do you mean?

SONNY: (*Deadly serious.*) My entire life has been an act. I've
   decided to come out of the closet.

BUDDY: (*Suddenly suspicious.*) *Oye, cabrón,* you didn't come
   back here to tell us you've gone, *¿tú sabes?*

SONNY: Gay?

BUDDY: You said it, I didn't.

CONNIE: (*Objecting.*) Buddy!

BUDDY: But it isn't true, right? (SONNY *smiles noncommitally.*)
   Right?

SONNY: (*Superior air.*) What if it is? What's wrong with being
   gay?

BUDDY: (*Reacting.*) WHAT? YOU WANNA GIVE ME A HEART
   ATTACK?! (*He lunges after* SONNY, *who backs up defensively;* CONNIE *goes after* BUDDY, *grabbing his arm.*)

CONNIE: *Viejo,* don't! Stop it!

BUDDY: (*Swiping at* SONNY.) Is that your big news, *baboso?*
   THAT YOU'RE A PALOBLANCO? (SONNY *blows a kiss
   at* BUDDY. BUDDY *chases* SONNY *through the kitchen
   and out into the backyard and ends up being held outside
   the french doors by* CONNIE, *as* SONNY *runs back into
   the den.*)

SONNY: (*Shouting.*) NO! DAD, WAIT! I'm not GAY, all right?

CONNIE: Then you knocked somebody up.

SONNY: And I didn't get anybody PREGNANT! And I'm not
   fleeing from the LAW! May we dispense with the family
   melodrama, PLEASE? What's Anita going to think?

BUDDY: (CONNIE *lets him inside.*) Anita again? What the hell
   does Anita have to do with this?

SONNY: Just sit down.

BUDDY: Who's Anita?

SONNY: Be rational, please. I'll explain everything.

CONNIE: (*Anxious.*) Yes, Buddy. Let's all sit down and be calm
   about this. *Ándale, hombre. Siéntate, por favor.* (BUDDY
   *and* CONNIE *sit down. There is a tense pause.* SONNY
   *takes a deep breath.*)

SONNY: (*Nervously.*) Thank you. Now the reason I've returned is ... (*Pause.*) Well, the simple fact of the matter is ... (*Pause.*) I quit.

CONNIE: Quit?

SONNY: (*Simply.*) Quit.

BUDDY: (*Swallowing hard.*) You quit Harvard?

SONNY: Dropped out. As of last week, I am no longer enrolled as a pre-law student at Harvard University. (BUDDY *and* CONNIE *sag on the couch, as* SONNY *begins to pace—a lawyer before his jury.*) I know this must come as bit of a shock. However, judge me harshly, if you wish. Find me guilty of irresponsibility, if you will. I won't dispute you. I simply enter a plea of *nolo contendere.* No contest. For I am finally, completely, joyfully, and irrevocably through with academic life. In short, I am a free man! The defense rests.

BUDDY: (BUDDY *and* CONNIE *in hysterics.*) He quit Harvard. After two years and twenty thousand dollars down the drain, he quit Harvard.

BUDDY AND CONNIE: YOU QUIT HARVARD?!

SONNY: (*Less assured.*) To follow my own destiny, Dad.

CONNIE: (*Deeply disappointed.*) Sonny, how could you? Your father and me were hoping ...

SONNY: (*Correcting her.*) Your father and I.

CONNIE: Your father and I were ... (*Stops.*) Don't correct me *cabrón*! Don't you realize what you've done? All our dreams, our hopes, our aspirations—you've thrown them out the window!

BUDDY: Not to speak of the money.

CONNIE: (*Emotionally.*) All these years—what have me and your Dad worked for? The money? ... the money's not important. For you, m'ijo!, for your future, the future of both our children, our children's children's future ... How can you just come back here and tell us you've quit? Just like that—no sign, no warning, nothing ... and from Harvard! Do you know how many Chicanos get the chance to go to Harvard?

SONNY: (*Aloof.*) I was there, Mom.

CONNIE: (*Impassioned.*) You're one in a million, *m'ijito*! Millions! You're a jewel, a rare jewel, our crown jewel. Look at you—young, handsome ...

BUDDY: Stupid.

CONNIE: The valedictorian of your class in high school and the university. Our pride! That's what you're throwing out the window. Our very pride! (CONNIE *goes to the fridge, opens a beer, chugs it down in a theatrical display.* BUDDY *is sagging on the couch.* SONNY *maintains a superior attitude. Short silence.*)

BUDDY: (*Baffled.*) Why? That's what I don't understand. Why did you do it?

SONNY: (*Shrugging.*) I was bored. Tired of being a ... *Ha'va'd* man. Just ... burned out.

BUDDY: Bullshit! What about all the Koreans around here—and all the boat people. You don't see their kids burning out. Hell no. They're going like Zippo lighters.

SONNY: I'm not admitting defeat.

BUDDY: That's what you said when you went from anthropology to sociology to Englishology to who knows what cacaology!

SONNY: Thirteen years, Dad. That's how long I've been in school. That's almost my entire lifetime.

CONNIE: (*Quietly intense.*) You sister went through all that, too. High school, University, Medical School. She never quit. *Suma Cum Laude, Suma Suma Cum Laude, Maxima Suma Cum Laude*!

SONNY: (*Stung.*) Lucy thrived on the pressure! She was born competitive. You never saw what she used to do to frogs in our backyard, did you? She'd dissect them just for the fun of it. Once when I was eating a peanut butter sandwich, she even made me throw up. "Sonny?" she says in that obnoxious, smart-alecky voice she used to have. "You wanna see the fastest dissection in the world?" Then she stuck a straw up a frog's ass and blew it apart! (BUDDY *inadvertently cracks up laughing.* CONNIE *cools him with a look.*)

BUDDY: Yep. That's Lucy all right.

SONNY: (*Painfully.*) She was always making me cry.

BUDDY: (*Hitching his pants.*) Yeah, well, that was a long time ago. You're a man now, and I didn't raise you up to be a *chillón*. You're a winner. (*Proudly.*) Look at all your trophies— basketball, baseball, football!. Shit. You could've been an All-American quarterback. Another Jim Plunkett ... except you were only twelve and 4'11" in high school.

SONNY: (SONNY *looks at his trophies without emotion.*) Most of these are for debate.

CONNIE: Precisely! The mark of a true lawyer, if there ever was one.

SONNY: (*Solemnly.*) I never wanted to be a lawyer, Mom. (BUDDY *stares at* SONNY, *then laughs in disbelief.*)

BUDDY: That's a lotta baloney. Remember how much you loved "Witness for the Prosecution"? We saw that video dozens of times. Why? Because your mom kept renting it? *Chale.* It was because you loved Charles Laughton. And wanted to be a great barrister, just like him.

SONNY: Well, I looked like Charles Laughton then. After I saw "Saturday Night Fever," I wanted to be like John Travolta. Mom even bought me a little white disco suit, when I lost all that weight. Remember? Then came Indiana Jones in "Raiders of the Lost Ark," and we went to Mexico, to the Yucatan. You never realized who talked you into that trip, did you? A stumpy, brown Harrison Ford seeking lost Mayan gold.

CONNIE: (*Slightly alarmed.*) Sonny, this is crazy, *m'ijo.* What are you trying to tell us?

SONNY: I'm saying the time has come for me to be honest with myself . . . and with you. Even on the debate team, what I really wanted was to compete in dramatic interpretation, but I didn't think you'd approve.

BUDDY: Why wouldn't we approve?

SONNY: Too close to home, maybe? I wanted to save you the embarrassment.

CONNIE: (*Genuinely puzzled.*) What are you talking about?

SONNY: (*Emotionally.*) The truth! I knew you and Dad didn't want me to be an actor. You wanted me to be somebody. Lucy was a doctor, so I had to be a lawyer. Acting just wasn't respectable enough. Or even masculine.

BUDDY: (*Recoiling.*) Oh, *sí*! And what does that make me? A *pinche vieja*? I'm an actor and I'm proud of it.

CONNIE: So am I. And I'm just as proud to be a *vieja*. *¡Pinche viejo!* (BUDDY *and* CONNIE *begin to act like they will start a fist fight.* SONNY *breaks them up, laughs cynically and starts to pace again, cruelly expressing his true feelings.*)

SONNY: Come on, Mom, Dad. You know what you are. Let's be honest. You're nothing but glorified Hollywood extras. Bit players who have managed to eke out a comfortable existence for yourselves—for me and Lucy. But, let's face it, in the larger scheme of Hollywood, you're only

marginal. Atmosphere at best. Invisible, for all intents
and purposes. (BUDDY *and* CONNIE *are astonished.*)

BUDDY: Invisible?

CONNIE: Marginal?

SONNY: (*Pompous but sincere.*) I just want to add, with all due
respect, I appreciate all you've done for me, Mom. However, I am now prepared to take my own chances in the
school of hard knocks.

BUDDY: (*Bristling angrily.*) Hard knocks, eh? I'll give this idiot
some hard knocks!

CONNIE: Be my guest. (BUDDY *once again chases* SONNY
*around the room. They rush* CONNIE *both of them spinning her crazily.*)

BUDDY: (*Incensed.*) You're going back to law school, *cabrón*! And
you're going back to-DAY! I'm taking you to the airport!
(SONNY *keeps backing off, hiding behind the couches,
staying out of* BUDDY's *reach.*)

SONNY: (*Throwing words at him.*) It won't work anymore, Dad.
I've grown INURED to your VITUPERATIVE displays
and threats of physical PERSUASION! I know it's only
bad ACTING!

BUDDY: (BUDDY *throws a cushion at him.*) INURED, MA-
NURED! (ANITA *enters quietly down the hallway, dressed
in a floppy robe, still wet from her shower.* SONNY *spots
her immediately; his face drops.*) Some Chicano progress!
(*Steaming.*) My son, the Harvard drop-out! Maybe you
should've been born into a family of BOAT PEOPLE!

CONNIE: (*Seeing* ANITA.) Buddy?

BUDDY: At least all those CHINOS know how to apply themselves. They never QUIT, that's for damn sure! I may
have fought in Korea, but I'll be the first to admit it, the
GOOKS are taking over Monterey Park, because ...

CONNIE: (*Pinching him.*)    Enough, *señor*! (CONNIE *gives*
BUDDY *a small, hard pinch and he recoils, rubbing the
spot.*)

BUDDY: *¡Ay, jodido!* What was that for?

CONNIE: We have company. (BUDDY *turns and finally sees*
ANITA. *He fumbles and mumbles and goes speechless.*

SONNY: (*Red-faced.*) This is Anita—Anita Sakai from Brooklyn,
New York.

BUDDY: That's Anita. (BUDDY *and* CONNIE *nod together, un-
consciously bending slightly at the waist, Japanese style.*
ANITA *smiles, blissfully stoned on tranquilizers.*)

ANITA: (*Speaking Japanese.*) *Doi tachi mashite.*

SONNY: Welcome to the "Teahouse of the August Moon!" (BUDDY *and* CONNIE *self-consciously snap right up.* SONNY *reassumes his haughty, superior air.* ANITA *just smiles.*)

ANITA: You must be Buddy and Connie. Hi ya!

SONNY: Sorry you had to walk into this little domestic scene, Anita. My parents and I seem to be embroiled in a typical middle-class squabble. My Dad was only trying to drag my ass to the airport and ship me back East. Right, Pop?

CONNIE: (*Chagrined.*) *Ay,* Sonny ...

BUDDY: ... That's a hellava thing to say.

ANITA: (*Cheerily.*) Hey, don't mind me. I'm just passing through. *Hasta la vista.* I'll leave you alone to talk.

SONNY: (*Calling urgently.*) We're only acting! You know how it is. A show business family? (*Turning to his parents.*) Anita's a dancer and an actor as well. She's even danced on Broadway ... and now she's here to make it in Hollywood. Right, Anita?

ANITA: I don't belong in this conversation, Sonny.

SONNY: (*Sotto voce.*) On the contrary, I need you to save my *gluteus maximus.* (*Putting* ANITA*'s hands on his butt.*) Come on, everybody, make friends! (BUDDY, CONNIE *and* ANITA *look at each other, puzzled and feeling awkward. Short pause.*)

SONNY: (*Wryly.*) Well, come on—we're all Americans! (CONNIE *steps forward trying to be civil at least.*)

CONNIE: Won't you sit down, Anita? I'm sorry we didn't hear you come in.

ANITA: Didn't Sonny tell you?

SONNY: (*Quickly.*) She was upstairs taking a shower.

CONNIE: There's a lot Sonny doesn't tell us.

ANITA: (*Feeling no pain.*) I had to borrow this robe. I hope you don't mind? Our last stop was, uh, breakfast in Vegas, and we drove straight through. Actually, I was just going to drop Sonny off, and head for Pacific Palisades, where my brother lives, when he's not in Hawaii or some such place, but my Peugeot crapped out on me and left me stranded, and I really felt stressed out and just needed to relax with a hot shower, you know what I mean? Great shower, by the way. Big Thanks for the hospitality. Am I talking too much? Why don't I just go back up and come down again? (*She climbs stairs and re-enters.*) Hi ya! You must be Buddy and Connie. Boy am I tired. (BUDDY *looks at* CONNIE, *subtly raising an eyebrow.* SONNY *catches it.*)

CONNIE: *Pobrecita ...* you must be exhausted! Please, make yourself at home. Are you two hungry? (BUDDY *comes forward, somewhat intrigued by* ANITA*'s presence.*)

BUDDY: How about some wine, Anita? Beer?

ANITA: I'll have some wine now. (BUDDY *gets the wine.* CONNIE *is starting to fix dinner, masking her emotions.* SONNY *is watching her, waiting to seize the moment.*)

CONNIE: Have you two eaten? Buddy and I have to go to a banquet tonight, but I can easily pop a chicken into the microwave, make a salad. Why don't I do that?

SONNY: Actually, Mom, I've invited Anita to spend the night in Lucy's room. Okay? (CONNIE *pauses, suddenly overtaken by maternal jealousy.*)

CONNIE: Sure ... fine! Whatever you wish, *m'ijo.* What do you say, Buddy? Shall we all stay home?

SONNY: Hey, don't change your plans on my account.

CONNIE: No problem.

SONNY: Really?

CONNIE: Your father didn't want to go, anyway.

BUDDY: *Whoa.* Don't blame it on me. *Douzo, douzo.* (BUDDY *brings* ANITA *her glass of wine, bowing graciously: the genial host.*)

ANITA: *Domo aregato gozaimus.*

BUDDY: Don't touch your mustache, too. (ANITA *laughs.* SONNY *takes a beer from* BUDDY*'s hand, a little jealous.*)

SONNY: Thanks, Dad.

ANITA: Sonny's been telling me about all your experiences in "the industry," Buddy. You've done a lot. When did you start making movies?

BUDDY: 1948—thereabouts.

ANITA: How about you, Connie?

CONNIE: (*Pointedly.*) Only since 1980 when Sonny finished elementary school.

SONNY: Don't let the false modesty fool you, Anita. Together they've been in hundreds of films. How many would you say you've made, Dad?

BUDDY: With or without TV shows?

SONNY: Movies. Let's start with the big stuff.

BUDDY: Maybe two, two hundred and fifty pictures. To tell the truth, I lost count after "JAWS."

ANITA: (*With admiration.*) You were in that?

SONNY: (*Tongue in cheek.*) Was he ever! He was one of the first guys to get eaten!

ANITA: (*To* CONNIE.) May I help you with anything?

CONNIE: No, thank you. Just sit.

SONNY: Tell her what else you've done, Dad.

BUDDY: "Close Encounters of the Third Kind," "Raiders of the Lost Ark," "E.T." ... I've been in most of Spielberg's biggest block-busters.

ANITA: Wow! Great!

SONNY: (*Subtly sarcastic.*) Can you beat that? And nobody knows it.

CONNIE: (*Sharply.*) Somebody knows it. He keeps on working.

BUDDY: Damn right. Bought me my restaurant.

ANITA: You have a restaurant, too?

BUDDY: BUDDY'S HOLLYWOOD VILLA over on Garfield. Chinese-Mexican cuisine. Nothing fancy, but it pays the bills, between pictures, know what I mean?

SONNY: I'll have to take you there sometime, Anita. You oughta see the walls. Dad's covered it with blow ups of himself, posing with all the stars he's ever worked with. Bogart, Cagney, Raft, next to Bandit, Wino, Wetback. What is it you call yourself, Dad? The silent something or other?

BUDDY: (*Pause.*) The Silent Bit King.

SONNY: Right. The Silent Bit *King* and *Queen* of Hollywood ... So! These are my folks, Anita. My roots and heritage. They're the reason I went to Harvard, and they're the reason I've returned—to vindicate their silence. (*There is an uncomfortable, funny silence.*)

CONNIE: (*Coming back.*) What silence? They're offering us speaking roles now. Your Dad and I left the Extras and joined the Screen Actors Guild. You know what SAG is, don't you, Anita? You're a dancer?

ANITA: Choreographer. A little classical Japanese dance, as well as modern, jazz, ballet ... actually, my plans are to concentrate on acting. TV, movies, HBO, whatever. (*Pause.*) I hear there's lots of work during pilot season, which is now, right?

BUDDY: (*Playfully sarcastic.*) Sure, sure, there's work if you're not choosy. As an extra, I used to work all the time, nighttime, daytime, overtime. Now she's got us killing time by the phone waiting for speaking roles. SAG, is right.

CONNIE: (*With an edge.*) Some of us are getting offers? Don't
    listen to him, Anita. I can show you the ropes. The im-
    portant thing is not to pigeon hole yourself. Go for it!
    The sky's the limit.

ANITA: (*Stoned.*) I like your energy. (ANITA *hugs* CONNIE, *high
    on life.*)

CONNIE: (*Disarmed.*) Are you into energy? Positive energy, that's
    my motto! Our daughter's an M.D. .... in Phoenix. "Out
    on a Limb?"

ANITA: Shirley Maclaine. "Gradual Awakening"?!

CONNIE: Steven Levine!

CONNIE & ANITA: Passages!

SONNY: (*Laughing.*) Sky's the limit! (*Another pause. They all
    stare at* SONNY, *who smiles back.*)

CONNIE: What are your plans, *m'ijo*?

SONNY: I was, uh, coming to it. Especially with all this positive
    show biz energy. Anita already knows, so it's cool, know
    what I mean? The stage is a world, the world is a stage
    ... of entertainment.

BUDDY: (*With carrot.*) So, what's up, Doc?

SONNY: (*Dramatically.*) What's up is ... I've finally discovered
    my real purpose in life, Dad.

BUDDY: And that is?

SONNY: To follow in your footsteps.

BUDDY: What ... do you mean ... my footsteps?

CONNIE: You quit Harvard to become an *extra*?

SONNY: (*Superior.*) On the contrary, I'm not that foolish. No,
    Mom, the only way I can ever justify my leaving Harvard
    is by ... (*Matter-of-factly.*) becoming the newest superstar
    in Hollywood.

CONNIE: (BUDDY *and* CONNIE'*s mouths drop open.*) Sonny,
    you can't be serious.

SONNY: Deadly serious. You always told me I could be anything
    I ever wanted in life, and this is what I want. I'm going to
    act, write, direct, produce and generally turn this town on
    its tinsel ear. In short, you're looking at the next Woody
    Allen. I didn't realize it until I met Anita, but I've been
    an auteur all my life ... Right, baby? I'm going to make
    stars out of all of us, All American All Stars!

BUDDY: Sonny, you can't mean it.

CONNIE: Of course, he doesn't mean it.

ANITA: He means it.

BUDDY and CONNIE: (*Simultaneously.*) ¡¡¡Me lleva la chingada!!!

ANITA: (*Rising.*) I'll drink to that. L'chaim! I think I'll go bring in the rest of my bags. (*She drains her glass.*)

SONNY: I'll help you.

ANITA: No, no thank you. I can handle it. (ANITA *exits with* SONNY *right behind her.*)

CONNIE: I'm gonna nuke a chicken.

BUDDY: (*Sagging on the couch.*) I feel like Marlon Brando in "The Godfather." When his youngest son decides to go into the mob? "I didn't want this for you, Michael. I wanted more—Senator Corleone, Governor Corleone—but there just wasn't enough time ... "

SONNY: (*Overhearing on his way back in.*) I'll be all right, Dad.

BUDDY: That's what Al Pacino said. Look where he ended up.

SONNY: It made him a star.

BUDDY: He's Italian, *baboso*! The wop's have been in since all those crime pictures in the 30's. They're still doing the mob, except now they get to play big shots. We don't have any big shots!

SONNY: Don't worry about it, Daddy-O! The Wild One is here. (*Outside we hear the sound of a car starting up. Turning.*) Hold it! What the hell ... ? That's Anita's car. (*Panicking.*) ANITA! (SONNY *bounds out of the den and down the hallway.* BUDDY *and* CONNIE *look at each other totally frustrated.*)

BUDDY: What the hell's going on?

CONNIE: (*Puzzled.*) I don't know! Maybe he's head over heels in love? Like father, like son.

BUDDY: What's that supposed to mean?

CONNIE: Figure it out.

BUDDY: (*Disturbed.*) I hope you're not talking about Korea? That was a long time ago—before I even met you!

CONNIE: Forget it, Buddy. It was just a bad joke. Maybe Sonny's, right. Maybe all he needs is a couple of months to come back to his senses, to experience Hollywood for himself, to get it out of his system. But ... that older woman? (I just can't see her in the sack with my baby!) (SONNY *comes rushing back in again, looking disoriented.*)

CONNIE: Where's Anita?

SONNY: (*Embarrassed.*) Coming in. My mistake ... I ran halfway down the block before I realized it was the neighbor's car ... I, uh, better help her upstairs with her luggage.

CONNIE: (*Concerned.*) *M'ijo*, are you all right? (ANITA *enters with her bags and goes directly upstairs.*)

SONNY: (*Smiling poignantly.*) Don't worry about it. I'll keep this
   situation comedy from turning into a soap opera. In fact,
   let's make it a prime time series ... before a live studio
   audience ... (*He finds this strangely hilarious and exits
   clucking like a chicken.*)
CONNIE: (*Confused.*) Live studio audience? I don't know whether
   to laugh or cry.
BUDDY: (*Shaking his head.*) He's the fruit of my loins, but something's gone rotten ... Where's the *chingas?*
CONNIE: The what?
BUDDY: The remote. I gotta turn on the tube for sanity's sake.
   (BUDDY *finds the remote control and aims it toward the
   invisible TV console at extreme downstage right. The faint
   sound of the set comes on, as* BUDDY *sits in his easy chair.*
   CONNIE *sits beside him deep in thought.*)
CONNIE: Situation comedy? Buddy that's not funny.
BUDDY: (*Muttering.*) Hah! I wish our life was a situation comedy. At least we'd be working steady! *He turns up the
   volume on the TV. Music comes up full; on the background
   monitors, closing credits are rolling on an old re-run of "I
   Love Lucy." The show's theme swells to a climatic flourish
   and fades out. Fade to black.*)

# ACT TWO

...................... SCENE ONE ......................

*Two hours later. Early evening. In the dark, we hear* SONNY*'s voice bark out commands with an imperious, directorial air.*

SONNY: QUIET ON THE SET ... ! ROLLING ... SPEED ... SLATE! HOMEBOY HOME MOVIE, SCENE FOUR, TAKE TWO. ACTION!

*Music: We hear a song opening in stereo, as the lights come up full on* CONNIE *and* BUDDY *in Mexican regalia, posing for* SONNY*'s video camera in the den. They go through a musical comedy routine, as* SONNY *"shoots" and* ANITA *watches, drinking wine and laughing with amusement.* BUDDY *and* CONNIE *mime a hold-up, with outrageous stereotypical accents.* SONNY*'s outrageous shots appear live on the studio monitors.*

SONNY: Dance! (CONNIE *and* BUDDY *dance. They finish with a final glint of the eye and a flash of the teeth in a musical comedy flourish.*)
SONNY: CUT! Reloading ... That's a print, folks. (SONNY *reloads his camera, all business with the technical stuff.* CONNIE *and* BUDDY *laugh, relaxing their final pose.* ANITA *applauds.*)
ANITA: Ole! Bravo, mucho bueno!
BUDDY: ¿No que no? I told you we'd still remember it!
CONNIE: I can't believe Sonny actually talked us into doing this! Look at us! A couple of stereotypes! We're such suckers for the camera.
ANITA: Aren't we all?
CONNIE: We did this number three years ago, Anita, at the LALA banquet? What a disaster, it totally misfired!
BUDDY: Did Mel Brooks misfire with "Blazing Saddles?" This routine could have been the start of something big!
CONNIE: Yeah, like another refried bean commercial. It took us till this year to have the courage to go back to another banquet, and here we are instead, doing "Blazing Frijoles."

BUDDY: (*Mugging.*) As my compadre Mel Brooks would say ...
    (*Lifts leg and blows a Bronx cheer.*) More wine, ladies?

CONNIE: Sure, why not? I've lost all shame. How about you,
    Anita?

ANITA: I'm not driving tonight, that's for sure. (BUDDY *goes to
    the breakfast bar, and opens another bottle of wine.*)

CONNIE: The things we do for our kids ...

ANITA: That's what my mother used to say all the time.

CONNIE: Oh? Was she a dancer, too?

ANITA: Traditional odori. When she was young.

CONNIE: Back in Japan?

ANITA: No, actually it was here, in L.A.

CONNIE: I thought you were from Brooklyn.

ANITA: It's a long story. (BUDDY *comes back with the wine bottle,
    singing operatically to the tune of "'O Solo Mio."*)

BUDDY: (*Singing.*)    There's no tortillas, there's only bread.
    There's no tortillas, that's why I'm so sad. My grief I
    cannot hide. There's no tortillas. For my refried. (*Speak-
    ing with Italian accent.*) *Su vino, señorina.* A delicate
    Tokay from Tokyo. Just kidding. It's a white Zin from
    the Sa-napa Noma country. Enjoy!

ANITA: *Molto grazie.*

BUDDY: And you, *bella mia*?

CONNIE: (*Italian accent.*) Just a half a glass, Luciano. I still have
    to wash the dishes. You oughta watch it too.

BUDDY: I'm watching it, I'm watching it. It isn't every day a
    son fulfills his jefe's dreams. I feel like Pancho Villa when
    he raided Columbus, New Mexico. The only other way
    a Mexican can shoot gringos and get away with it is by
    becoming a Hollywood director. Right, Sonny?

SONNY: Whatever you say, jefe.

BUDDY: What are you calling our movie, anyway?

SONNY: TYPES IN STEREO.

BUDDY: (*Pause.*) *¡Cantinero! ¡Otro tequila para el General!*
    (BUDDY *heads back to the breakfast bar, doing a Mexi-
    can General. He pops open a bottle of tequila.*)

CONNIE: Weren't you only going to have one shot of that stuff?

BUDDY: *¡Viva Villa, chingao!* (BUDDY *downs the whole shot
    glass, and* CONNIE *is not happy.* SONNY *hoist the cam-
    era on his shoulder, obsessed, as he turns toward* ANITA.)

SONNY: Okay, folks, here we go again. Mom, playback. Rolling
    ... speed ... Your turn, Anita. Slate! SCENE FIVE,
    TAKE ONE! ACTION, sweetheart.

ANITA: (*Doing Ingrid Bergman.*) I love you Rick ... and I will
    always love you, but you must stay here in Casablanca,
    and I must fly off to a new life or there's no end to this
    movie ...

SONNY: (*Shooting.*) Great, Ingrid. Now how about a little Anita
    Sakai? A little classical Japanese dance? Jazz, modern?
    Better yet, just tell us about yourself. Cinema verite! How
    did you end up in Brooklyn?

ANITA: (*Laughing.*) I was born there.

SONNY: When? (SONNY *waits with bated camera, still rolling,*
    *on* ANITA, *close-up.*)

ANITA: Hate to spoil the shoot, Sonny, but I'm not really into this.
    My life is enough of a soap opera.

SONNY: Tell us about your radish legs.

BUDDY: Her what? Did he say radish legs?

ANITA: (*A little hurt.*) Sonny, that's a really personal story.

SONNY: (*Seriously.*) That's why I want it. Trust me, baby. I'm still
    rolling. (ANITA *pauses a beat, taking a breath, looking at*
    SONNY.)

ANITA: All right. As a kid, they used to call me radish legs. *Di-*
    *akoniashii.* Like the Japanese radish? That's because I
    had these big thick ankles and calves I couldn't stand. So
    I became a dancer. I fell in love with ballet. I was classi-
    cally trained from the age of seven ... By the time I was
    thirteen, I was dancing on point, graceful as a swan.

SONNY: So how did you learn Japanese dance?

ANITA: Before I could study ballet, Mama always insisted that
    I first learn classical Japanese dance. I resented her for
    it. It had nothing to do with anything I saw around me
    in Brooklyn. I didn't realize until I was much older that
    my mother was trying to help me become a woman, a
    woman able to draw from the well-springs of her own life.
    Okay? (BUDDY *and* CONNIE *have been listening with*
    *rapt attention.*)

CONNIE: Okay! I mean, it's true. It's a very personal story.

SONNY: How about that dance?

ANITA: Sorry. My music's packed away. In the Peugeot.

BUDDY: (*Feeling good.*) So, unpack it! Come on, be a sport.

CONNIE: (*Dryly.*) Anybody for some more chicken salad? If not,
    this scullery maid is going to clean up the kitchen.

ANITA: I'll help you wash the dishes.

SONNY: (*With bullhorn.*) And CUT! (ANITA *helps* CONNIE
    *pick up plates, heading up to the kitchen.* SONNY *low-*

*ers his camera, looking angry, intense and preoccupied.*)
Listen, PEOPLE. We're seriously SHOOTING A MOVIE
here. Would you MIND giving me your undivided attention and a little GODDAMN COOPERATION? Is that
TOO MUCH to ASK?! ... Sorry, I didn't mean to shout.
(BUDDY, CONNIE *and* ANITA *are momentarily aghast.*)
Nevermind. I'll get the friggin' music myself! It's in that
little red suitcase behind the green trunk, right? Take
a break, and rest your honkers. I'll be right back. (*He
storms out the back, toward the garage.*)

BUDDY: He's good at bossing people around, isn't he?

CONNIE: This is getting out of hand, Buddy. He's never talked to
us with such disrespect before. Who does he think he is?
Otto Preminger?

BUDDY: (*Angered.*) Look, whose idea was it to let him pull out
all the video equipment? Now let's get it straight. Do you
want to humor the idiot genius or do you want me to talk
to him? Let me slap some sense into him man to man.

CONNIE: Don't hurt him.

BUDDY: When I was his age, I still had to kiss my father's hand.
I'll show that *mocoso* who his *padre* is! (BUDDY *puts on
his sombrero, grabs* CONNIE *and kisses her theatrically,
then walks off with comic macho bravado, his prop gun in
hand.* CONNIE *and* ANITA *are left alone in the kitchen
for the first time. There is a pause.*)

CONNIE: So.

ANITA: So?

CONNIE: So how long have you known Sonny? If you don't mind
my asking?

ANITA: (*Pauses, she smiles.*) About a week. He answered my ad
in "The Village Voice" for a driving companion, and he
seemed like a safe bet.

CONNIE: I'll bet he did.

ANITA: He's a sweet kid. I've grown very fond of him in seven
days.

CONNIE: Anything happen on the trip I should know about?

ANITA: Why? Did he say something?

CONNIE: He's just acting strange ... stranger than when he left
for Harvard, I mean. It's hard to tell with Sonny. He was
always a little eccentric. Brilliant but absurd, as one of
his teachers said. But he was always shy, especially with
girls. Something must have happened to him. He's acting
awfully cocky for sixteen.

ANITA: Sixteen?

CONNIE: Technically. His 17th birthday isn't until next month. Not that it matters. He's not a virgin anymore. Is he? I saw it in his eyes right away. They aren't innocent anymore. They glistened with that horny look men get. My baby!

ANITA: (*Feeling bad.*) Gee, I'm sorry. (CONNIE *stares at her without malice.*)

CONNIE: I knew it had to happen sooner or later ... Anyway, I'm glad I heard you say what you said about your mother? It's a nice thing for a daughter to recognize her mom.

ANITA: It was a while ago. When she still talked to me. (CONNIE *registers interest in following the topic, but she doesn't want to be obvious about it. She pours more wine for both of them.*)

CONNIE: You say your mom grew up in L.A.?

ANITA: (*Sadly.*) Born in Japan, and brought here as a four-year-old. My Dad was born in East Los Angeles, though, in a place called Dogtown. Can there be such a place?

CONNIE: (*Amazed.*) Wait till I tell Buddy. He'll hound you to death about the place.

ANITA: Of course, that was before World War II.

CONNIE: Of course. The 50's were more my time, but I saw all the John Wayne movies. "WAKE ISLAND," "SANDS OF IWO JIMA," "GUADACANAL DIARY" ... Which camp was your family concentrated into?

ANITA: None. (ANITA *suddenly chokes with emotion. It's been welling up inside her all evening and now the dam is about to break.*)

CONNIE: Excuse me?

ANITA: They escaped!

CONNIE: I'm sorry. I mean, that's okay. I understand. You don't have to talk about it. (ANITA *lets some tears go, but she takes control of herself, blowing her nose and shaking her head.*)

ANITA: No, I'm fine. It's better that I talk about it. It's no big deal. It's just my fucking anonymous life ...

CONNIE: Your 'effing' what?

ANITA: Anonymous life. Yeah, it'd make a great movie on PBS. Instead of waiting for the Army to pack them up, my old man packed up his wife and son and musical instruments and headed East in his 1936 Chevy. It was called voluntary self-evacuation in those days.

CONNIE: Voluntary self-evacuation?

ANITA: Permissible by law, but my family's trek made headlines clear across the country. It was even on nationwide radio. Daily reports of their whereabouts as they crossed city, county and state lines.

CONNIE: At least they were famous.

ANITA: Oh yeah. "The Japs are coming, hide the kids!" When they finally arrived in New York City, my dad got my mother and brother and settled in Brooklyn, hoping just to live in quiet anonymity ... I wasn't born until 1960, but I grew up in that anonymity. (*She fondles the Valium container.*)

CONNIE: (*Moved.*) I know what you mean. Have you ever been married? What about your Mom?

ANITA: She grew old at home. My Dad eventually got a job playing the cello with the New York Philharmonic. My brother ended up chasing football fields around the country ... I figured it was time for me to come back to L.A.

CONNIE: (*Blunt but not kind.*) Why? Now, I mean.

ANITA: (*Straight in the eye.*) I just broke up with my boyfriend. We lived together for five years. He was a black choreographer. (*Looks at the Valium.*) I don't need this shit!

CONNIE: You've got a lot of guts, girl. (SONNY *calls from the hallway and comes running in, carrying* ANITA's *red suitcase of audiotapes.*)

SONNY: (*Enters on a skateboard.*) HO! Here we go-o! Thumbs up on the *música*! We'll just lay these puppies down right here. (*He lays the tapes down and picks up his camera, adjusting the lights and slapping a cassette into the stereo.*)

CONNIE: Where's your Dad?

SONNY: You'll find out. Pick up the camera, change the mood, add a little soundtrack ... and this movie outfit is back in action! Mom, you're in the shot. Mom, you're still in the shot! I want this whole area clear! Anita, be my dolly grip.

ANITA: Your what?

SONNY: Push the skateboard. Mom, playback ... ROLLING ... SPEED ... GO FOR IT, DAD! SCENE SIX, TAKE ONE ACTION!! (*We hear music from the soundtrack of "Treasure of the Sierra Madre." BUDDY enters, his bandit costume all disheveled, his face dirty. He pulls out his .22 pistol.*)

CONNIE: Buddy, what is this? What are you doing with that pistol?

SONNY: QUIET ON THE SET, MOM. PLEASE? It's a PROP, okay? Come ahead, Dad. We're still rolling. ACTION! (BUDDY *shrugs at* CONNIE *and keeps going toward* SONNY*'s camera.*)

CONNIE: Did you check to see if it was loaded?

BUDDY: (*Stopping.*) Sorry, Boss, I lost it.

SONNY: CUT! SHIT!

CONNIE: Watch your language, young man! Who the hell do you think you're talking to? Rodney Dangerfield? What happened to the "man to man" talk, boss?

BUDDY: (*Pause.*) We had it, *verdad, m'ijo*? We got to talking about the old days, when he was just a squirt, and we used to do that scene from my favorite movie. Anita, did I ever tell you the story of my favorite picture?

CONNIE: Here it comes. I knew we'd get to it sooner or later. (BUDDY *crosses to the poster.*)

BUDDY: "The Treasure of the Sierra Madre," starring Humphrey Bogart ... It was my first job. I was only eighteen then and still living in Dogtown.

CONNIE: So was Anita's Father.

BUDDY: (*Oblivious.*) In downtown L.A. there were still signs saying "No Dogs or Mexicans Allowed," so the thought of working with Bogart made my head spin ... But the main guy for me turned out to be Alfonso Bedoya. He was the leader of the *bandidos* see? With that toothy smile and greasy look he built his career on, and the rest of us Mexicans, well, we were his men ... Right Sonny? Start your cameras rolling *m'ijo* ... Remember how we used to do it? Anita, he used to do Bogey. (SONNY *who has been studying the gun, lifts the camera and starts to roll.*)

SONNY: (*Doing Bogart.*) ¡ALTO! Sweetheart.

BUDDY: (*Doing Bedoya.*) ¡Ay jijo! Mira la palomita que me encontré en su nido.

SONNY: Don't come any closer!

BUDDY: *Oiga señor*, we don't try to do you any harm, why don't you try to be a little more polite? Give us your gun and we'll leave you in peace.

SONNY: I need my gun myself!

BUDDY: Ah. Throw that old iron over here. We'll pick it up and go on our way. We're not federales.

SONNY: If your the police, where are your badges?

BUDDY: Badges? We ain't got no badges. We don't need no badges. I don't have to show you any stinking ... (*The phone rings.*)

SONNY: GODDAMIT! CUT!!

BUDDY: (*To* ANITA.) Your father used to live in Dogtown? (SONNY *storms out into the patio.* ANITA *goes out to talk to him.* CONNIE *answers the phone.*)

CONNIE: Hello? Oh ... hello, Betty. Yes, we're still here. (*Cupping the speaker.*) She sounds pissed ... Oh no, no, just relaxing. We had some unexpected company, and decided not to go ... Sonny, our Harvard dropout? What? Yes, yes I know, Betty, but really, it's so late, and ... who's there? (*Cupping the speaker.*) The casting director from the Nicholson picture! He's looking for Hispanic faces at the banquet. What? He wanted to see Buddy? For a speaking role? The part of a Costa Rican General? Buddy!

BUDDY: A General?

CONNIE: Betty, it's already past nine o'clock. We'll never make it on time.

BUDDY: The hell we won't. In my red hot 'Vette? Monterey Park to Beverly Hills? Gimme forty five minutes and a lead foot. A job's a job.

CONNIE: Can you hold him for an hour? We're on our way! (CONNIE *hangs up.*) My God. How are we going to do it? We're not even dressed!

BUDDY: We'll dress at the hotel! I know the waiters. (CONNIE *and* BUDDY *head for the hallway.*)

SONNY MOM! DAD! Aren't you forgetting something?

CONNIE: (*Stopping, calm for a second.*) Of course. Our clothes! We forgot to pick up our clothes, Buddy.

SONNY: NO!

CONNIE: No? OH! Anita, how rude of me, please excuse us. We're just going to drop in on the LALA banquet for a moment. It's a movie, you see. Gotta see a man about a horse.

BUDDY: (*Happy.*) A general's horse!

ANITA: Go for it.

CONNIE: Now behave yourselves, you two. We'll be back by midnight. *Viejo*, shouldn't we take my LTD instead? (BUDDY *and* CONNIE *exit to the bedroom.* SONNY *looks at* ANITA, *like a spoiled child.*)

SONNY: Do you see? Do you see what's going on here? They forgot completely about my movie.

ANITA: Those are the breaks. Parents grow up, just like everybody else.

SONNY: I don't see you spending quality time with your parents. They won't even talk to you, because of your black boyfriend.

ANITA: Are you deliberately being nasty, or is that just more juvenile angst? (SONNY *picks up his camera.*)

SONNY: What if it is? Half the successful directors in Hollywood are juvenile assholes, why should I be any different?

ANITA: Because you are different. Or at least I thought you were. (SONNY *follows her with the camera.*)

SONNY: Remember Little America, that truck stop in Wyoming? The one with all the redneck cowboys? It was like a scene out of a movie, wouldn't you say?

ANITA: I suppose.

SONNY: Which movie?

ANITA: I don't know ... "Easy Rider?"

SONNY: The sixties flick? With Jack "The Border" Nicholson? How about "The Geisha and the Greaser," crossing the Western Divide in a snow covered Peugeot? (ANITA *looks at* SONNY *with impatience.*)

ANITA: Are you kidding me?

SONNY: Too unreal or just uncommercial?

ANITA: Too weird.

SONNY: Precisely. Rednecks won't pay to see us making love. Unless it's a porno.

ANITA: (*Pause.*) I'm not buying any of this bullshit, Sonny.

SONNY: (*Sarcastically.*) The real question is will anybody in the movies buy you? Or will you just settle for the local anchor spot on the Eleven O'Clock News? (ANITA *looks at* SONNY, *furious and hurt. He continues to shoot.*)

ANITA: Stop this, will you?

SONNY: Am I getting to you?

ANITA: You're messing with me.

SONNY: Well, I'm a Messican.

ANITA: Fuck You! This is Nancy Nissan, signing off! (ANITA *hits aside* SONNY's *camera, and storms upstairs.* SONNY *holds for a moment, trying to laugh.*)

SONNY: (*Lowering his camera.*) CUT! ... bad cut. (CONNIE *and* BUDDY *come out of the bedroom, carrying their clothes, shoes and make-up kits, heading toward the garage.*)

CONNIE: Okay, *m'ijo*, this is it! We're on our way.

BUDDY: Wish us luck, eh? The part of a Mexican general, *fijate*! Opposite my buddy, Jack Nicholson.

CONNIE: The general is Costa Rican. Not Mexican.

BUDDY: Did you ever meet a casting director who could tell the difference? (BUDDY *and* CONNIE *exit down the hall, and they are heard getting into their car and driving away.* SONNY *studies his camera, and then turns around to face himself. He records his close up.*)

SONNY: (*Changing shirts.*) Greater East Los Angeles. February 20th. 9:30P.M. Continuing script and production notes RE: HARVARD HOMEBOY MOVIE... (*Putting his wool cap on.*) You're fucking up, homeboy! You're not fooling anybody, *ese.* You didn't fool nobody in Harvard, and you ain't fooling jack shit here, *bato!* (SONNY *starts talking to himself, as if he is a group of cholos, raking him over the coals.*) We're the echo from the barrio streets of your mind, loco! We know you're middle class; pussy, aye. Harvard and all that shit. Well, you're nothing, dude. A little Mexican-American fart, still sucking Momma's tit. Or is it Moby's Dick? What about that fine woman up-stairs? You oughta be up there right now banging the bitch sideways, and you're down here, thinking about how you hurt her feelings ... ? Pussssyyy ... (*Disgusted with himself.*) Get out into the streets, and find something real to do, motherfucker. Don't just sit there, going out of your fucking mind. OUT INTO REALITY! (SONNY *turns off the camera and picks up the gun. He pauses for a beat, then pocketing the gun, picks up the skateboard and exits, strutting with street-wise cool. Fade to black.*)

.................... SCENE TWO ....................

*In the dark, we hear a soundtrack of police calls and siren, overlaid with rap music. It holds for a few moments, then fades out. The music of tiko drums, giving way to melody: "Odori" played by Hiroshima. The lights come up to reveal* ANITA *dancing a graceful odori in the den. It is midnight, and she is alone. Presently,* SONNY *appears in the shadows from the hallway, still dressed as a cholo and carrying a fast food hamburger bag. He watches her, until* ANITA *senses his presence.*

ANITA: (*Stopping.*) Sonny? Is that you?

SONNY: Simón. Go on. (ANITA *throws the fan at him and changes into modern dance. In the midst of the dance she stops, hugs* SONNY, *and turns off the stereo.*)

SONNY: That was fuckin' beautiful. What'd you stop for?

ANITA: I've been waiting for you. What time is it? Jesus, it's past midnight. My ride oughta be here in a few minutes.

SONNY: Ride?

ANITA: My brother called me back again. The service has been trying to reach me. Turns out my *kuso tare* brother was still home, waiting for me. He's bringing a tow truck.

SONNY: How did your brother get this number? (ANITA *pauses, realizing* SONNY *is not buying it.*)

ANITA: I left it with them, didn't I? All right ... So it's a gypsy friend from Santa Monica. What's the difference? May I leave some presents with you? (ANITA *goes to the coffee table, where she has laid out gifts.*) This is a gift for your mom. And this is for Buddy. It's a *daruma* doll. Tell him to make a wish and paint in the right eye, and when it comes true, paint in the left eye. And I want you to have one of my fans.

SONNY: What's with the gifts?

ANITA: It's *omiage.* Thank you gifts for all their hospitality. I'll be going now.

SONNY: Just like that?

ANITA: No, not just like that. I'm going to miss you. But it's obvious you need some time alone with your parents. I should have known you were only sixteen. Anyway, I'm proud and happy to have been your first lay. (SONNY*'s face hardens into a cholo mask.*)

SONNY: You mean like ... ? "I'm glad to be in AMERICA, so fine to be een AMEERICAA! Aiee, Aiee!" (*His face hardens into a cholo mask.*) What's that again, aye?

ANITA: You heard me, aye.

SONNY: *¿Sabes qué?* Pity the existential condition of the dude, eh? *Sayonara.* (ANITA *studies him a little regretfully.*)

ANITA: I was hoping we could part friends.

SONNY: (*Sarcastically.*) Maybe I could buy you dinner sometime. Over at the local crap-in-the-box? See, I've always suspected they put something in this garbage to give you ... a feeling ... of emptiness. (SONNY *empties the hamburger bag. Styro-foam containers, empty soft drink cups, and as-*

*sorted wrappings fall out. He kicks them around. Exploding.*) And want! And CONFUSION! AND ANOMIE!!

ANITA: (*Shocked.*) Sonny, what? What are you doing! (*She starts to pick up an empty container.* SONNY *drops into his cholo stance.*)

SONNY: No! Don't touch it—leave it!

ANITA: But what will your Mom say when ...

SONNY: (*Fiercely.*) I SAID LEAVE IT, *ESA!* (ANITA *freezes.* SONNY *advances, sauntering and lapsing into his cholo accent.*) Did I scare you? Sorry. It's just that this is all ... creative garbage ... and evidence. We're all on trial here, see? In a decidedly precarious pseudo-psycho-juridical conundrum. Can you dig it?

ANITA: Is this some kind of joke?

SONNY: Fuckin'ey. A case in point. What's the difference between a chicken and a Chicano? A chicken is born out of one egg, the Chicano out of two ... (*Grabs his balls.*) ... and that's schizoo ... (*We hear the sudden siren of police cars as they roll down the street outside, shinning a spotlight, on the house.* SONNY *dives for the switch, and kills the kitchen lights.*) Shit! Get down, be quiet, it's the cops.

ANITA: (*Wilting.*) Cops? Sonny, I can't handle this.

SONNY: Fuck! Somebody must have seen me running into the house. Assholes! Just because I wear a Pendelton, I'm some kind of burglar! Don't they know I live here?

ANITA: Why don't you just go out and tell them?

SONNY: (*Pause.*) I robbed the local Crap-in-the-Box.

ANITA: (*After a beat.*) Come again?

SONNY: (*Surprisingly clear.*) I pulled a heist. It was over before I knew what happened. I just walked in there, with my Dad's little .22 and held up the joint. Two Fat Jacks and a Big Bopper. Is that weird? Do I seem dangerous to you? Criminally dangerous or merely Hispanic?

ANITA: Let me get this straight you robbed a burger joint? (SONNY *laughs with a brooding undertone.*)

SONNY: (em Pulls off cap and glasses.) I was ACTING! I'm acting-see? No more threatening East L.A. cholo. Check it out. Here's my straight on, neutral shot with an innocuous shit-eating smile all casting directors require? See?

ANITA: What's the matter with you? What are you doing robbing Crap-in-the Boxes, for Christ's sake! Do you want to go to prison? (SONNY *puts on his blue beanie again.*)

SONNY: What's the difference? Here's the main event: the indispensable illiterate cholo gang member-heroin-addict-born-to-lose-image, which I suppose could account for 99% of my future employment in TV land. Just look hostile, dumb, and potentially violent. Preferably with rape on the mind, know what I mean? (*He gives* ANITA *a lascivious leer—overacting—wiping his mouth with his hand.*)

ANITA: Sonny, stop it. What are you up to?

SONNY: (*Grabbing* ANITA.) ACTING! Am I being CONVINCING?

ANITA: Let me GO! Are you OUT OF YOUR MIND?

SONNY: (*Struggling with her.*) Are you—AFRAID—I'LL RAPE YOU? Is that it? Do you—EXPECT ME—to act the type?

ANITA: LET ME GO!!! (ANITA *grabs* SONNY'*s arm and flips him completely over.*)

SONNY: What ... was that ... martial arts?

ANITA: Modern dance. Seriously, Sonny. What's going on?

SONNY: Have I been screwing up, fortune cookie?

ANITA: No, just screwed up, bean dip!

SONNY: (*Pause.*) I'm having a spiritual hernia. A cathartic outburst below the belt. I'm a scholastic disgrace. Thanks to you.

ANITA: No you don't. Don't start pretending you left Harvard because of me. I told you back in New York this was a mistake. Whatever your problem is, it's gotten worse since we arrived in L.A. Come back to reality, Sonny.

SONNY: Which reality? Your particular suspension of disbelief? Look around you. Does any of this look real to you? I knew what I was getting myself into—coming here. I grew up in this low-rated situation comedy! (*Looks out at audience.*) You can almost imagine a studio audience out there ... sitting, watching, waiting to laugh at this cheap imitation of Anglo life. Superficial innocuous bullshit that has to conceal its humorless emptiness with canned laughter! (SFX *We hear more police cars coming up, sirens blowing. Street sounds, traffic, then the voices of men. Then canned laughter.*) ¿Órale? Did you hear that? (ANITA *sneaks to to the kitchen window and looks out.*)

ANITA: My God! The place is surrounded by cops. They're standing across the street, looking this way! (*Spotlights trace the side of the house.* ANITA *ducks. More canned laughter.*)

SONNY: There it is again. Canned laughter.

ANITA: Cut the act, will you? Get a hold of yourself. Honestly, you sound like you're going off the deep end. What are we going to do?

SONNY: You wanna make love. (ANITA *looks at him lovingly, in spite of the circumstances.*)

ANITA: You're hopeless. I really have a talent for finding the basket cases.

SONNY: (*Gently.*) My Dad fell in love with an Asian girl, when he was in Korea. Wanted to marry her, but the Army discouraged him ... So he came back to the states, promising to send for her. He never did. The family pressure was so against it, he ended up marrying my Mom instead. Rumor has it he might even have left a son behind ... I guess he'd be older than me now—poor bastard. A Korean Chicano ... (*The front door bell chimes, followed by a solid pounding.*)

ANITA: They're knocking at the front door! (SONNY *snaps to life again, wielding his pistol.*)

SONNY: Stay put. Don't move! Nobody here but us chickens ... (*More knocking. A police bullhorn blares outside.* SONNY *carefully opens the side door.*)

BULLHORN: (*Offstage. Sounding like Bogart.*) THIS IS LIEUTENANT SMILEY, L.A.P.D. WE KNOW YOU'RE IN THERE, KID. DO US ALL A BIG FAVOR: THROW OUT YOUR WEAPON AND COME OUT WITH YOUR HANDS OVER YOUR HEAD. REPEAT. YOUR HANDS OVER YOUR HEAD! WE HAVE YOU SURROUNDED.

SONNY: (*Yelling outside.*) SCREW YOU, COPPERS! REPEAT, SCREW YOU!! YOU'LL NEVER TAKE ME ALIVE! (SONNY *fires off the twenty two—pop! pop! pop!—then slams the door.*) HIT THE DECK! (ANITA *hits the floor beside* SONNY, *just as a barrage of gunfire smokes the outside of the house. We hear the sound of shattering glass. Pause.*)

ANITA: Sonny ... ? (ANITA *starts punching him with a vengeance.*)

ANITA: (*Fuming.*) What's the matter with you, man? Just what the fuck is your problem?

SONNY: I'm trying to break through this ridiculous situation comedy into some contact with reality, goddammit! Real life! You know what I'm talking about. Come on, let it out.

ANITA: Let what out?

SONNY: Your emotions. Your guts. Your chaos! Don't you ever take off that Kabuki mask? Don't you ever explode?

ANITA: (*Tears.*)   NEVER! A good Japanese girl learns to control her feelings. A good Japanese girl learns to control her guilt. You *gaman*, you endure! (ANITA *stares into* SONNY'*s burning eyes, then out of care or compassion or both, she leans into his arms and they kiss—passionately—slowly sinking to the floor. Short pause, then the sound of the bullhorn blows again.*)

CONNIE: (*Offstage. On the bullhorn.*) SONNY? THIS IS YOUR MOTHER, *M'IJO*, OUT HERE WITH THE POLICE. YOUR FATHER AND I JUST DROVE UP A FEW MINUTES AGO. MY GOD! THEY SAY YOU JUST ROBBED A FAST FOOD PLACE! *POR DIOS, M'IJO!* WHAT HAVE YOU DONE? *¿QUÉ CHINGADOS HAS HECHO?*

SONNY: *¡Yo no speako Españole!*

BUDDY: (*Taking the bullhorn.*)   SONNY, THIS IS YOUR FATHER, BUDDY VILLA.

SONNY: Why is he telling me his name? I know who he is ... unless ... ?

BUDDY: TURN ON THE TV IN THE DEN, *M'IJO*. YOUR MOM AND I ARE ON 'LIVE'—COAST TO COAST—ON CNM. (SONNY *turns on the imaginary TV set. The monitors go on.* BUDDY *is drunk but trying to control it, performing for the camera.*)

REPORTER: (*Live footage camera crew, outside Villa home.*) ... That's right, Blair, I'm right here at the scene, as this drama unfolds directly behind me. The details as we know them at this moment are sketchy, but we have been able to piece together this scenario. Earlier this evening, the suspect, now barricaded in this house and, as you can see, completely surrounded by police, was identified as local sixteen year old, SONNY VILLA, "the skateboard bandit" who terrorized employees and patrons at a local fast-food restaurant. His parents, BUDDY and CONNIE VILLA alleged "show-biz" folks, were alerted by the police and called away from the gala LALA banquet in Hollywood, and are now pleading with their son to give himself up. Ah ... here's Mr. and Mrs. Villa now ... Mr. Villa, do you know what this is all about?

BUDDY: I DON'T KNOW WHAT'S GOING ON HERE, SON, BUT I JUST WANT AMERICA TO KNOW THAT I FOUGHT IN KOREA, AND THAT WE'RE PROUD TO BE MED-SICAN AMERICANS. OUR SON IS

AN HONOR STUDENT AT HARVARD UNIVER-
SITY, AND LIKE RICHARD NIXON, HIM IS NOT A
CROOK!

CONNIE: GOD BLESS YOU, M'IJO. WE'RE COMING IN!

BUDDY: THE POLICE ARE GIVING US A CHANCE TO TALK
TO YOU, SONNY.

CONNIE: DON'T SHOOT. (CONNIE *and* BUDDY *walk away
from the CNM cameras.* SONNY *is incredulous.*)

REPORTER: And there you have it, Blair. A tense and highly
volatile situation, probably gang-related, here in Monterey
Park in East Los Angeles. Reporting live, this is Chico
Chingón for CNM, The Chicano Media News Network.

SONNY: Can you believe this? I can't break out of this INANE
situation comedy! MOTHERFUCKERS!!!! (SONNY *gets
out another couple of pops! A barrage of gunfire slams into
the house again.* SONNY *and* ANITA *eat dust. Pause.
The phone rings.* SONNY *answers it with a heavy street-
wise accent.*) Simón? What can I do for you, man? I
mean, ma'am ... uh, *esa* ... no *chale, La* Connie's not
here. She and Buddy went out tonight. Who's this? Lucy?
Lucy, my *carnala*? ... *¡Órale!* This is Sonny! (*He gives
the phone the finger.*) All right, all right, Lucy ... Hold
it a second. Before you jump ... wait, give me a chance
... WAIT, GODDAMMIT! I DON'T CARE IF IT'S ON
CMN! I don't care if you're disgusted. GO ON, GO ON,
call me a failure! I don't give a damn! I'VE GOT CON-
TROL OVER MY OWN LIFE, LUCY! YOU STAY OUT
OF IT—IT'S MY PRISON TERM! FUCKIN' EY!—Stick
that up a FROG'S ASS AND BLOW IT, SISTER—I LOVE
YOU TOO! GOODBYE! (*He hangs up.*)

CONNIE: (*Offstage. Cheerily.*) Yoo-hoo? It's me kids. Are you
decent?

ANITA: (*Hiding his gun.*) Shit. Don't say anything about this—be
cool. (SONNY *collapses onto the kitchen floor, spread-
eagled and faking mortal injury.* CONNIE *enters, dressed
to the nines and looking like a million bucks in a formal evening gown, high heels, jewelry, imitation mink and
sweeping glamorous hairstyle. She screams, but proceeds
past* SONNY *to the mess in the den.*)

CONNIE: *¡Santo Niño de Atocha!* What hit this place? Punk rock-
ers?

SONNY: (*The cholo again.*) I had to set the scene, Mom! (CON-
NIE *comes down into den, dismayed, shaking her head.*)

CONNIE: *Mira nomás* ... It looks like you've been feeding dogs in here!

ANITA: We can clean it up in a second. It's all empty garbage.

SONNY: I said leave it, *esa!*

CONNIE: *¿Esa?* What do you think this is? "Hill Street Blues"? TV cholos are a dime a dozen.

SONNY: (*Cryptically.*) I'm a Korean Chicano ... part of the Chinatown suicide prevention squad. Right, Anita? (CONNIE *signals* ANITA *to let her carry the ball.*)

CONNIE: Forget it. I've got a real job for you. On the Big Screen! Are you ready for this, *m'ijo?* I just landed you a role in your first movie!

SONNY: (*Stunned.*) Me? How?

CONNIE: (*Picking up trash.*)  At the LALA banquet.  We sat with Betty, our agent, and Jack Nicholson's casting director. You should have seen the main room of the Beverly Hilton. It was packed! And the stars—everywhere! Ricardo Montalbán, Mario Moreno "Cantinflas," Katy Jurado, Raquel Welch, Martin Sheen (aka Ramón Estevez), Linda Ronstadt, the Lennon Sisters ... Did you know their grandmother was Mexican? (CONNIE *looks at the garbage in her hands, stuffed into a hamburger bag.*) What am I doing? This is your job, Sonny. Slowly but surely all these Hollywood stars with brown roots are coming out of the closet. If the gays can do it, why can't we? Right, Anita?

ANITA: Right on.

CONNIE: At least once a year we can get togther to hand out awards and put on the dog. How do you like my stole?

ANITA: (*Distracted, watching* SONNY.) Um?  Oh ... I love it. Mink?

CONNIE: Dog. Just kidding. It's imitation mink. I wouldn't kill a rat for it's fur.

ANITA: (*Looking.*) Where is Buddy? Wasn't he with you?

CONNIE: He stopped to throw up. (SONNY *kneels in the kitchen and ritualistically stabs the burger bag hari-kiri fashion. Trash spills out. There is a pause.*)

ANITA: So what's the movie about, Connie? I mean, does Sonny have a good role?

CONNIE: It's not bad.

SONNY: Is it any good, Mom?

CONNIE: (*Philosophically.*) It's a movie—what do you want? And on international location—in Panama! A lot of guys would

give an arm and a leg for chance like that. Starring with
Jack Nicholson? You'd better believe it!

ANITA: (*Impressed.*) Jack Nicholson? Sonny, that's great.

CONNIE: Or maybe Sylvester Stallone. They haven't nailed down
the main lead yet.

SONNY: (*Suspiciously.*) What part do I play?

CONNIE: (*Cautiously.*) Sort of a soldier ... A *guerrilla.* The
story takes place in Central America, see? And there's
this American Marine who's down there advising the *con-
tras.* Well, you're one of the boys he's training.

SONNY: (*Sharply.*) To overthrow what, Nicaragua?

CONNIE: Who said anything about Nicaragua?

SONNY: Who's financing this thing, the Sandinistas or the CIA?
Why doesn't it have Arnie Schwarzenegger?

CONNIE: (*Perplexed.*) No, you don't understand ...

SONNY: (*Angry.*) I'm not participating in any reactionary facsist
film.

CONNIE: (*On the defensive.*) *M'ijo,* you've got it all wrong. It's a
comedy, sort of a funny love story set in El Salvador.

SONNY: (SONNY *glances at* ANITA. *Pauses.*) So what's your role,
*Consuelo?*

CONNIE: (*Peeved.*) Sort of a hostess, and don't call me Consuelo.

SONNY: (*Snide.*) What kind of hostess?

CONNIE: (*Evasively.*) A hostess with the mostess. I run the canteen in the mountains.

SONNY: (*Bitterly.*) Canteen or *cantina?*

CONNIE: (*Shrugs.*) I sell the gringos a few drinks. So what?

SONNY: What else do you sell them—"gorls"?

CONNIE: It's only a movie, for Pete's sake.

SONNY: It's a whorehouse isn't it?

CONNIE: It's a job!

SONNY (*Seething.*) And what am I suppose to be—one of the
customers, too, or just a pimp? I probably don't even
speak English, do I?

CONNIE: (*Affronted.*) You don't even get to speak at all.

SONNY: So I'm an EXTRA, is that it? An extra in a goddamn CIA
WHOREHOUSE? That's sick, Mom. SICK! How much
is a FUCKING MOVIE worth?

CONNIE: WHAT?

SONNY: I don't want your fucking job, and I don't need your
fucking agent!

CONNIE: (*Slaps* SONNY.) Don't you use that language with me,
*cabrón*! *¡Soy tu madre! Pos mira* ... What's the matter

with you? I didn't want to do that, especially in front of Anita, but it's time you showed some respect and appreciation for what I've tried to do for you, eh? Being your mom doesn't mean I'm your dishrag! I've got hopes and dreams for myself, just like you, and I need my space to do it. You hear what I'm saying? Grow up! (SONNY *turns and pathetically exits up the hall. There is a pause.* CONNIE *is distraught.*) He's getting worse, isn't he?

ANITA: (*Anxiously.*) That's putting it mildly. He's got Buddy's gun, Connie. He could hurt himself.

CONNIE: (*Guilty.*) But how-why? Buddy and I have done everything for that kid and his sister. He's had a great life, a middle-class life. Is it our fault he doesn't know what to do with it!

BUDDY: (*enters, tipsily rocking to and fro, with a gloriously drunken smile on his lips, impeccably attired in a TUXEDO. With his tie straight and every hair on his balding head in place, he nevertheless looks quite dapper. Slurring.*) Cheerio! Good evening.

CONNIE: (*Insensed.*) Señor, are you still drunk? (BUDDY *smiles and suddenly straightens out, dropping his drunken routine, but in high spirits.*)

BUDDY: (*Almost British.*) No, actually. I'm quite in control of my faculties, after a bit of an upchuck. López is the name, Nigel López. (*Lisping.*) Señorita princesa, ¿cómo está usted? (*He nods to* ANITA.)

CONNIE: (*Disgusted.*) You're ridiculous.

BUDDY: Would you prefer a little Noel Coward? Where's Sonny?

CONNIE: For your information, Mr. Coward, your son is upstairs with a gun about to blow his brains out, for all we know, with your gun!

BUDDY: (*Relieved.*) That old thing? It hasn't been fired in twenty years. (*A gunshot goes off. Silence.* BUDDY, CONNIE *and* ANITA *look at each other horrified.*)

CONNIE: (*Screaming.*) SONNY!!! (BUDDY *leaps out of the den and runs up the hallway, followed by* CONNIE *and* ANITA. *Long pause. The den remains empty.* BUDDY, CONNIE *and* ANITA *return slowly, backing down the hallway, with their arms slightly raised in caution.* SONNY *has the gun aimed at them. Smiling insanely, he is wearing shades and a green beret.*)

SONNY: (*Sings.*)

"Put silver wings on my hairy chest
make me one of America's best ... "

BUDDY: (*Bewildered.*) What's going on, Sonny? Is this some kind
   of game?

SONNY: (*Sick smile.*) The only game in town, a little game of life
   and death.

CONNIE: (*Emotionally.*) Are you CRAZY?!

BUDDY: (*Turns to her anxiously.*) ¡Cállate, mujer! He isn't being
   serious. Right, Sonny? You're acting, aren't you, *m'ijo*?

SONNY: (*Spaced out.*) Do you really think so?

BUDDY: (*Humoring him.*) That outfit you're wearing, isn't that
   part of my costume for "The Green Beret's"?

SONNY: (*Shakes his head vigorously. Wild-eyed.*) Screw John
   Wayne! I'm going to Central America to make my own
   movie! YO!

BUDDY: (*Glares at* CONNIE.) Central América?

SONNY: (*Laughing crazily.*) It's a comedy, Dad. A laff riot set in
   El Salvador. We're going down there to kick some brown
   ass and have a ball, huh Mom?

BUDDY: What have you been ... ? Did you offer him a job in the
   Nicholson picture?

CONNIE: (*Helpless.*) I was only humoring him, *hombre.*

SONNY: (*Fiercely intense.*) It appears both of you are having trouble taking me seriously. Would it help if we played a little
   game of Russian roulette a la Robert DeNiro in "The Deer
   Hunter"?! Motherfucker, Huh? Motherfucker! (*He spins
   the chamber on the gun and holds it up.* BUDDY *stands
   tall before his son shielding* CONNIE *and* ANITA.)

BUDDY: Come on, *m'ijo!* Enough's enough. Settle down and give
   me the gun.

CONNIE: (*Fearfully.*) M'ijo, por el amor de Dios, what are you
   going to do?

SONNY: (*Stepping on hearth with an insane smile.*) One of us may
   not get out of here alive. The only question is which one?
   The maid, the gardener, the ballerina or me?

ANITA: You're ill, Sonny seriously ill.

SONNY: (*Holding up the gun to his own throat.*) SHUT UP!! Or
   the beaner gets it. Now SIT DOWN!

BUDDY: (*Standing steadily.*) If you're going to shoot me, you may
   as well do it now, Sonny, I don't take orders in my own
   house.

SONNY: (*Bitterly.*) Right, the Silent Bit King in his castle! What about all those cops outside, King? Are you going to close up the moat and keep them out? Or did you come to talk me into surrendering? What chance do I have of going back to Harvard now, huh, Pop? Your prince and heir? They're going to throw my ass in prison, Daddy-O! I'm going to do EXTRA time!

BUDDY: (*Angered.*) So who told you to leave Harvard? Sonny, you had it made!

SONNY: (*Desolate.*) You still don't get it, do you? What it's like being a Chicano at Harvard? The sense of isolation and guilt.

CONNIE: (*Emotionally.*) No more, *m'ijo,* please.

SONNY: (*Shaking his head morosely in desperation. Anguished.*) Do you know how many times I've denied you? Lucy used to do it all the time. Do you think she gave a damn? I'm talking about SHAME! HUMILIATION!— all those scum-sucking roles you've played in the movies all these years! DRUNKS and WHORES and ASS-LICKING GREASERS! And for what? So Lucy and I could make something of ourselves? Well, we have, Dad! We've become SOMEBODY ELSE! Anybody else but your CHILDREN!—ACTORS faking our roles to fit into the GREAT AMERICAN SUCCESS STORY: go away, move away, change your name and deny your origins, change your SEX if need be, but become NEUTER, like everybody else! You see, in order to ACT TRULY AMERICAN, you have to kill your parents: no fatherland, no motherland, no MEXICAN, Japanese, African, Jewish, Puertorrican, Philipino, Armenian, Latvian, Chinese, Indian, Arabian, Norwegian, old-country SHIT! Well, I damn near succeeded ... Thanks to good old Anglo Saxon Protestant, MONROE JAMES! (*Music: We hear Mozart's "Rondo in C" in underscore.*)

BUDDY: Monroe who?

SONNY: (*Obsessively.*) My roommate at Harvard ... He was everything I ever wanted to be. Tall, rich, blonde, but he wasn't much company, so I preferred to do my homework in the library. One night I was working on a paper— writing with all my conscious skill to make the syntax of my English sentences as perfect as they could be. I couldn't tolerate the thought of being anything less than brilliant, you see. If you're not white, you have to be brilliant, just to be considered acceptable. Well, I got stuck ... on one paragraph ... First, I restructured the sentences, hoping to eliminate a certain kind of circular logic in the paragraph. I hate being REDUNDANT ... Then the linear order of the words began to bother me. MY ENGLISH WAS BREAKING DOWN! Then I couldn't tolerate the space between the words. Finally, I got stuck on a hyphen, a lousy hyphen, so I scratched it out. And the HOLE between the two words became an unbridgeable GAP, and I FELL! ... into a sea of nothingness. So I ran, I ran like my life depended on it all the way back to the dorm. Then ... when I opened the door to our room, I spotted Monroe, holding a gun to his head. Neither of us said anything. He just smiled, and pulled the trigger. My fucking role model! He blew his brains out! (*He collapses in silent tears. There is a pause.* CONNIE *crosses to* SONNY, *and sits beside him, overwhelmed with maternal concern, also in tears.*)

CONNIE: Whatever we've done, *m'ijo*, it's been for you. We wanted to be proud of you, but more than anything we wanted you to be at peace with yourself. I just don't honestly know what's gone wrong. You had everything going for you!

ANITA: It's time to grow up, Sonny. Accept your parents for what they are and maybe you'll accept yourself. We're all only human.

BUDDY: You know, Sonny. After a while, making movies can be just like any other job, but it's never been scum-sucking work. You don't like the roles we've played? That's tough. You see, *m'ijo* ... Bedoya was right. Inside yourself you know your own worth. And I should know. I'm your father and I don't have to show you any stinking badges. NOW, GIVE ME THE GUN! (BUDDY *holds his hand out for the gun.* SONNY *is about to hand it to him when the LAPD interrupts and brings* SONNY *back to his craziness. The LAPD bullhorn blares out again in front of the house.*)

BULLHORN: THIS IS THE LAPD. TIME'S UP! YOU'VE GOT TWO MINUTES TO COME OUT WITH YOUR HANDS UP, OR WE'RE COMING IN!

SONNY: Nice try, Dad, but it won't work! Your speeches were a bit too predictable.

CONNIE: Sonny, please!

BUDDY: Let's have it cabrón. (BUDDY *reaches for the gun.*

SONNY *backs off, raising the pistol to his head.*)
SONNY: DON'T, DAD! OR I'LL SHOOT!!   (BUDDY *stops.*
ANITA *comforts* CONNIE.)
ANITA: Sonny, why are you torturing your parents like this?
SONNY: (*Laughs insanely, his face a tragicomic mask. With sui-
cidal irony.*) Toture? ... You mean I'm finally being convincing? ... I don't know if I'm acting or not anymore ...
Am I being melodramatic? I don't know ... and I don't
care ... I only know that I'm not going to prison and that
the white whale must die. Would you believe I'm going
after white whale—inside my head? I now understand
why, so if the gun is still loaded, this is GOODBYE! (*He
places the barrel of the gun between his eyes, shutting his
eyes tight.*)
CONNIE: (*Pleading.*) *M'ijo* ... please ... don't.

*Blackout.*

.................... SCENE THREE ....................

*In the dark, immediately following, we hear a recording of Los
Lobos singing "Will the Wolf Survive?" Half lights come up. A
STAGEHAND walks onstage, takes the gun from SONNY and be-
gins to clear props.*

SONNY: (*Opening his eyes.*) Hey, wait. Stop it, I said. CUT!!!

*Lights black out, except for a single spot on SONNY. BUDDY,
CONNIE and ANITA sit in the background. There is a pause. We
suddenly hear the DIRECTOR's voice—Speaking to SONNY from
the booth, his face on the studio monitors, looking and sounding
exactly like SONNY!*

DIRECTOR: WHAT'S THE MATTER, SWEETHEART?
SONNY: (*Talking to the booth.*) It's not working out, man. You're
messing with the tragic implications of my entire story
here. What happened to the final shot.
DIRECTOR: (*Offstage.*) WE GOTTA KEEP IT LIGHT. ENTER-
TAINING, ESE.
SONNY: (*Intensely.*) Don't *ese* me! It's idiotic! This isn't reality!
DIRECTOR: WHO SAID ANYTHING ABOUT REALITY?
THIS IS TELEVISION. FRANKLY, REALITY'S A BIG

BORING PAIN IN THE ASS. WE'RE IN THE ENTER-
TAINMENT BUSINESS. LAUGHS, SONNY, THAT'S
MORE IMPORTANT THAN REALITY. LOTS OF
LAUGHS.

SONNY: (*Pained.*) You promised to respect my script.

DIRECTOR: (*Offstage.*) AND I MOST CERTAINLY DO. I JUST
CAN'T USE IT. NOT IN THIS PILOT SHOW. LATER
PERHAPS? ONCE WE'VE EARNED SOME DECENT
RATINGS.

SONNY: What if I disappear for a while. I go away for six months
back to Yucatan, to the sacred pyramids of the Mayan
jungle. I go through my own psychic death and rebirth
in Mexico. I plummet to the schizophrenic depths of my
own cosmic root and emerge from the dark side of my own
soul cleansed and enlightened. Would that be amusing?

DIRECTOR: IN A SITUATION COMEDY? 'FRAID NOT,
SONNY. PERHAPS YOU CAN FASHION AN ART
FILM OUT OF THOSE EXPERIENCES.

SONNY: And the politics? I go on to Guatemala and Nicaragua.
What about all the stuff on American Foreign Policy in
Latin America?

DIRECTOR: DITTO. WRITE AN EDITORIAL. THE ONLY
LATINS OUR AUDIENCES CARE ABOUT ARE
THOSE WHO DANCE AND SING AND STAMP
THEIR FEET ... AND SAY FUNNY THINGS,
CROSSOVER VALUE, SONNY! IF IT CAN'T COME
ACROSS IN BUFFALO, YOU CAN FORGET IT. THE
COSMIC TRUTHS ARE FINE, BUT DOWN HERE ON
EARTH, PROGRESS MOVES LIKE A SNAIL. GIVE IT
A CHANCE. NOW, SHALL WE WRAP THIS MOTHER
UP? FOR THE SAKE OF PROGRESS?

SONNY: (*Cagily.*) Can you get rid of the cops? And the burglary
rap at the Crap-in-the-Box?

DIRECTOR: (*Pause.*) WHY SHOULD I?

SONNY: (*Passionately.*) Because you can change the ending if you
want to ... It's our story. Right? We can't leave all these
high school drop-outs with this downer, man! Give the
people some hope. Save the Harvard Homeboy. Be honest with yourself, Sonny. Am I talking to myself?

DIRECTOR: (*Offstage.*) TO THE BONE, SONNY BOY. TO THE
BONE.

SONNY: (*Confidently.*) All right, then I wanna make this ending
my own. A spectacular ending!

DIRECTOR: (*Offstage.*) OKAY! OKAY, FINE. IT'S ALL YOURS, JUST DON'T SCREW IT UP. MAKE IT EMOTION-ALLY SATISFYING, HOMEBOY.

SONNY: BELIEVE. (*He turns and slowly starts to exit down the hall, then stops and turns.*) ACTION!!! (*He hurries out as the lights fade to black.*)


...................... EPILOGUE ......................

BUDDY *and* CONNIE*'s dream.*

*In the dark: The* DIRECTOR*'s voice comes over the audio system.*

DIRECTOR: (*Offstage.*)  LADIES AND GENTLEMEN, WE WOULD LIKE TO TAKE THIS OPPORTUNITY TO THANK YOU FOR PARTICIPATING AS A LIVE STU-DIO AUDIENCE IN THE TAPING OF THIS SHOW. WE HOPE THAT YOU WILL FIND OUR ENDING POSITIVELY HILARIOUS.

*Music: Lights come up on the den to reveal* BUDDY *and* CON-NIE *asleep, still wearing their evening clothes.* BUDDY *is in his chair, and* CONNIE *is on the couch, covered with her imitation mink. They stir to the sound of the driving music of hypnotic flutes, shamisens and drums. Out in the patio, through the night mist, a body of great flashing lights descends from the heavens, indicating the arrival of an extra-terrestial object.* BUDDY *rises and goes to the patio doors, and looks out with utter amazement.*

BUDDY: GOD BLESS AMERICA *¡y que viva México, chingao!*

CONNIE: (*Getting up.*) What is it?

BUDDY: Come and look at this beautiful sight, *viejita!*

CONNIE: (*Looks out, with equal amazement.*) My God. It's a flying saucer!

BUDDY: (*Laughing like a child.*) A GIANT, SOMBRERO FLY-ING SAUCER! Didn't I tell you? There it is! It wasn't just a crazy movie idea, it's real! Isn't it?

CONNIE: Are we dreaming?

BUDDY: How can we both be having the same dream? (SONNY *and* ANITA *come down the stairs, dressed and ready to travel, carrying suitcases. Their New Age American look is stunning, the stuff of the 21st Century.*)

SONNY: Mommy-O and Daddy-O? It's my dream. We're on our
    way.

CONNIE: You're leaving? Where are you going?

BUDDY: What are you doing, Sonny?

SONNY: (*Seriously.*) Trying to give this situation a fantastic solu-
    tion. To do that I've got to convince you that my recent
    misadventures were only abberations of my stressed-out
    over active brain. You see, we're only as real as we believe
    ourselves to be. In show-biz terms, I'm asking you to sus-
    pend your disbelief in me and to believe me when I tell
    you I'm mentally, physically and spiritually okay. *Mens
    sana in corpore sano.* I have found my own mind again.
    Are you ready for this? I'm going back to Harvard, to
    finish what I started.

CONNIE: (*Delighted.*) ¡M'ijo!

ANITA: Sonny, that's wonderful!

BUDDY: I knew you'd come through, *m'ijo!* (BUDDY *puts his
    arm around him.*)

SONNY: (*Thoughtful.*) I've been thinking a lot about this, Dad.
    To be honest, I still don't know what the hell I'm going to
    be, but I'm going to make you proud of me, whatever I
    become. Lawyer, filmmaker or cosmic lowrider.

BUDDY: Cosmic lowrider?

SONNY: I'm only sorry I put you all through this melodramatic
    violence. I just had to come back to the Twilight Zone to
    find out who I was.

BUDDY: (*Head up.*) And so ... who are you?

SONNY: (*With maturity.*) Your spaced-out-son, for one. (*There is
    a quiet moment.* BUDDY *embraces* SONNY, *then* CON-
    NIE *joins them, then* ANITA.)

BUDDY: (*Ironically.*) Well, at least we've managed to save our
    *pinche* dignity, *chinago!*

CONNIE: I'm beginning to see a happy ending to all of this!
    (*A whirring sound is heard offstage, the great light starts
    to glow out in the patio.* SONNY *puts his arm around*
    ANITA.)

SONNY: Anita's coming back to the East Coast with me, for a
    while anyway.

ANITA: (*Excited.*) I'm going back to see my folks. It wasn't right
    of me to leave without saying goodbye, so I'm going back
    to say hello and mend some broken fences. The Peugeot
    is going with us, by the way. Thanks for the fantastic ride
    Sonny conjured up.

SONNY: Actually, it was my Dad's idea. He deserves all the credit.

BUDDY: (*Proudly.*) The Flying Saucer Sombrero ... how does it fly, Sonny?

SONNY: Heliotropic waves. Aztechnology. Mayan Solar Lord stuff. The stuff of dreams and science fiction. Everybody's got a right to star in their own movie, right? This one's mine. From now on, we're going nowhere but UP. Straight up, into the brightest stars of our wildest dreams. Ready to go, baby?

ANITA: Hey, after the crazy cholo, I'm ready for anything.

SONNY: Then let's go, Mom, Dad? (BUDDY *and* CONNIE *both embrace their son.* ANITA *holds back.*)

CONNIE: (*Tears.*) Go on, now. Your Father and I have our own dreams and world to conquer. We're perfectly happy staying in our own home. Right, *viejo*?

BUDDY: Sure.

SONNY: Sure sure?

BUDDY: Don't sweat it. Get going!

SONNY: (*Laughs and kisses* CONNIE *on the cheek.*) Thanks, Mom, Dad. It's great to be home for a while. I just want you to know you're both a fine pair of human beings. And that I LOVE YOU!

ANITA: (*Joining the embrace.*) That goes for me, too.

BUDDY: *Sayonara.*

ANITA: *¡ADIÓS!*

SONNY: *¡Ay los watcho!* (*Offstage.*) *Ese,* Scotty, beam me up, homes! (SONNY *and* ANITA *step out into the patio, glowing with light. The flying saucer sombrero takes off, in a spectacular ascent, making a great whoosh as it flies away. There is a pause.* BUDDY *is standing in the den. They look at each other.* BUDDY *heads to the fireplace mantle and picks up the daruma doll.*)

CONNIE: What are you doing?

BUDDY: Filling in the left eye. *¿No que no?* Our wish came true! Sonny went back to Harvard. Well, *vieja*, shall we call it a day or work up a little more sweat? We gotta be in shape, you know, if we're gonna make that anti-war Nicholson movie together.

CONNIE: Forget it, Buddy. I'm hitting the showers.

BUDDY: I'll join you.

CONNIE: We won't fit.

BUDDY: I'll make us fit ... Come on.

CONNIE: (*Tempted.*) Let's go for a real Hollywood ending, like in
all those movies in the 40's.

BUDDY: Let George do it.

CONNIE: (*Loving it.*) *Cómo eres señor*—look at you. The middle-
aged father of an established doctor and an up-and-coming
cosmic lowrider. Well, Nigel, what do you have to say for
yourself?

BUDDY: (*With monocle, British accent.*) What else? I don't
have to show you no stinking badges! (*He turns on the
tape deck, which plays "Rhapsody in Blue." BUDDY and
CONNIE cross slowly and romantically towards each other,
meeting center stage. BUDDY holds CONNIE in his arms
and they do an old-fashioned kiss as the lights fade to
black.*)

*Curtain.*